The Calamitous and Lamentable 'Arab Spring

An Analysis of The Illiteracy and Hypocrisy of an 'Arab Muslim

The Calamitous and Lamentable 'Arab Spring

An Analysis of The Illiteracy and Hypocrisy of an 'Arab Muslim

By

'Allāma Dr. Sāni Şālih Musṭapha

Strategic Book Publishing and Rights Co.

.تحسبهم جميعا وقلو بهم شتى ذالك بأنهم قوم لا يعقلون

"You think they are united but their hearts are divided. That is because they are a people who understand not." Qur'ān 59:14.

Strategic Book Publishing and Rights Co.
12620 FM 1960, Suite A4-507
Houston TX 77065
www.sbpra.com

ISBN: 978-1-61204-790-4

DEDICATION

I am blessed by Allāh having lived under the care and training of my parents. I hope Allāh will accept my intercession on their behalf.

Other works by 'Allama Dr. Sani Salih Mustapha
Muhammad Rasūlullah and the People of the Book
Reviving as-Ṣalāt of the Holy Apostle: The Gateway to Paradise.
Necessitates and calls for the second ocuupation of Makka
(Ka'ba)
The Sciences of Hadīth Literature
'Ilm-al-Uṣūl-al-Fiqh

TABLE OF CONTENTS

ABOUT THE AUTHOR

Dr. Sāni Sālih Muṣṭapha, a "moderate" Islāmic preacher, was born in Kano, Nigeria, in 1946. He received elementary Islāmic education under his grandfather, Ahmad; he never graduated, but he was lucky to learn 'Arabic up to the secondary school level.

While in medical school, he wanted to opt out, but was urged not to by an Islamic scholar and Grand Qādi, the late 'Abūbakar Mahmood Gumi, who told him, "Western education is more important than Islamic education because as a doctor if you are kind and gentle, you can easily attract others to Islām. But as a judge, people will run away from you."

After completing his post-graduate studies in Community Health, he continued his personal studies of Islam. In the mid-1980's, he was rebuked by the local Islamic preachers for not knowing Islam and for reading books written in English. This irritated him, but he remembered what his 'Arabic teacher had told him: "Arabic is an evaporating language. You must read it every day, or else you will forget it. Have a dictionary by your side, for even I, an 'Arabic teacher, will come across a word I have to look up for its meaning." He then turned to reading Islamic jurisprudence from 'Arabic texts.

ABOUT THE BOOK

This book attempts to unveil the ignorance and hypocrisy of the followers of Muhammad Rasūlullah in this century. They do not portray Muhammad Rasūlullah as a Messenger of peace. They make their Jihād to precipitate chaos, corruption, and tyranny in the world. If the Levi tribe could go through the history of their ancestors who lived in Medina, based on the description they found in the then Torah (Talmud) of the arrival of the Messiah, they will find that Muhammad, the son of 'Abdallah, was sent as a bringer of glad tidings and mercy to mankind. That remains so today.

The world can enjoy peace, stability, progress, and prosperity only if the Levi tribe of the Children of Israel preaches to their tribe and persuade them to demand a return to the status quo of 623-629 A.D. The Muslim world should recognize and appreciate the role the Levi tribe of the Children of Israel had in establishing and consolidating the Sharī'a, rather than accusing them of disbelief. They were punished according to the Sharī'a and therefore have been forgiven. They are now in Paradise! The punishment of the followers of Muhammad will be the severest on the Day of Judgment, for they deliberately refused to take heed of the lessons from the Children of Israel: from the Exodus to the apparent crucifixion of Jesus, the son of Maryam.

PREFACE

In the name of Allāh, Most Beneficent, Most Merciful, praise be to Allāh, the Lord of the Worlds, and peace be upon the Master of the Apostles, his family, and companions.

Mankind was created by Allāh on Friday as the last of the creations of Allāh. Allāh describes the creation of mankind in many verses of the holy Qurʿān as "best and perfect." In 40:64 He says, "Allāh, it is He Who has made for you the earth as a dwelling place and the sky as a canopy, and has given you shape and made your shape good (looking) and has provided you with good things. That is Allāh your Lord: so Blessed be Allāh, the Lord of the ʿĀlamin (mankind, jinn and all that exists)."[1] This verse applies to what mankind knows, sees, recognizes, and comprehends, as well as to that which he does not know, cannot see with the naked eye or comprehend, from that very Friday Allāh created Adam. These decreed events are living witnesses of the *reality* of Allāh: that whatever situation in which one finds himself must necessarily be his own doing. Man has nothing but that which he strives for.[2]

Genesis 3:23 of the Holy Bible mentions the expulsion of Adam and Eve out of the Garden of Eden, as in many places in the holy Qurʿān. Unlike the Talmud, the holy Qurʿān mentions the advice or warning from the moment of expulsion to their

---

[1]   See The Holy Bible, Promise Study Edition, CEV. (Nashville, TN: Thomas Nelson. 1996), 67. The Book of Genesis 1:1-31. Here Allah looked at what he had done, and it was good.
[2]   See holy Qurʿān 53:39.

landing on earth. When Prophet Adam (AS) and his wife, and by extension the whole of mankind and jinn, were expelled from the Garden of Eden, Allāh reminded us, as we were about to descend down to earth, of what happened between Him and Shaiṭan (the devil, Satan) in holy Qur'ān 18:50, "And (remember) when We said to the angels: 'Prostrate yourselves unto Adam.' So they prostrated themselves except Iblīs (Shaiṭan). He was one of the jinn; he disobeyed the Command of his Lord. Will you then take him (Iblis i.e., one who disobeyed the Command of his Lord) and his offspring as protectors and helpers rather than Me while they are enemies to you? What an evil is the exchange for the Zālimūn (polytheists, and wrong-doers)."[3] That uncontestable incident calls on logic and common sense to believe in its application to the office of the 'Representative' of Allāh, that Allāh will always remain our 'Ruler.'

Reminding us of the covenant we undertook with Him while we were in the loin of our father Prophet Adam (AS), Allāh says in holy Qur'ān 2:38, "And if, as is sure, there comes to you guidance from Me, whosoever follows My guidance, on them shall be no fear, nor shall they grieve. But those who reject Faith, and belie Our Signs, they shall be Sahābas of the Fire, they shall abide therein." The companions of the holy Apostle confess that "The holy Apostle mentioned what mankind needs for his worldly needs and those of the Hereafter." Unfortunately, his followers are far away from the guidance.

These Decreed events must have stood according to the Laws of Allāh. Allāh says in the holy Qur'ān 53:39, "And that man can have nothing but what he does (good or bad). And that his deeds

---

[3]   See the holy Qur'ān 51:56. The jinn are like human beings. We were given the power of choice- between good and evil, prosperity and adversity, to believe or to disbelieve. This Law or warning from Allāh came even before the commissioning of Apostle Adam as a prophet and was further explained in the Book of Genesis 4: 21-24 and the explanatory notes of Reverend Matthew Henry.

will be seen. Then he shall be recompensed with a full and the best recompense." We experience variable weather conditions. When they set in, we just fold our scientific instrument and attribute the cause and events to 'Nature.' We also experience earthquakes, drought as a result of Allāh withholding that good thing from the sky. We equally fold our instruments and attribute that event to 'Nature. We can today predict earthquakes and measure their strengths, but cannot prevent them. We have identified the most vulnerable points of earthquakes but cannot shift their positions. In fact in every point and location of the universe, there are signs indicating the *absolute control*, *power*, *will*, and *plan* of Allāh.

Allāh challenges mankind at the moment their beloved ones are dying in the holy Qur'ān, 56:83-87: "Then why do you not (intervene) when (the soul of a dying person) reaches the throat? And you at the moment are looking on. But We (that is the angels who take the soul) are nearer to him than you, but you see not. Then why do you not--if you are exempt from reckoning and recompense (punishment) bring back the soul (to its body), if you are truthful."

Again in the holy Qur'ān 75:26-27, Allāh says, "Nay, when (the soul) reaches to the collar bone (that is up to the throat in its exit) and it will be said, Who can cure him (and save him from death)?" And he (the dying person) will conclude that it was (the time) of parting (death) and one leg will be joined with another leg, the drive will be, on that day, to your Lord (Allāh)!" These realities are not appreciated and apprehended by all of us. The medical personnel know more about death than the non medical personnel. They are the witness and executors of "one leg will be joined with another leg. The drive will be, on that Day, to your Lord" aptly applies to the relations and friends on the burial day. If this is understood, then why should one dispute what Muhammad said? The message of Muhammad Rasūlullah should not be limited to what one reads in the holy Qur'ān.

There is no justification in creating discord and disharmony by extracting a part of the holy Qur'ān and comparing it with what was revealed to any prophet before Muhammad Rasūlullah. Such details in the book of that prophet may not be available in the holy Qur'ān. Its unavailability in the holy Qur'ān does not mean that it was not a revelation, or that it will not be of any value to us today. How old is the physical world? The rain and the flood experienced by the people of Prophet Noah have the same origin as the rain and flood experienced by the people of Queensland. The tornado and hurricane experienced by the citizens of the United States of America has the same origin as the tornado and hurricane experienced by the people of 'Ād.

From the above premise, mankind is divided into two: those who perceive, appreciate, and realize practically what they read and those who perceive but do not have the appreciation and practical meaning of what they read. If there is disagreement between them and a third person joined in the argument, he is bound to support one of them, not both. He can be an arbitrator also in explaining where they differ. This must take place in a language understood by both parties. The most important arbitrator is the use of a common background--language, and knowledge common to all. The case of Prophet Joseph with his inmates is a good example.[4]

Likewise, in any matter relating to man's survival, based on the claim of Allāh that He has provided to mankind whatever he needs in this world for his survival, the final arbitrator in any dispute is the common language and knowledge in understanding our common need. This is acclaimed by Allāh in the holy Qur'ān 14:4, "And We sent not a Messenger except with the language of his people, in order that he might make (the Message) clear for them. Then Allāh misleads whom He wills (but only after He sent the Message) and guides whom He wills. And he is the All-Mighty, the All-Wise."

---

[4]   See Genesis. 39.

In the holy Qur'ān 41:44, Allāh explains why He sent messengers in the language of their people, "And if We had sent this Qur'ān in a foreign language (other than Arabic) they would have said: 'Why not its verses explained in detail (in our language)? What! (A Book) not in 'Arabic and (the Messenger) an 'Arab?' Say: It is for those who believe a guide and a healing. And as for those who disbelieve, there is heaviness (deafness) in their ears, and it (the Qur'ān) is blindness for them. They are those who are called from a place far away (so they neither listen nor understand)."

The 'Arabs have no ground, no excuse for behaving the way they are behaving today, for they are far away from obeying Muhammad Rasūlullah. The non-'Arab speaking Muslims who follow them blindly equally have no excuse to offer in the Hereafter. The followers of Muhammad Rasūlullah are the ones described in this verse, because they do not hear the warning. If they disagree, they cannot escape from the description of the holy Qur'ān 2: 93, "We have heard and disobeyed." If, in this verse the Levi tribes were described as believers merely for worshipping the calf, is it not the same for worshipping power, money, lust, and desire?

The Heavenly Scriptures are available today, all except one, in foreign languages. The only available one in its original linguistic form is the magnificent holy Qur'ān, described by Allāh in the holy Qur'ān 39:28, "An 'Arabic Qur'ān, without any crookedness (therein) in order that they may avoid all evil Which Allāh has ordered them to avoid, fear Him and keep their duty to Him." Indeed the Message in the holy Qur'ān deserves to be listened to by all since it is a call to mankind to avoid evil, which Allāh has ordered them to avoid. In effect, Allāh is saying again that the carbon element he composed us from is free from any tint of evil, but it has the capacity to be tinted with evil. The Message thus carries an element of precaution, which is in that element of choice endowed on mankind by Allāh.

Allāh demanded us to always perform a litmus test to ascertain the truth for our benefit. If the Message had been made clear by the holy Apostle and was applied in his time for the salvation of the then civilization, do we have any means and method of ascertaining its truth? That is, did historians write anything on the life of Muhammad Rasūlullah confirming beyond any doubt that what he demonstrated to the then civilization, as practical guidance from Allāh has stood the test of that time? In other words, did he succeed in bringing peace, prosperity, and tolerance among the then nations or chaos and anarchy?

Historians criticizing the teaching of Muhammad Rasūlullah and accusing him of all that they accuse him of, do so out of ignorance, prejudice, and hatred. I have come across such writings, which some Muslim scholars regard as insulting. I never considered such ideas insulting, for the character of the holy Apostle is indeed told in the holy Qur'ān. These critics have never for one moment disagreed with the holy Apostle on his descriptions in the holy Qur'ān of the following:

Detailed exposition of past nations and civilizations.
An exposition of what will happen after him.
A decision on our way of life.
A distinguisher and never a jester.
A Message (and personality), which, if abandoned by any overweening person, will never succeed.
Seeking guidance elsewhere so that Allāh will lead him astray.
Allāh's stalwart rope, the wise reminder, the straight path.
That which desires do not swerve, the tongue does not confuse, and the learned cannot grasp completely.
That which is not worn out by repetition--nor do its wonders ever cease.
That which is free from any ambiguity.
A meaning that cannot be exhausted.

The firmament that is the firmament of the heavens.
That which is always shining.

It is that message that compelled the jinn's to say, "Verily, we have heard a wonderful recitation. It guides to the Right Path, and we have believed therein, and we shall never join (in worship) anything with our Lord (Allāh)." {The holy Qur'ān 46: 30-32}

Whoever stands by it is truthful.
Whoever executes its command is rewarded.
Whoever judges by it, judges with equity.
Whoever calls people to it will guide to the Straight Path.

The holy Qur'ān is a Message to mankind for their salvation, progress, and all that they need in the world. It is not possible then for man to stand and work against what he has no grounds for rejecting or finding another way to accomplish his desires, wishes, and needs. We can solve our problems only by following its guidance. It is like a blind man who needs someone to direct him? That one must be one who can see. Physical sighting requires the eyes with their intact healthy anatomical structure and a functional central nervous system. Of course, there must be the object to sight or a goal. Usually it what is immediately in front of man that is constantly preoccupying his mind. However, when one goes to sleep, everything is cut off from all the signs he knows. He is virtually dead. After a while, he may be awakened due to a distended bladder, a noise, or the natural instinct that it is dawn.

In the holy Qur'ān, 16:10-16, Allāh lists the following objects and physical signs:

the sky from which He sends down water for drinking
the growth of vegetables for feeding cattle
the growth of crops, olives, date-palms, grapes, and every kind of fruit. (It is interesting to observe Muhammad Rasūlullah describing what is not available in Makka!)

night and day, the sun, moon, and stars—all created by
Him
varying colors (botanical life) and animals (zoological
life)
the sea for providing fresh, tender meat, as well as
ornaments. (We see ships ploughing through the sea.)
mountains, which he has fixed with rivers and roads
(Was Muhammad then a construction engineer?)
vegetation on which our cattle pasture
landmarks and the stars guiding mankind

After enumerating the above facts, His creations that would
draw our attention to understanding the Straight Path, He calls
on us in the holy Qur'ān 16:17, "Is then He Who creates, as one
who creates not? Will you not then remember?"

The above physical signs cover a wide range of professions,
and irrespective of their diversity all show the existence of only
one source of Power, Will, and Knowledge. Man has very little
to say and cannot alter the course or do anything to change
or prevent their characteristics and form. However, we have
come to understand and tamper with whatever He created in
the heavens and earth for our benefits. This does not mean that
mankind is able to change His plan, power, and will, or the base
knowledge of that substance. We must draw this distinction
between Allāh and us, understand it, respect it, and stay within
our ability of comprehension. We must leave what is for Allāh
to Him and to take what is our due. This is not a matter of
balancing, but rather that of *right, cognizance,* and *obedience.*

What is the significance of "remembering," and what does
one remember in the above verse? Essentially, remembering
something enables one to know his limits, opportunities, strength,
and whether he can succeed or fail in an endeavor. Remembrance
is never intended to suppress, intimidate, or thwart one's efforts
and thinking. On the other hand, it encourages one to think, be
resilient, confident, and above all humble. This opens the gate

of competition, development, and growth, leading to what is written in the holy Qur'ān, 2:152, "Therefore remember Me, I will remember you, and be grateful to Me (for My countless Favors on you) and never be ungrateful to Me." "Remembrance," then, consists of remembering what is in the physical world that leads ultimately to remembering Allāh.

In the holy Qur'ān, 39:45, Allāh mentions the attitudes of mankind when He is mentioned (when something causes Him to be remembered) and when some signs in the physical world are mentioned (perceived, recognized, and comprehended): "And when Allāh Alone is mentioned, the hearts of those who believe not in the Hereafter are filled with disgust (from the Oneness of Allāh) and when those (whom they obey or worship) besides Him are mentioned, behold, they rejoice." How could this happen or be possible, when Allāh in the holy Qur'ān, 33:4 says, "Allāh has not made for any man two hearts inside his body."

It was reported that one day the holy Apostle was praying, and he got muddled while reciting. The hypocrites responded to this saying, "He has two hearts; one with you and the other with them." Then Allāh revealed it. Generally, it is understood to mean that Allāh did not create us to have inconsistent and undefined attitudes towards Him--serving Him and at the same time serving one of His signs in the physical world. This sign of the physical world refers to no one other than a system-- that of the Caliphate. In the Caliphate, it is Allāh who is obeyed and worshipped, as described and explained in Allāh in the holy Qur'ān, 7:201, "Verily, those who are Al-Muttaqūn (the pious) when an evil thought comes to them from Shaiṭan (Satan), they remember (Allāh), and (indeed) then they see (aright)." On the other hand, when a Muslim Umma takes to the contrary in instituting a rule other than that of the Caliph, they according to the holy Qur'ān 7:202, (i.e. the devils) "plunge them deeper into error, and they never stop." What is then the position of the Muslim Umma today? How are they going to face Allāh on the Day of Judgment? Whom are they going to blame for their misgivings and misfortunes? The answer is not easy. We claim to differ in understanding the injunctions of Allāh in the holy Qur'ān, which are a sign from Allāh, like the sea, river, light, sun, and all his physical creations. For example, who does not ask for water if he is thirsty? Incidentally, I entered a restaurant in London serving a buffet dinner that evening. I was the first to enter the restaurant. According to my custom I went to inspect what was on the food table for there were no labels. I was actually hungry. I saw a beautiful bowl of meat balls, and I took some as my starter. They tasted sweet, soft, and tender. When I went for my main course, I asked a waiter if there was pork on the table. He pointed to the bowl from which I had taken my appetizer I just laughed! I was exhilarated! Yes! I have committed a sin; but Allāh will not punish me for this carelessness, for I did not commit it with resolve and daring. I was hungry and there was no label on what was on the table.

How is one going to face Allāh, after Allāh has emphasized in the holy Qur'ān 30:57, "So on that Day no excuse of theirs will avail those who did wrong (by associating partners in worship with Allāh and by denying the Day of Resurrection), nor will they be allowed (then) to return to seek Allāh's Pleasure (by having Islamic Faith with righteous deeds and by giving up polytheism, sins, and crimes with repentance)."

How many Muslims have ever read the Holy Bible and the Talmud with the sincere intention of comparing their content with that of the holy Qur'ān? Has the story of the holy Apostle, the life history of the Sahābas, indicated that one is not allowed to read them? I am probably among those who never believed that a follower of Muhammad Rasūlullah is not supposed to read them. I believe that reading them is as important as reading the holy Qur'ān. One has to fear Allāh before understanding the Sunna of Muhammad Rasūlullah, which is the holy Qur'ān's explanation of the rituals as simply acts of worship. Unlike the commentary of the holy Qur'ān, which came to us through the

Sahābas and their immediate pupils, the interpretation of the Sunna of the holy Qur'ān is the sole prerogative of Muhammad Rasūlullah. There are also some resemblances of his Sunna in the Bible and the Talmud.

I found reading the Bible and the Talmud increased my faith and my fear of Allāh. Imagine Allāh saying to the children of Israel in the time of Prophet Moses, "If even one of you worship idols you will be like the root of a fruit that produces bitter poisonous fruit."[5] Worshipping idols means obeying one other than Allāh. In the Bible, worshipping idols was restricted only to inanimate objects. I do not commit any of the major sins, even though I know that I will be forgiven after I receive the punishment for that sin in this world, but on account of the explanation given in the Bible for why Prophet Moses died before seeing the Promised Land. In an explanation to Deuteronomy 34:4-10, the author of the Promise Study Edition Contemporary English Version said, "Moses did not go to enter Canaan because he had disobeyed God. Sometimes we think that a small bit of disobedience is no big deal to God, but sin always has consequences. When we disobey God, he will forgive us if we turn away from our sin and turn back to him. We still must live with the consequences of that sin, though God forgave Moses because of his trust in God, but Moses missed one of the greatest goals of his life--living in the land God had promised the Israelites."

The Holy Bible, for a period of about 1450 years, never mentioned an incident that contradicted the fixed law, that is, the written law--the Ten Commandments of Prophet Moses. As for the oral law, there could be some variations according to the needs of that law in the time of that Prophet of Allāh. Every incident in the Old Testament or Talmud is a lesson for the followers of Muhammad Rasūlullah, whether it is repeated or otherwise in the holy Qur'ān.

---

[5]   See Deut.29:18.

Such incidents often happen during the time of Muhammad Rasūlullah. For example, why did Muhammad receive injury during the battle of Uhud? This injury is similar to the inability of Prophet Moses to enter the Promised Land and a juridical analogy according to Islamic jurisprudence. This, in essence showed that the Sharī'a of Muhammad Rasūlullah in some cases did not differ fundamentally from the Sharī'a of Prophet Moses. What mankind claims as differences in the Sharī'a of Allāh are all made by man and not by Allāh.

How I wish Allāh would turn the hearts of those with sincere intention to obey the Allāh (G-d) of Abraham, Ishmael, Isaac, and Jacob and have them listen to this simple and basic convincing argument and do away with all those prejudices and wrongs that are making an 'Arab decapitate and slaughter a Jew and vice-versa. For example, when Moses called a meeting of all the people of Israel, so he could teach them the words to the song that the Lord (L-rd) had given him, he told them, as written in Deut. 31:6-8 (Latinized form), "Israel, the LORD is your Father, the one who created you, but you repaid him by being foolish. Think about past generations. Ask your parents or any of your elders. They will tell you that God Most High gave land to every nation."

The Talmudic version (the Hebrew or, probably the original Aramaic version) is: "Is this how you repay the Lord, you disgraceful, unwise people?! Is He not your Father, your Master? He has made you and established you. Remember the days of old; reflect upon the years of [other] generations. Ask your father, and he will tell you; your elders, and they will inform you. When the Most High gave nations their lot, when He separated the sons of man, He set up the boundaries of peoples according to the number of the children of Israel."

The Qur'ānic version is as follows: In the holy Qur'ān, 43:45, "And ask (O Muhammad) those of Our Messengers Whom We sent before you: Did We ever appoint alihah (gods) to be worshipped besides the Most Glorious (Allāh)?" The reference to Muhammad is insignificant for he is to ask only Moses and Jesus for they are the only two Messengers of the Children of Israel. Now during the ascension of Muhammad to the heavens he met Moses and Jesus. Moses advised him to beseech Allāh to reduce the number of prayers from fifty to five. Muhammad did. Now, obviously, we do not know what Moses told Muhammad when he asked him if Allāh ever appointed an alihah to be worshipped. Now, if the followers of Muhammad worship alihah what will the followers of Moses do?

In the holy Qur'ān 5:20, Prophet Moses appealed to the Children of Israel, "O my people! Remember the Favor of Allāh to you when he made you Prophets among you, made you kings and gave you what He had not given to any other among the Ālamin (mankind jinn, in the past)."

One can keep on enumerating the similarities between the Messages Allāh sent to different generations, on all aspects of the life of mankind as an indication that there is only One Allāh and one Way of life. Despite this, one gets nothing but an outright and outward rejection of the proofs, evidence, and signs, which are as clear as the rising of the sun on the fourth hour on a clear blue horizon. There is comfort and relief to the one who is rebuffed whenever he calls people to worship Allāh.

Worshipping Allāh means living comfortably in peace, prosperity, and security. One does not even need to work to get what he needs. The Children of Israel did not request Allāh to give them shade, clouds, dew and doves, after the Exodus. When they complained about the bitterness of the water at Mur, which means "bitter" in 'Arabic, the water turned palatable and sweet. The then Children of Israel knew about Allāh more than any race in the world. The majority of them survived and taught their people always to obey Allāh and be grateful to Him.

I am not unaware of the position of the Levi tribes in ensuring that the Torah is read weakly. What is happening today should be compared with the past. Then there would be no contention between the Children of Israel and any race today that worships

Allāh. The Children of Israel would have no grounds for dealing with anyone who does not believe in the Allāh of Abraham, Ishmael, Isaac, and Jacob. I am of the strong belief that the sermons of Moses, Joshua, Samuel, and all the Prophets who came after them had always taught to obey Allāh.

Since Muhammad Rasūlullah did not alter the written law--the Ten Commandments, the followers of Prophet Moses and Muhammad Rasūlullah must therefore live together in peace and prosperity. The Jews, according to their history, always return to the LORD (L-rd) when the truth is revealed to them. The destruction of Babylon by Nebuchadnezzar and Titus mentioned in both the Torah and the holy Qur'ān, further strengthened my argument on the similarity if not the uniformity of the law. The Jews never intentionally refused to obey Allāh. Their disobedience was under Irādatul Kawniyya Diniyya.

Today, however, the Jews have deviated from the teaching of the Torah, which was discovered by Hilkia. The law prohibits them from dealing with any heathen nation. If they deal with one, they will lose, for the God of Abraham will abandon them. Probably, this law is no longer binding or has been abrogated by Jesus, the son of Maryam. However, this is very unlikely. Therefore, if the Jews still believe in the Torah, then the question is: Why are they under siege by their neighbors?

Muhammad Rasūlullah did not come to remove the influence of the Levi tribe or to banish them from their strongholds in Medina. He indeed strengthened their position, lifting their honor; for he reminded them from time to time over a period of six years what they had forgotten of their ancestors. He did not deny their position as the chosen ones. His way of life, the much disputed Sharī'a he practiced, was definitely of Talmudic origin.

It never happened during the six years contact with the Levi tribe of the Children of Israel in Medina that anyone interfered or disallowed another to follow what Allāh revealed as one's way of life. If you agree with my premise, then you and I will agree that Allāh, his messengers, or any of their sincere followers never caused mischief, by way of injustice, corruption, or other vices in Muhammad's community. The Children of Israel, as stated earlier, never disobeyed Allāh on their own volition right after their freedom from the pharaoh. In contrast, the Sahābas besides Abūbakar Siddīq disobeyed the holy Apostle, but with full sincerity that they were following his instructions. Without the intercession of the holy Apostle, they were all forgiven by Allāh.

When Muhammad Rasūlullah died, 'Umar ibn Khaṭṭab proclaimed, "Revelation has seized, and we are to be judged by the Sunna. We shall punish anyone who commits an offense punishable by the Sunna." This shows that the Umma must select someone who will definitely continue the mission of Muhammad Rasūlullah, this time under *indirect* Divine guidance, not under *direct* Divine guidance as was the case with Prophet Joshua. I am sure, only the insane believe that the followers of Muhammad Rasūlullah accept his Sunna over the Qur'ān. Let us understand that the Qur'ān is what is in one's heart, while the Sunna is outside one's heart. We do not feel the electric conductivity of our heart muscles, but we see it on paper by connecting electrodes to our chests.

An Egyptian scholar, 'Abdul Qādir Audah, who was condemned to death by the Egyptian President 'Abdel Gamel Nasser, on 29 August, 1966, observed that eighty percent of the then Muslim Umma was illiterate. The remaining twenty percent was made up of the Muslims with a Western education, who understand Islam historically and scientifically. However, on the question of Islamic jurisprudence, they are no better than the masses.[6] The observation of Audah is actually what this book is attempting to convey to readers—that the followers of Muhammad Rasūlullah are nearly one hundred percent ignorant of the Sunna of Muhammad Rasūlullah. If you want to convince

---

[6] Maudūdi, S. Abul Ala. The Meaning of the Qur'ān. Lahore, Islamic Publications. 1993. Vol.6:162.

yourself, ask anyone of them to tell you the exact time of the noon and afternoon prayers in his city. His response will be that he does not know. In my country, they will look at the sky and tell you it is when the sun passes overhead! But the holy Apostle did not mean that. The time for prayers was measured, even during his time.

Therefore, if the history of the Children of Israel tells us that the Law/Sharī'a is the backbone of stability, security, peace, progress, and all that the mind and the body needs, it is impossible to get into an atmosphere where the followers of Muhammad Rasūlullah are leaders. This line has already been drawn, explained, and proved beyond any doubt by Muhammad Rasūlullah. He said: "Allāh eradicates by the power of government those evils, which are not eradicated by the teachings of the Qur'ān." In fact, this is actually the explanation of what happened between Hilkiah, the high priest, and Prophet Josiah. If preaching the Torah, that is, reading it by the Levites, is enough to ward off evil, Hilkiah could not have sought the help of Prophet Josiah.

One of the greatest problems of the followers of Muhammad Rasūlullah is their reduced capacity in realization and appreciation of the truth. They are so clever that they fail to understand the minutest similitude intended to awaken them. For example, it says in the holy Qur'ān 62:5, "The likeness of those who were entrusted with the (obligation of the) Taurāt (Torah) (i.e. to obey its commandments and to practice its laws), but who subsequently failed in those (obligations), is as the likeness of a donkey which carries huge burdens of books, (but understands nothing from them." But this did not happen when Hilkiah accidentally found the Torah. So, who are those referred to in the verse?

In a hadīth Quddusi, the holy Apostle said, "Indeed Allāh is Pure. He will not accept any sacrifice but that which is pure. Indeed Allāh has commanded the believers with what He commanded the Messengers." This hadīth does not need any explanation, for it is a general hadith referring also to the

Children of Israel. You must necessarily command that which is commanded and forbid that which is forbidden, or else Allāh will visit you with torments and disasters. He will allow you to be ruled by tyrants and merciless rulers. If you ask for Allāh's help, he will not help you.

But the followers of Muhammad will never agree, although it is the truth. The followers of Muhammad Rasūlullah are servants who will never believe, according to the holy Qur'ān 10:96-97, "Truly! Those, against whom the Word (Wrath) of your Lord has been justified, will not believe. Even if every sign should come to them, until they see the painful torment." Their mentality is: No one knows the Sunna of the holy Apostle except the 'Arabs, no one is worthy of following except the one who does not know, or knows but does not practice what he knows.

You may doubt the gross arrogance and ignorance of the followers of Muhammad Rasūlullah. This is my proof: Observing the five daily obligatory prayers is one form of worship that the followers of Muhammad ought to have perfected by now, for they have prayed 2,606,240 times from the Hijrah. If you were to ask them the exact time of the beginning of the prayers, they will just guess. No one of the one billion or more population will ever produce a graph on the relation between the length of a rod and the time of the Zuhr and afternoon prayer. They do not know the time of the Isha', and Fajr prayers according to the Sunna. The three million or so attending the annual pilgrimage does not observe the short prayer. There is no amount of preaching you will do to them, to convince one that he is wrong.

Now, tell me, how can you show the clear path for believers to those with such a mentality? If they do not know about the prayers, how can they know about something that was never practiced in any of their countries? Peace, progress, security, and all that man desires and needs can only be attained by him after following the commands of his Lord. The command of Allāh in the final message entails two forms:

For the enjoyment of the life in this world. This is a general command and not specific to the followers of Muhammad Rasūlullah.

For the enjoyment of the life in the Hereafter. This is applied only to the followers of Muhammad Rasūlullah, but do not follow his actions. Even in this, one is supposed to be on his own.

It is written in the holy Qur'ān 2:256, "There is no compulsion in Islām. Verily, the right path has become distinct from the wrong path. Whoever disbelieves in Ṭāghut (e.g., following tyrants and unjust rulers) and believes in Allāh then he has grasped the most trustworthy handhold that will never break. And Allāh is All-Hearer, All-Knower."

I want to assure the reader that this is not an opinion, but what I will stand on the Day of Judgment to be judged on. This book is not a criticism, but the Way of the Righteous. My aim is to stimulate you to think of the Hereafter and fear the Punishment on that Day. You can fear Allāh by reading the Holy Bible and not necessarily the Qur'ān. Begin from there. You need *Matthew Henry's Complete Commentary on the Whole Bible* to help you. (See footnote 8.) If you convince yourself that you are a servant of Allāh and that you wish to worship him, you have to study and understand the Sunna of the holy Apostle. Try to learn the 'Arabic language. True believers need you to understand Allāh and help in establishing the Caliphate. It is the foundation of everything.

The present disposition of the Muslim Umma cannot bring peace, for if Allāh is a just Judge and He punishes anyone who disobeys Him, the followers of Muhammad today are yet to be punished by Allāh according to the Sharī'a. Understand that if the first born of the Children of Israel were not selected by Allāh for His special service because they worshipped the golden calf, how could Allāh accept the followers of Muhammad who have committed the same crime for His special service? It is the warnings, threats, and the law in the Torah, as well as examples of success and failure, that prompts me to call on you to believe in Allāh and follow the actions of Muhammad in at least removing corruption, tyranny, and injustice. I want to know your understanding of Josh. 1:8: "If you obey it completely, you and Israel will be able to take this land." My understanding is similar to my understanding when Muhammad Rasūlullah told 'Umar ibn Khaṭṭab: "On this occasion ten such verses have been sent down to me, that the one who measures up to them will most surely go to paradise."[7] Was there choice or selection in the Sharī'a?

I am not calling on you to pray, fast, or perform the annual pilgrimage. Please, do not observe them. Read carefully Genesis.1-2 and reflect on this beautiful commentary of Reverend Matthew Henry: "That man was made last of all creatures, that it might not be suspected that he had been, any way, a helper to God (Allāh) in the creation of the world: that question must be forever humbling and mortifying to him. . . . Yet it was both an honor and a favor to him that he was made last: an honor, for the method of the creation was to advance from that which was less perfect (although in the holy Qur'ān this defect was not mentioned) to that which is more so; and a favor, for it was not fit he should be lodged in the palace designed for him till it was completely fitted and furnished for his redemption."[8]

There are two categories of "revolution" that the Muslim Umma, the followers of Muhammad must do:

The "revolution" to make the world a safe place for all. This does not necessarily mean strictly abiding by the Sunna of Muhammad Rasūlullah. Allāh forbids injustice. It is known by all and sundry. A just disbeliever can rule people to enjoy their

---

[7] Maudūdi, Abdul A'la. The Meaning of the Qur'ān.(Lahore: Islamic Publications Ltd. 1993),chapter 23.

[8] See Matthew Henry's Complete Commentary on the Whole Bible. (USA. Hendrickson, 1998), 6, Genesis.1:26.

worldly life, by providing employment, housing, security, and a clean environment.

The "revolution" for the comfort of life in the Hereafter. This is not done by the followers of Muhammad Rasūlullah. It can be achieved only through establishing the Caliphate and following the Sunna on the rituals. The two are inseparable.

I am not using 'Arabic names of the apostles, but rather their Latinized-Greek names, for the book is addressing Westerners. I have omitted sending Salāt on the holy Apostle (usually written SAW) when his name is mentioned, because that is to be done only during Salāt. Also, almost every sentence is a reference.

I have used the current translation of the holy Qur'ān, by Dr. Muhammad Taqī-ud-Dīn Al-Hilāli and Dr. Muhammad Muhsin Khan, as well as on one or two occasions that of 'Abdullāh Yūsuf 'Āli. I find the commentary of 'Abdul 'Ala Maududi very useful as well as that by Imām Shawkani. I hope, I have not exceeded the permission to quote one thousand words from the Contemporary English Version of the Promise Study Edition of the Holy Bible. I am grateful once again, to Donna Green for permitting me to quote from *Matthew Henry's Commentary on the Whole Bible*.

Introduction

Mankind in the Holy Qur'ān

Allāh explained the purpose of creating mankind in the holy Qur'ān 51:56: "I only created jinn and mankind to worship Me." The jinn understood the holy Qur'ān to be a recitation from Muhammad Rasūlullah that is worthy of being heard. When the holy Apostle finished reciting the holy Qur'ān, they went to their people, as it says in the holy Qur'ān 46:31-32, "Verily we have heard a Book sent down after Moses confirming what came before it: it guides to the truth and to the Straight Path. O our people! Respond (with obedience) to Allāh's Caller (that is Muhammad Rasūlullah) and believe in him. He (Allāh) will forgive you of your sins, and will save you from a painful torment. And whosoever does not respond to Allāh's Caller, he cannot escape on earth, and there will be no Auliyā' (lords, helpers, supporters, protectors) for him besides Allāh. Those are in manifest error." Thus, the jinn in their confession believed that one needs Allāh's protection, support, and help. It is wrong for one looking for protection to seek it from someone else. They also made the following confessions:[9]

Allāh has no son or wife.

That some fools among them used to utter against Allāh what was an enormity in falsehood.

That men and jinn would not utter a lie against Allāh.

There were men among mankind who took shelter with the males among the jinn, but the jinn increased mankind's sin and

---

9   See the holy Qur'ān 72.

transgression. They were referring to those people in Yemen and the Bani Hanifata.

There were men also who thought that Allāh wouldn't send any Messenger (to mankind or jinn).

That they used to ascend to the heaven and sit in stations hearing the Message of Allāh; but with the arrival of Muhammad Rasūlullah, this privilege was stopped.

That obedience to Allāh is necessary for one to prosper in this world. The source of this prosperity is water--that very substance or element forming a component of mankind and that very element or substance that destroyed the disbelievers of Prophet Noah. Water is the primary source of man's wealth and is yet to be synthesized by man. How could one then turn his hopes, aspirations, and wants to one other than Allāh?

This confession should serve in ending our disputes about Allāh. It is an added springboard for all to comply with the Message delivered by Muhammad Rasūlullah, on behalf of the Messengers and Prophets, mentioned in the scriptures. This is the only way to avoid crises and bring an end to our sufferings. Let us look at the absurdity and stupidity of those accusing Muhammad Rasūlullah with all that they accuse him of, and disbelieving in him, or finding an alternative way for their sustenance.

Why did they not criticize this incident: the confession of the jinn of the Prophet hood of Muhammad Rasūlullah? Did the critics not realize earlier on that Allāh did not need their confession? We should address this confession seriously: Why did the jinn compare the Torah, the Ten Commandments, with what they heard Muhammad Rasūlullah reciting, that is, the holy Qur'ān? Which period were they referring to? How could an event that happened before the destruction of Jerusalem be disputed later by those who believe in what the jinn believed in? Is the story in the holy Qur'ān 34:12, "And we caused a fount of (molten) brass to flow for him, and there were jinn that worked for him by the Leave of his Lord" a lie? Was their belief in the Message of Muhammad Rasūlullah as a recitation from the Torah unequivocally and unerringly meant to be the same as what is in the Injeel, which is the New Testament? Apart from the jinn, Allāh informed us in the holy Qur'ān 17:44 that "The seven heavens and the earth and all that is therein, glorify Him (Allāh) and there is not a thing but glorifies His Praise. But you (mankind) understand not their glorification. Truly, He is Ever Forbearing, Oft-Forgiving."

There is every fraction of information in the holy Qur'ān, detailing us on the absolute existence of Allāh, His Authority, and that obedience to Him involves total submission to His rules and regulations. Certainly, there is very detailed evidence that Allāh has no partner in His Authority. For this, mankind should not be arrogant and feel secure in disobeying Allāh. He is ever, at all times, responsible and accountable for his deeds, both here and in the hereafter. Mankind's collective (negative) responsibility is what is responsible for his downfall in this world. In the Hereafter, the opposite is true. On that Day, no one can plead against his crime and disadvantaged vintage position in failing to fight against injustice and oppression. In this earthly world, one is punished only after solid proofs of his crimes have been established against him. Only deliberate and purposeful crimes are punished. If one confessed to his crime immediately before a judge, the judge is usually lenient and passes mild punishment. But those who are adamant and develop a military attitude of deflection get the maximum penalty. The same is true with the judgment by Allāh. The door of repentance and forgiveness is ever open and available to those with a sincere heart who after their ignorance heard the truth and turned to Allāh.

Those with inadequate knowledge of the message of the holy Apostle always attribute their wickedness and evil deeds to the influence of the devil that is Shaiṭan. There is no excuse for one to apportion blame on Shaiṭan for one's misadventures and misfortunes.[10] This is explained in the holy Qur'ān 15:34-42, in

---

[10] See Exod. (inset) 7:3-5, the Promise Study Edition. Contemporary English Version, 67.

a conversation between Allāh and Shaiṭan, after Shaiṭan refuses to prostrate to Adam:

Allāh said, "Then get out from here, for verily, you are Rajīm (an outcast or a cursed one)."

Shaiṭan said, "O my Lord! Give me respite till the Day they (the dead) will be resurrected."

Allāh said: "Then verily, you are of those deprived. Till the Day of the time appointed."

Shaiṭan said, "O my Lord! Because you misled me, I shall indeed adorn the path of error for them (mankind) on the earth, and I shall mislead them all. Except Your chosen (guided) slaves among them."

Allāh said, "This is the Way which will lead straight to me. Certainly, you shall have no authority over My slaves, except those who follow you of the Ghāwun (Mushrikūn, and those who go astray, criminals, polytheists and evil-doers)."

On the Day of the Hereafter, Shaiṭan will finally absolve himself from misleading one in this worldly life, as in the holy Qur'ān 14:22 it is written, "And Shaiṭan will say when the matter has been decided: "Verily, Allāh promised you a promise of truth. And I too promised you, but I betrayed you. I had no authority over you except that I called you, and you responded to me. So blame me not, but blame yourselves. I cannot help you, nor can you help me. I deny your former act in associating me (Shaiṭan) as a partner with Allāh (by obeying me in the life of the world). Verily, there is a painful torment for the Zālimūn (polytheists and wrong-doers)."

Again, Allāh described the relationship between those who were deemed weak (the governed) and the arrogant (their governors/rulers) in the holy Qur'ān 34:31-32. Those who were deemed weak will say to those who were arrogant: "Had it not been for you, we should certainly have been believers!" And those who were arrogant will say to those who were deemed weak: "Did we keep you back from guidance after it had come to you? Nay, but you were Mujrimīn (polytheists, sinners, disbelievers,

criminals)." Those who were deemed weak will now confess to
their knowledge of the truth that Muhammad Rasūlullah brought
and will say as in the holy Qur'ān 34:33, "Nay, but it was your
plotting by night and day: when you ordered us to disbelieve in
Allāh and set up rivals to Him!"

It is hard to believe how anyone educated, free, and
mentally sound could be unable to distinguish between truth
and falsehood. One is expected to know how to save and make
his life comfortable in this earthly world. Saving one's life is
the primary objective of the message of Allāh, requiring one to
believe in Him alone. Belief in Allāh as the sole authority does
not compromise one's survival. One's survival at that moment
becomes supreme over his belief. Faith in Allāh was never an
instrument to deprivation, impoverishment, or regret, but an
instrument of pleasure, prosperity, freedom, comfort, and above
all, the love of one another.

The faith of Prophet Abraham, according to the holy Qur'ān,
made him to be cast into the pit of fire. But Allāh saved him. He
was childless, but got one after migrating from the focus of evil
and idolatry. Likewise, despite the arrogant high-handedness of
the pharaoh, a believer from his family came out to challenge his
arrogance saying in the holy Qur'ān 40:28, "Would you kill a man
because he says: My Lord is Allāh, and he has come to you with
clear signs (proofs) from your Lord? And if he is a liar, upon him
will be (the sin of) his lie; but if he is telling the truth, then some
of that (calamity) wherewith he threatens you will befall on you."

Likewise, in the holy Qur'ān 36:20-27, is the discourse of
another believer: "O my people! Obey the Messengers. Obey
those who ask no wages of you (for themselves), and who
are rightly guided." That man, according to some Muslim
commentators of the holy Qur'ān, was a sculptor, curving idols.
The incidence happened at Antioch during the prophet hood
of Jesus, the son of Maryam. No one is to obey Allāh without
knowing Him. One must acquire the appropriate knowledge
and practical skill before one starts worshipping Allāh. Yes,

this requirement is exactly like all requirements in this earthly world, when one is required to acquire the appropriate skill and knowledge before he is given a job. We shall be graded in the Hereafter in the manner we are graded in this earthly world-- according to our inputs. We have three classes in this earthly world, while in the Hereafter we shall be classified under seven degrees, according to our educational background, action and skill.[11] In the Hereafter, practical skill carries more weight than educational background.

That one, who recognized the truth, must run away from falsehood. He must stand on his own and obey Allāh. The question of joining evil ones, therefore never arose in Islām. We are all responsible for our deeds and misadventures. This message and warning kept on recurring in the holy Qur'ān, like its recurrence in the Bible. In the holy Qur'ān 22:3-4, Allāh says "And among mankind is he who disputes concerning Allāh, without knowledge, and follows every rebellious (disobedient to Allāh) Shaiṭan. For him (the devil) it is decreed that whosoever follows him, he will mislead him, and will drive him to the torment of the Fire." Therefore, the road map for mankind to prosper, progress, and enjoy the good things Allāh provides for him, involves one's realizing his limitations. He was created from nothing--just mere soil.

There are many such challenges in the holy Qur'ān, calling man to reason and to surrender to Allāh. In the holy Qur'ān 22:5, Allāh engages us saying, "O mankind! If you are in doubt about the Resurrection, then verily We have created you (i.e. Adam) from dust, then from a Nuṭfah (mixed drops of male and female sexual discharge), then from a little lump of flesh--some formed and some unformed (as in the case of miscarriage)--that We may make (it) clear to you (i.e., show you Our Power and ability to do what We will). And We cause whom We will to remain in the wombs for an appointed term, then We bring you out as

---

[11]   The three classes are lower, middle, and high.

infants, then (give you growth) that you may reach your age of full strength. And among you there is he who is brought back to the miserable old age, so that he knows nothing after having known. And you see the earth barren, but when We send down water (rain) on it, it is stirred (to life), and it swells and puts forth every lovely kind (of growth)."

There is no scientist, however prejudiced and hateful he is toward Muhammad Rasūlullah, who will find fault or something doubtful and suspicious in the above plain and articulate exposition. Allāh is addressing only scientists, drawing their attention to the Day of Resurrection--the Day of Judgment--when one is called to account as to why he did not believe in Muhammad Rasūlullah (and by implication a prophet in one's time) and obey him. In the preceding verse Allāh added more weight to round off His call and argument saying, "And it is He Who is able to do all things." In one hundred and sixty words, Allāh explained the 950 and the 63 years spent by Prophet Noah and Muhammad Rasūlullah respectively. Is Allāh a liar? What evidence, sign, or proof is one waiting for to convince him of the might and majesty of Allāh and that He is indeed the LAWGIVER! In other words, I am calling on scientists to ponder on the conclusion of Allāh in the holy Qur'ān 3:6, "He it is Who shapes you in the wombs as He wills. None has the right to be worshipped but He, the All-Mighty, the All-Wise."

Belief in Allāh, obeying Him by following the Sunna of Muhammad Rasūlullah, that is, his actions does not depend upon the volume and depth of one's knowledge. If it is true that 'Abdallāh bin 'Abbas said that the Tafsīr of the holy Qur'ān consists of a part that one needs no one, and 'Abdallāh bin 'Umar said that each letter of the holy Qur'ān is saying to the one reciting the holy Qur'ān: listen to what I am saying to you and obey and heed what I am warning you of, could one listen to someone who is in the grave? Rejecting the warnings and command of a letter of the holy Qur'ān is equivalent to rejecting the warning and command of the 340,000 letters in the holy Qur'ān.

Probably, these observations and explanations by the foremost Sahābas sound untenable and ridiculous today.[12] If, again it is true that by the time one is holding the holy Qur'ān, Muhammad Rasūlullah is in front of him, listening to what one is reciting, is it appropriate for you and me to quote anyone as authority other than the holy Apostle? Then, how can one err? The plain truth is: we cannot read and understand the 'Arabic language; and even if we read and understood, we are not concerned with accountability or our stand in front of Allāh in the Hereafter in the rendering of our account.

---

[12] Secularization of Islam that is true, despite the objection of the followers of Muhammad.

Chapter 1

THE BEGINNING OF CIVILIZATION IN
EGYPT (CIRCA 7,000 B.C.)

Historians describe Egyptian civilization as falling under the following time periods: Ancient Egypt, Ptolemaic, Roman Era, Coptic Era, Islamic Era, Modern History, and Post-modern History. Egypt was once divided into Upper and Lower Egypt, which became united circa 3,000 B.C. Upper Egypt was comprised more of a homogeneous society made up by the Africans, while Lower Egypt was cosmopolitan because of the influence of the Mediterranean Sea, a trade route. Archaeological excavations have revealed much on the history of Egypt. What is relevant to this book is evidence of Prophet Muhammad's assertion that the holy Qur'ān is the solution and an answer to the problems and needs of mankind.

In the Holy Bible, the book of Genesis tells us that Egypt was founded by one of the sons of Ham, a son of Prophet Noah. Probably he migrated to Egypt and settled there. However, the Talmud does not mention the name Egypt. Nothing was mentioned about Egypt until during the visit of Prophet Abraham, after escaping from his people worshipping idols. Egypt, like Nineveh, was also a delta region where the river Nile formed by the union of the White and Blue Nile enters the Mediterranean Sea. Probably, the Nile valley at that time was a business center, helped by its agricultural proceeds and the beauty of the desert. The message Allāh revealed to the Egyptians between Egypt's beginning and the arrival of Prophet Abraham through the arrival of Prophet Joseph in Egypt was not known. The famine in Palestine forced the Children of Jacob to travel to Egypt to buy grains. On one such visit with his brothers, some of them made up their mind to kill Joseph by throwing him in a pit. According to the book of Genesis, his brother Reuben objected. According to the holy Qur'ān, Joseph was then sold to a king's official in charge of the palace of Potiphar for a paltry sum. This could have taken place around 1700 B.C.

The story of Joseph and his brothers is beautifully mentioned in the holy Qur'ān, to fit into the lesson intended for mankind as mentioned in the book of Genesis 41. The history of Prophet Joseph is the practical interpretation and meaning of the following verses:-

In the holy Qur'ān 58:11, "Allāh will exalt in degree those of you who believe, and those who have been granted knowledge. And Allāh is Well-Acquainted with what you do."

In the holy Qur'ān 39:9, "Are those who know equal to those who know not? It is only men of understanding who will remember."

In the holy Qur'ān 16:73, "And they worship others besides Allāh--such as do not and cannot own any provision for them from the heavens or the earth."

In the holy Qur'ān 10:31, "Who provides for you from the sky and the earth? Or who owns hearing and sight? And who brings out the living and the dead and brings out the dead from the living? And who disposes the affairs?" They will say, "Will you not then be afraid of Allāh's punishment (for setting up rivals in worship with Allāh?"

One will keep on seeing the truth, every time one reflects on the holy Qur'ān. This truth will never be exhausted according to the holy Qur'ān 18:109: "If the sea were ink for (writing) the Words of my Lord, surely, the sea would be exhausted before the Words of my Lord would be finished, even if We brought (another sea) like it for its aid."

The lessons behind the spiritual story of Prophet Joseph can be summarized as the fulfillment of the Sharī'a, which Allāh revealed to Prophet Noah. Prophet Jacob had eleven children. Allāh promised the righteous abundance of children, for they are a pleasure and delight to the eye. Prophet Joseph according to Muslim historians was one of the most beautiful youths in the world. Worldly desires, leading to jealously, are inadvertently caused by man's instinct for affection. Jacob loved Joseph out of the reality of the physical world. Children are loved more than youths.

In addition to forbidding killing, as in the case of Cain and Abel, Sharī'a also warns of the following:

No one knows the unseen. One should always be hopeful and upright.

Affection and love are part and parcel of human nature.

Shaiṭan will never have control on the righteous, since man is capable of warding off evil.

Illegal sexual relationship is the greatest and most attractive evil and destroyer of civilization.

A man of faith will always reveal openly his faith, as an invitation to others.

One should always rely on Allāh and be guided through the knowledge Allāh bestowed on him.

Mankind cannot exist in isolation. He is always in need of someone's help.

Cause and effect are under the mercy of Allāh. The famine was caused by Allāh. The solution was solved by Allāh only through his righteous servant.

Allāh gives leadership only to the righteous one.

Forgiveness is the hallmark of Islām.

Prophet Joseph

Much of what is known today of Egypt was the product of Egypt's record in monuments, inscriptions, and tombs. Prophet Joseph came to Egypt during the Hyksos Dynasties XV to XVIII. The Hyksos were from Syria, and probably Israelites, although

3

some historians regard them to be Phoenicians, Amalekites, or Hittites. According to 'Abdul Āla Maududi, they were regarded as foreign invaders, who got the opportunity of establishing their kingdom because of the internal feuds in Egypt. Those who believed the Hyksos to be Israelites argued that if they were not Israelites, Prophet Joseph could not have ascended to such a high position.[13]

We should not disregard its cosmopolitan nature and its agricultural potential, which made it a refuge for her neighbors during famine. It was, therefore, like the Western capitalist countries of today. The Hyksos' establishment was similar to that of Syria, with a seeming lordship over the native dynasties of Upper Egypt.

The Children of Israel lived in Egypt for nearly four hundred and fifty years. We are sure of the eighty years covering the birth of Prophet Moses and the Exodus. With an initial population of seventy inhabitants, they grew to more than six hundred thousand able-bodied fighters by the time of the Exodus. Prophet Abraham and Jacob practiced polygamy. This could be the reason why the offspring of Prophet Jacob populated Egypt.

The tribe of Prophet Joseph at the beginning of his reign was in a minority with no economic influence. The Egyptians were at that time living in affluence and had no experience in managing their resources in times of hardship. This was in contrast to Syria and adjacent provinces, often affected by draught. This could be inferred from the Prophet Joseph's interpretation of the dream of the King of Egypt, of seven fat cows and seven lean ones. There was never a place for nepotism, since a civilized and well-integrated community always looks for the best to be in charge of their affairs. It was never a democracy of the majority by the illiterates, but that of able-bodied, educated, moral, and Allāh fearing individuals.

---

[13] There is no place for partisanship in the Sunna of Muhammad Rasūlullah.

The Hyksos probably never experienced trust in leadership from Allāh. Prophet Joseph, being at that time the most educated, was given the responsibility of distributing the country's gross national and domestic product. He did this efficiently, faithfully, and effectively, so that within a short time, the people of Egypt and her neighbors enjoyed peace, stability, and prosperity. Prophet Joseph never thought of staying permanently in Egypt. It was Providence that brought him there. He knew the Promised Land to be their home at that time. So he told his brothers and sons, in Genesis 50:24-25, "I won't live much longer. But God will take care of you and lead you out of Egypt to the land God promised Abraham, Isaac, and Jacob. Now promise me that you will take my body with you when God leads you to that land."

Neither the Holy Bible nor the Talmud says anything about the Children of Israel immediately after the death of Prophet Joseph in Egypt. One could assume that they continued living in prosperity, irrespective of who was their leader. They were at least guided practically on the theory and practice of supply and demand in the time of distress and want.

It was suggested that an internal strife led to the overthrow of the Hyksos dynasty at the end of fifteenth century B.C. According to Maudūdi, the formation of a nationalist movement ignited the ultimate overthrowing of the Hyksos dynasty, and the exile of about two hundred and fifty thousand Amalekites. The force behind that formation has not been spelt out by historians. Most likely, it could have been arrogance and indifference on the part of those playing with the upper hand over the citizenry. The Children of Israel's influence was thus exposed and left unprotected. Indeed the holy Qur'ān mentions and emphasizes the streamline flow of Prophets, from the Children of Israel to guide the then nations. The wide gap between the change of the bodyguards and the birth of Prophet Moses was very sketchy, if not totally forgotten.

Why did the Israelites and those misunderstanding the holy Qur'ān, say nothing positive on this period? Is this silence not an indicator that once the holy Qur'ān is silent on an issue, the whole world is deaf, dumb, and blind on that issue? Could it be possible that someone introduced idol worship in Egypt, which was adopted by those in authority after the death of Prophet Joseph? Did the teaching of Prophet Joseph stop immediately after his death? What happened to the Children of Israel is an issue that can be best revealed by the Levi tribes.

According to 'Abdullāh Yūsuf Ali, the pharaoh who "knew not Prophet Joseph" looked upon the Israelites as contemptible slaves, not worthy of a thought except when they revolted, and then only as a despised race fit to be punished and kept in its place.[14] What is interesting is how power slipped from them, turning them into slaves within a short period.

Prophet Moses

Joseph and his brothers died, and the children of Israel multiplied in the land of Egypt. They could have held important positions, playing a role in the political, cultural, and economic life of the country. It would not be surprising if they stirred the jealousy of the native Egyptians, who felt outshone by the "foreigners."[15]

The old pharaoh died too, and a new king ascended the throne. He had no sympathy or love for the children of Israel and chose to forget all that Joseph had done for Egypt. He decided to take action against the growing influence and the high birth rate of the children of Israel. He called his council together, and they advised him to enslave these people and oppress them before they grew too powerful. The pharaoh limited the personal freedom of the Hebrews, put heavy taxes on them, and recruited their men into forced labor battalions, under the supervision of harsh taskmasters. Thus the Children of Israel had to build cities,

---

[14] A. Yusuf Ali: The Qur'ān: Text, Translation and Commentary. Maryland. Amana Corp, 1983. 405.

[15] The 'Arabs have forgotten this lesson.

erect monuments, construct roads, work in the quarries, and hew stones or make bricks and tiles. But the more the Egyptians oppressed them, and the harder the restrictions imposed upon them became, the more the Children of Israel increased and multiplied. Finally, when the pharaoh saw that forcing the Hebrews to do hard work did not succeed in suppressing their rapidly growing numbers he decreed that all newly born male children of the Hebrews be thrown into the Nile River. Only daughters should be permitted to live.

Thus, the pharaoh hoped to end the numerical increase of the Jewish population, and at the same time, to eliminate a danger, which, according to the predictions of his astrologers, threatened his own life in the person of one to be born to the Children of Israel.

The Levites

According to Jewish history, the only group of Jews that escaped enslavement was the tribe of Levi. Levi was the last of Jacob's sons to die, and his influence over his tribe was both great and lasting. They had taken over the Torah academy Jacob had established in Goshen, and they instructed the children of Israel in the knowledge of G-d and His holy teachings. They became preoccupied with spiritual matters and did not mix with the neighboring tribes, while many of their brethren had given up their old customs and way of life. Except for their language, clothing, and names, many of the children of Israel had become assimilated into the social and cultural environment of their Egyptian neighbors, and they were the ones to arouse the wrath of the Egyptians. Only the children of Levi, therefore, were spared the slavery and oppression, which the Egyptians imposed upon the rest of Israel.

Egypt after the Exodus

The pharaoh and his authority centering on idol worshipping eventually disappeared. It is to be noted that some of the

Egyptians were averse to the worship of idols. Their number is not known. Since all those drowned were the courtiers of the pharaoh, invariably signaling the end of idol worship, one can suppose that the Egyptians returned to the worship of the Allāh of Abraham, Isaac, and Jacob.

The holy Qur'ān alludes to the fact that Prophet Joseph did not change the Sharī'a. In the holy Qur'ān 12:75, Prophet Joseph proclaimed the following Sharī'a: "His penalty should be that he, in whose bag it is found, should be held for the punishment (of the crime). Thus we punish the Zālimūn (wrong-doers)." The same judgment also appears in the Torah: "But Joseph refused their offer and said that only the one in whose possession the cup had been found was to remain as slave; the others could return to their father in Canaan."[16]

The holy Qur'ān mentions Zul-qarnain, identified by some Muslim historians as Alexander the Great and by others as King Cyrus. 'Abdallāh Yusuf Ali had the strong belief that Zul-qarnain (The "two-horned") was Alexander the Great, as the description given in the holy Qur'ān fits into his record history. On the other hand, Maududi argued that he could only be Cyrus the Great, the Persian whose Empire extended east to west and south to Egypt and Libya. His rule was that of a pious believer, a King who treated all with justice and equality.

According to the Bible, Prophet Daniel saw in his vision that the united kingdom of Media and Persia was like a two-horned ram before the rise of the Greeks. The Jews had a very high opinion of the "the two-horned" one, because it was his invasion that brought about the downfall of the kingdom of Babylon and the liberation of the Israelites. Having visited Egypt and established his kingdom, the Egyptians must have

---

[16] If those passages in the Talmud and the Bible that resemble others in the holy Qur'ān were not extracts by their writers from the holy Qur'ān, why is it that wherever the holy Qur'ān is silent, the Talmud and Bible are also silent.

worshipped the Allāh of Prophet Abraham. The Persian and Assyrian invasions ultimately weakened the power of Egypt. The Persians held sway in Egypt until the Thirty-first Dynasty, when the last pharaoh fled to Ethiopia in 340 B.C. This was followed by the Macedonian Period--323-30 B.C. and the Roman Period--30 B.C-639 A.D., after which the 'Arab and Turkish conquests evolved into modern Egypt and Muslim Egyptian civilization.

Egypt then has had a checkered history. The influence of the Roman civilization and other countries on this region because of its important trade routes should not be forgotten. Abūl Hasan 'Ali Nadwi explains:

> In some cases sovereignty was considered to be the special prerogative of a particular group or country. It was an article of faith with the Romans that they were the sovereign race and all other races had been created to be subservient to them. The other races were like veins and arteries whose sole function was to carry the blood to and from the heart, which was Rome. The Romans could over-ride any law, violate any right and ravish any country. Community of religion or treaties of friendship with Rome were no protection against high-handedness of the Romans.
>
> The Roman dependencies had no legal status or administrative autonomy within the Empire. They were, so to say, like the she-camel, which gives milk and is used for transport, but receives, in return, only as much of fodder as might keep its back strong and udder full.

Quoting Briffault about the Roman Empire, Nadwi says,

> The intrinsic cause that doomed and condemned the Roman Empire was not any growing corruption, but the corruption, the evil, the adaptation to fact in its very origin and being. No system of human civilization that

9

is false in its very principle, in its very foundation, can save itself by any amount of cleverness and efficiency in the means by which that falsehood is carried and maintained, by any amount of superficial adjustment and tinkering. It is doomed root and branch as long as the root dooms what it was. The Roman Empire was, as we have seen, a device for the enrichment of a small class of people by the exploitation of mankind. That business enterprise was carried out with all honesty, all the fairness, and justice compatible with its very nature, and with admirable judgment and ability. But all those virtues could not save the fundamental falsehood, the fundamental wrong from its consequence.

Quoting Dr. Alfred Butler, he writes: "The whole machinery of rule in Egypt was directed to the sole purpose of wringing profit of the ruled for the benefit of the rulers. There was no idea of governing for the advantage of the governed, of raising people in the social scale, of developing the moral or even the material resources of the country. It was an alien domination founded on force and making little pretence of sympathy with the subject race."[17]

---

[17]   Nadwi, Abul Hasan Ali. Islam and the World. (Riyadh: International Islamic Publication house,1992), 34-35.

Chapter 2

SECULARIZATION, THE SECULAR, AND SECULARISM

According to Syed Muhammad Al-Naquib Al-Attas,[18] Jacques Maritain, a leading Christian philosopher and one regarded by Christians as among the foremost of this century, described how Christianity and the Western world were going through a grave crisis. It had been brought about, he thought, by contemporary events arising out of experience and an understanding and interpretation of life as manifested in the trend of neo-modernist thought emerging from among the Christians themselves and the intellectuals--philosophers, theologians, poets, novelists, writers, and artists--who represent Western culture and civilization. Some Christian theologians and Central European philosophers-sociologists, have envisaged the rise of science and the overthrow of religion, and believed, according to secular logic, that society has been "evolving" and developing from the primitive to the modern stages and that metaphysics is in transition from theology to science.[19]

From the moment Nietzsche began to cry that "God is dead, "which got mingled with "Christianity is dead," some influential

---

[18]   Al-Attas, Syed Muhammad Al-Naquib. Islam and Secularism. (Lahore: Art Printing Works, 1978).

[19]   In Islam, our thoughts and intentions are included in the knowledge Allah taught Prophet Adam. Studying the universe is part of our lives and is encouraged by Allah in the holy Qur'ān.

Protestant theologians started to initiate preparations for the laying out of a new theological ground above the wreckage in which lay the dissolute body of traditional Christianity, out of which a new secularized Christianity might be resurrected. They hypothesized that secularization has its roots in biblical faith and is the fruit of the Gospel; and therefore, rather than oppose the secularizing process, Christianity must realistically welcome it as a process congenial to its true nature and purpose. Their counterparts from America and Europe also found cause to call for radical changes in the interpretation of the Gospel and in the nature and role of the Church, which would merge them logically and naturally into the picture of contemporary Western man and his world envisaged in the secular panorama of life.

Even those Christians who are opposed to this new theory and thinking are themselves unconsciously assiduous accomplices in that very process to the extent that those aware of the dilemma confronting them have raised general alarm. There has now emerged with increasing numbers and persistence what Maritain called "immanent apostasy" within the Christian community. They realize and believe as a matter of historical fact that the ground itself will be ever-shifting, that by the very relativistic nature of their new interpretation a new version will ultimately gain prominence and even that will be replaced by another and so on, each giving way to another as future social changes demand. They visualize the contemporary experience of secularization as part of the revolutionary process of human history. They view it as part of the irresistible process of "coming of age," of growing into maturity when they will have to "put away childish things" and learn to have "the courage to be" a part of the *invisible* process of social and political change and the corresponding change in values, almost in line with the Marxian vision of human history.

These portents of drastic change aroused the consternation of the traditional Catholic theologians, whose appeal of distress caused Pope John XXIII to call for an *aggiornamento* to study ways and means to overcome, or at least to contain, the crisis in the Christian religion and theology. The Church attempted to resist secularization through the enunciation of the ecumenical movement and the initiation of meaningful dialogues with Muslims and others in the hope not only of uniting the Christian community but of enlisting our conscious or unconscious support as well as exorcising the immanent enemy. Nonetheless, they admit, albeit grudgingly, that their theology as understood and interpreted during these last seven centuries is now indeed completely out of touch with the "spirit of the times" and is in need of serious scrutiny as a prelude towards revision.

The term "secular," from the Latin *saeculum,* conveys a meaning with a marked dual connotation of *time* and *location*, time referring to the "now" or present sense of it and the location to the "world" or worldly sense of it. Thus *saeculum* means "the present time, which refers to contemporary events in this world. The term *secular* refers to the *condition* of the world at this particular time period.

This spatio-temporal connotation conveyed in the concept secular is derived historically out of the experience and consciousness born of the fusion of the Greco-Roman and Judaic traditions in Western Christianity. It is this 'fusion' of the mutually conflicting elements of the Hellenic and Hebrew world views, which have deliberately been incorporated into Christianity, that modern Christian theologians and intellectuals recognize as problematic, in that the former views existence as basically *spatial* and the latter as basically *temporal* in such wise that the arising confusion of world views becomes the root of their epistemological and hence also theological problems.

"Secularization" is defined by the Dutch theologian Cornelis van Peursen as the deliverance of man "first from religious and then metaphysical control over his reason and his language." It is the "loosing of the world from religious and quasi-religious understandings of itself, the dispelling of all closed world views, the breaking of all supernatural myths and sacred symbols . . . the 'defatalization of history,' the discovery by man that he has been left with the world on his hands, that he can no longer blame fortune or the furies for what he does with it . . . ; [it is] man turning his attention away from worlds beyond and toward this world and this time" [20]

Secularization encompasses not only the political and social aspects of life, but also inevitably the cultural, for it denotes "the disappearance of religious determination of the symbols of cultural integration." It implies "a historical process, almost certainly irreversible, in which society and culture are delivered from tutelage to religious control and closed metaphysical world views. It is a "liberating development," and the end product of secularization is historical relativism. . . . The integral components in the dimensions of secularization are the disenchantment of nature, the separation of religion from politics, and the deconsecrating of values.

By the "disenchantment of nature"--a term and concept borrowed from German sociologist Max Weber-- the Secularists mean as van Peursen means, the freeing of nature from its religious overtones; and this involves the dispelling of animistic spirits and gods and magic from the natural world, separating it from God and distinguishing man from it, so that man may no longer use nature for his needs and plans, and hence create historical change and "development."

By separating religion from politics the secularists mean the abolition of sacral legitimatizing of political power and authority, which is the prerequisite for political and social change, allowing for the emergence of the political process.

By the deconsecrating of values they mean the rendering transient and relative all cultural creations and every value system, which for them includes religion and world views having ultimate and final significance; man would be free to create the change and immerse himself in the "evolutionary" process. This

---

[20]   Al-Attas, Syed Muhammad Al-Naquib. Islām and Secularism. (Lahore: Art Printing Works, 1978. 15)

attitude towards values demands an awareness on the part of secular man of the relativity of his own views and beliefs; he must live with the realization that the rules and ethical codes of conduct that guide his own life will change with the times and generations. This attitude demands what they call "maturity," and hence secularization is also a process of evolution of the consciousness of man from the infantile to the mature states, and is defined as "the removal of juvenile dependence from every level of society . . . the process of maturing and assuming responsibility . . . the removal of religious and metaphysical supports and putting man on his own."[21]

They secularist say that this change of values is also the recurrent phenomenon of "conversion," which occurs "at the intersection of the action of history on man and the action of man on history." They call it "responsibility, the acceptance of adult accountability."[22]

According to Al-Attas, the definition of secularization which describes its true nature to our understanding corresponds exactly with what is going on in the spiritual and intellectual and rational and physical and material life of Western man and his culture and civilization; and it is true only when applied to describe the nature and existential condition of Western culture and civilization. The claim that secularization has its roots in biblical faith and that it is the fruit of the Gospel has no substance in historical fact. Secularization has its roots not in biblical faith, but in the *interpretation* of biblical faith by Western man; it is not the fruit of Gospel, but is the fruit of the long history of philosophical and metaphysical conflict in the religious and purely rationalistic *worldview* of Western man. The interdependence of the interpretation and the worldview

---

21 Ibid., p. 16
22 Ibid., p.17

operates in history and is seen as a 'development'; indeed it has been so logically in history because for Western man the truth, or God Himself, has become incarnate in man in time and in history. [23]

Of all the great religions of the world Christianity alone shifted its center of origin from Jerusalem to Rome, symbolizing the beginnings of the *westernization* of Christianity and its gradual and successive permeation of Western elements that in subsequent periods of its history produced and accelerated the momentum of secularization. There were, and still are from the Muslim point of view, two Christians: the original and true one and the Western version of it.

Original and true Christianity conformed to Islām. Those who before the advent of Islām believed in the original and true teachings of Jesus (on whom be Peace!) were true believers (*mu'min* and Muslim). After the advent of Islām they would, if they had known the fact of Islām and if their belief (Iman) and submission (Islām) were truly sincere, have joined the ranks of Islām. Those who from the very beginning have altered the original and departed from the true teachings of Jesus (Peace be upon him!) were the creative initiators of Western Christianity, the Christianity known to us. Among the People of the Book, and with reference to Western Christianity, those who inwardly did not profess real belief in the doctrine of the Trinity, the Incarnation, and the Redemption, as well as other details of dogma connected with these doctrines, who privately professed belief in God alone and in the Prophet Jesus (on whom be Peace!), who set up regular prayer and did good works in the way they were spiritually led to do, who while in this condition of faith were truly and sincerely unaware of Islām, were those referred to in the holy Qur'ān as nearest to the Believers in Islām.[24]

---

[23]   End quote. Reference Ibid. pp.17-21

[24]   See the holy Qur'ān 5:85-88.

The separation of the Church and state, of religious and temporal powers, was never the result of an attempt on the part of Christianity to bring about secularization; on the contrary, it was the result of the secular Western philosophical attitude set against what is considered the anti-secular encroachment of the ambivalent Church based on the teachings of the eclectic religion. The separation represented for Christianity a *status quo* in the losing battle against secular forces; and even that status quo was gradually eroded away so that today very little ground is left for the religion to play any significant social and political role in the secular states of the Western world.

Moreover, the Church when it wielded power was always vigilant in acting against scientific enquiry and purely rational investigation of truth, which is seen in the light of present circumstances brought about by such "scientific" enquiry and "rational" investigation as it developed in Western history is, however, partly now seen to be justifiable. Contrary to secularization, Christianity has always preached a "closed" metaphysical worldview, and it did not really deconsecrate values, including idols and icons; it assimilated them into its own mold. Furthermore, it involved itself in sacral legitimatization of political power and authority, which is anathema to the secularizing process.

The westernization of Christianity, then, marked the beginning of its secularization. Secularization is the result of the misapplication of Greek philosophy in Western theology and metaphysics, which in the seventeenth century logically led to the scientific revolution enunciated by Descartes, who opened the doors no doubt to skepticism; and successively in the eighteenth and nineteenth centuries and in our own times, to atheism and agnosticism, to utilitarianism, dialectical materialism, evolutionism, and historicism. Christianity has attempted to resist secularization but has failed; and the danger is that having failed to contain it, the influential modernist and theologians are now urging Christians to join it. Their fanciful claim that the historical process that made the world secular has its roots in biblical faith and is the fruit of the Gospel must be seen as an ingenious way of attempting to extricate Western Christianity from its own self-originated dilemmas. While it is no doubt ingenious, it is also self-destructive, for this claim necessitates the accusation that for the past two millennia Christians, including their apostles, saints, theologians, theorists, and scholars, had misunderstood and misinterpreted the Gospel, had made a grave fundamental mistake thereby, and misled Christians in the course of their spiritual and intellectual history.

If what they say is accepted as valid, how can they be *certain* that those early Christians and their followers throughout the centuries who misunderstood, misinterpreted, mistook, and misled on such an important, crucial matter as a secular message of the Gospel and secularizing mission of the Church, *did not also* misunderstand, misinterpret, mistake, and mislead on the paramount, vital matter of the religion and belief itself; on the doctrine of the Trinity; on the doctrine of Incarnation; of the doctrine of Redemption, and on the *reporting* and *formulation* and *conceptualization* of Revelation?

Since it ought to be a matter of absolute, vital importance for them to *believe* that the *report* of the very early Christians about God, Who revealed Himself to them was *true*, it would be futile for them to overcome this problem by resorting to belief in human "evolution" and historicity and the relativity of truths according to the experience and consciousness of each stage of human history, for we cannot accept an answer based merely on subjective experience and consciousness and "scientific" conjecture where no criteria for knowledge and certainty exist. What they say amounts to meaning that God sent His Revelation or revealed Himself to man when man was in his infantile stage of evolution. "Infantile" man then interpreted the revelation and conceptualized it in dogmatic and doctrinal forms expressing his faith in it. Then when man matured, he found the dogmatic and doctrinal conceptualizations of "infantile" man no longer adequate for him to express his faith in his time, and so he

18

must develop them as he develops; otherwise, they become inadequate. Thus they maintain that the dogmatic and doctrinal conceptualizations evolve, but they evolve not because they are from the very beginning necessarily inadequate, but because as man develops, they become inadequate if they fail to develop correspondingly.

Western man is always inclined to regard his culture and civilization as man's cultural vanguard; and his own experience and consciousness as those representative of the most "evolved" of the species, so that we are all in the process of lagging behind them, as it were, and will come to realize the same experience and consciousness in due course. It is with this attitude that the secularists, believing in their own absurd theories of human evolution, view human history and development and religion and religious experience and consciousness. We reject the validity of the truth of their assertion, with regard to secularization and their theories and interpretation of knowledge based on their experience and consciousness and belief, to speak on our behalf.

Religious belief certainly refers to the existence of a supernatural power that has overall control on the affairs of the world. Fundamentally, this supernatural power refers to GOD. With all due respect to Latinized Greeks, god is the same name as Allāh in the Semitic language of the 'Arabs. Who else will blame a blind man for falling into a pit? Secularization as defined and explained by Al-Attas should in no way ever make an imprint into someone's thought, lest that be discussed and written in our news media, broadcast on our television and radio stations.

There is no harm in the definition of secularization relating to man's awareness of his environment and the necessity for him to do whatever is necessary to maintain his living and existence. The threat of his environment was present at that time, but not recognized as a threat to his existence. We have now the concepts of "time," "now," "present," "location," "world," and "worldly" challenging us. Whatever steps one would have to take to neutralize the threats must be from something at his disposal that he can manipulate with such precision as to neutralize them. Neutralization is the first step that can lead to the elimination or containment of a threat.

We are not created as leviathans, but as animals given all the necessary tools and materials for cultivating the soil and looking after our animals. No one can say that the devastation done by lions to the sheep of Abel or what the ravaging insects did to the farmland of Cain were their works. Abel could not bury Cain without the intervention of YHWH--the Lord. Prophet Noah never knew how to construct a ship, but only by the command and guidance of Allāh. Prophet Abraham was the first to practice circumcision. How did Prophet Moses know the shrub to use to neutralize the bitterness of the spring water after they crossed the Red Sea? Man cannot be independent of Allāh. Did Allāh right from the beginning not provide all that man needs for his survival? There is no difference between today and yesterday. Everything goes back to Allāh. Those civilizations received inspirations during their time, but today our inspirations are in the laboratory. Allāh has made this clear, in the holy Qur'ān 45:13, "And has subjected to you all that is in the heavens and all that is in the earth, it is all as a favor and kindness from Him. Verily, in it are signs for a people who think deeply."

If one looks at some Ahādith of the holy Apostle, one can immediately see the Islāmic aspect and concept of secularization. Indeed, the Final Message was never historically new. What it did was only to streamline the facts and make clear what was misconceived, misunderstood, misinterpreted, and hidden due to prejudice and hatred. Faith was an indelible ideology full of logic that resisted adumbration of the past. This is the essence in sending Muhammad Rasūlullah to mankind. He can technically be said to have brought "secularism," since he is the seal of the Apostles, the Imām of the Messengers. His Sunna did not project a closed world view and an absolute set of values in line with an ultimate historical purpose having a final significance for man.

For example, Huzaifa bin Yamani asked the holy Apostle:

'O the Messenger of Allāh! Will there be a time when people will forget this blessing and plunge themselves into evil?'

The holy Apostle replied, 'Yes! That will be the time when they will forget my instructions and practice and guide people not in accordance with the way and manner I guided you.'

Huzaifa asked, 'Will there be a time worse than this?'

The holy Apostle replied, Yes! People will be inviting people to do acts that will lead them to the Hell-fire.'

Huzaifa asked again, 'What are their characteristics?'

The holy Apostle said, 'They are those who resemble us as they will be speaking "Arabic." That is they will be explaining my Sunna to their people in their language.'

Huzaifa asked, "What then do you command me if I lived to that time?'

The holy Apostle replied, 'Always be in the company of Jama'a of three believers and their Caliph.'[25]

Huzaifa asked, 'But what of, if they do not have a Caliph and therefore have no Jamā'a (community of three people obeying the Sunna of Muhammad)?'

The holy Apostle replied, 'Leave that sect completely, and be on your own, even if you cling to the trunk of a tree, until death overtakes you.'[26]

---

[25] See the Torah, the history of prophet Ibrāhim. "Jama'a" does not carry the meaning of a multitude. It refers to a righteous man. This referred to prophet Ibrāhim.

[26] Shātibi, Allāma Muhaqq Abī Ishāq Ibrāhim bin Mūsa bin Muhammad Lahmi. Al-'Itisām. Manama. Maktabat Tawhīd. 2000. P. 105

Arising from the adulteration of the original teaching of Prophet Moses and Jesus, the son of Maryam, through the migration of the Injeel (the New Testament) from Jerusalem to Rome, Islāmic secularism is the reversal of that concept. The world must learn and stand by the teaching of Muhammad Rasūlullah.

Secularization, as it applies to the holy Qur'ān, refers only to the sciences describing the physical world and its animal kingdom. We are continuously doing research to understand the nature of the universe and mankind. The Sunna covering the rituals is also not totally beyond secularization. For example, we can use aerosol water to perform ablution. We use a geo-magnetic compass to locate the Ka'ba. Saving life is as important as any article of faith. Man must be honored and respected.

Secularization Applied to Muslims

The Western Christian world never claimed to be fighting Islām. This is a sound statement, whose import and meaning the Christians do not understand. They are indirectly saying that they have recognized the continuity of the message of Muhammad Rasūlullah and that his Allāh (God) is the Allāh of Abraham, Ishmael, Isaac, Jacob, and the tribes. Their claim should be: They are fighting the extremists among the Muslims. By this, I understand them to be referring to those self-proclaimed followers of Muhammad Rasūlullah who do not have the qualifications to speak on the duties and actions of Muhammad Rasūlullah, and yet claim to be his followers.

Therefore the ones the West claim to be fighting among the followers of Muhammad Rasūlullah are those that Allāh, Muhammad, the angels, the sincere followers of Muhammad Rasūlullah, and all creatures are cursing. Allāh made this plain in the holy Qur'ān 2:159, "Verily, those who conceal the clear proofs, evidences, and the guidance, which We have sent down, after We have made it clear for the people in the Book, they are the ones cursed by Allāh and cursed by the cursers." Unfortunately these are the ones the Western Christian world is befriending and supporting. The thinking of the West is therefore a paradox.

Islām, in particular the Sunna of the holy Apostle, is facing a crisis more serious and devastating than what Christianity suffered subsequent to its migration from Jerusalem to Rome. The final Message is universal and cannot therefore be expected to stay only in Makka and Medina. Had not Allāh promised to protect it, that is the Sunna of the holy Apostle, it could have disappeared in 40 A.H. In fact, the Sunna of the holy Apostle has virtually disappeared except as described by him, from the very few of his followers who have climbed the mountaintop with their grazing sheep.

The distinction between the holy Qur'ān and the Sunna of the holy Apostle was made by 'Āli ibn Abī Tālib, when he sent 'Abdullāh bin 'Abbas to convince the then party fighting him over the Caliphate. He instructed him not to engage them with the holy Qur'ān, for it has many sides and faces. He should engage them with the Sunna of the holy Apostle, for it has only one side and face. The followers of Muhammad Rasūlullah are confused about the nature of Muhammad, as the earlier Christians were confused about the nature of Allāh (God).

The crime of past generations is easily forgiven by Allāh, while that of the followers of Muhammad will never be forgiven, unless one gets the prescribed punishment here. The activities performed by Muhammad Rasūlullah are the ideals and standard, couched in such a manner that no one will ever claim that he is unable to perform them. But his followers are continuously claiming inability to follow them, but that Allāh will forgive them.

The association of Western Christians with Muslims not elected according to the democratic process set up by the holy Apostle, and their acceptance of the distortion of the meaning and import of the Sunna of the holy Apostle from the preachers and jurists close to the door of power, has confused the West. Because of their ignorance and their friendship with tyrannical

Muslim authorities in order to benefit from Muslim wealth, especially oil and the sales of arms, Western authorities regard anyone calling for the establishment of the Sunna of Muhammad Rasūlullah a terrorist and an extremist. But Allāh has by today proved them to be wrong, for if their tyrannical friends were on the Straight Path, the current uprising in Tunisia, Egypt, Yemen, Bahrain, Jordan, Qatar, and other countries could never have surfaced.

The Western Christians should better open their eyes and read the meaning of the holy Qur'ān. Muhammad never forbade the Jews in Medina to read the holy Qur'ān; rather, he would refer and inform them of whatever Sharī'a is revealed. The revelation of the Sharī'a lasted for six years after the Hijrah, to answer the challenges of the Levi tribe of the Children of Israel in Medina. Nobody ever stole in Medina; nobody was given the punishment of amputating the limb. The case of stoning Mā'iz was done according to the Torah and not the Sunna of Muhammad Rasūlullah at that time. The difference is regarding secularism--the demand in that time for mercy, justice, individual rights, education, and finally confession.

Chapter 3

THE FORMATION OF
THE MUSLIM UMMA

An Umma means a group of people, living in a particular area, comprising three people living under the Sunna of the holy Apostle. A pre-Islāmic 'Arab poet, an-Nābigha adh-Dhubyānī, defined Umma in his poetry, saying:

"I swear by it, and leave behind
No suspicion in your soul.
Can a man with *Umma* then go astray?[27]

The Muslim Umma was established with the migration of Muhammad Rasūlullah to Medina. The first thing he did was to compose the Medina Covenant, as he was invited to come and settle the disputes between the Levi tribe of the Children of Israel and the tribes of Aws and Khazraj. The covenant, well recorded by historians, ran something like this:

In the name of Allāh, the Compassionate, the Merciful. This is a document from Muhammad the Prophet governing the relation between the believers and the Muslims of the Quraysh and Yathrīb, and those who followed them and joined them and labored with them.[28] They are one community to the exclusion of

---

[27]   Helmut Gätje. Qur'ān and its Exegesis: Selected Texts with Classical and Modern Muslim Interpretations(London: Routledge &Kegan Paul Ltd. 1976) 93.

[28]   This is a very important statement and the wordings should be as they were. A believer is that one who believes in the articles of

all men. The Quraysh emigrants according to their present custom shall pay the blood wit within their number and shall redeem their prisoners with the kindness and justice common among believers. Believers shall not leave anyone destitute among them by not paying his redemption money or blood wit in kindness.

A believer shall not take as an ally the freedman of another Muslim against him. The Allāh-fearing believers shall be against the rebellious or him who seeks to spread injustice, sin, enmity, or corruption between believers; the hand of every man shall be against him even if he be a son of one of them. A believer shall not slay a believer for the sake of an unbeliever, nor shall he aid an unbeliever against a believer. Allāh's protection is one; the least of them may give protection to a stranger on their behalf.

Believers are friends one to the other to the exclusion of outsiders. To the Jew who follows us belongs help and equality. He shall not be wronged, nor shall his enemies be aided.[29] The peace of the believers is indivisible. No separate peace will be made when the believers are fighting in the way of Allāh. Conditions must be fair and equitable to all. In every foray, a rider must take a rider behind him.

---

belief. A Muslim is a believer, once he has followed the Sharī'a of the existing messenger. The holy Apostle described the people of Medina as believers and Muslims, as he was sent to mankind. It is only after clear proof has been presented to an individual beyond any doubt, and he accepts it but then refuses to follow it that he is called a Kāfir. See the author's book, 'Salāt of the Holy Apostle.

[29] I could have achieved the purpose of this book even if I stopped here. Let the world understand that Muhammad never discriminated against any believer. The attitude of the Muslim Umma should be looked upon only on the Model of the holy Apostle. If they fall short of this Model, then they cease to be called as Muslims. They should be warned by all believers to amend their ways. Islam is one and is centered on humanity, justice, kindness, and protection of life and property. This is the duty of every man irrespective of his practice.

The believers must avenge the blood of one another shed in the way of Allāh. The Allāh-fearing believers enjoy the best and most upright guidance. No polytheist shall take the property or person of Quraysh under his protection, nor shall he intervene against a believer. Whosoever is convicted of killing a believer without good reason shall be subject to retaliation unless the next of kin is satisfied (with blood-money), and the believers shall be against him as one man, and they are bound to take action against him.

It shall not be lawful to a believer who holds by what is in this document and believes in Allāh and the last day to help an evildoer or to shelter him. The curse of Allāh and His angel on the day of resurrection will be upon him if he does, and neither repentance nor ransom will be received from him. Whenever you differ about a matter, it must be referred to Allāh and to Muhammad.

The Jews shall contribute to the cost of war as long as they are fighting alongside the believers. The close friends of the Jews are as themselves. None of them shall go out to war save with the permission of Muhammad, but he shall not be prevented from taking revenge for a wound. He who slays a man without warning slays himself and his household, unless it be one who has wronged him, for Allāh will accept that. The Jews must bear their expenses and the Muslims their expenses. Each must help the other against anyone who attacks the people of this document. They must seek mutual advice and consultation, and loyalty is a protection against treachery. A man is not liable for his ally's misdeeds. The wronged must be helped. The Jews must pay with the believers so long as war lasts. Yathrīb shall be a sanctuary for the people of this document. A stranger under protection shall be as his host doing no harm and committing no crime.

A woman shall be given protection only with the consent of her family. If any dispute or controversy likely to cause trouble should arise, it must be referred to Allāh and to Muhammad the Apostle of Allāh. Allāh accepts what is nearest to piety and goodness in this document. Quraysh and their helpers should not be given protection. The contacting parties are bound to help each other against attack on Yathrīb. If they are called to make peace and maintain it, they must do so; and if they make a similar demand on the Muslims, it must be carried out except in the case of a holy war. Everyone shall have his portion from the side to which he belongs; the Jews of al-Aus, their freedmen, and they have the same standing with the people of this document in pure loyalty to them.

Loyalty is a protection against treachery. He who acquires anything acquires it for himself. Allāh approves of this document. This deed will not protect the unjust and the sinner. The man who goes forth to fight and the man who stays at home in the city are safe unless they have been unjust and sinned. Allāh is the protector of the good and Allāh-fearing man, and Muhammad is the Apostle of Allāh.

That was the covenant the holy Apostle wrote, as the spiritual and political leader of the newly established Islāmic State, inviting not only the inhabitants of Medina to come to common terms with him, but indirectly the whole of 'Arabia. **The covenant did not expressly stipulate that Muhammad Rasūlullah as the messenger of Allāh must be obeyed. Even before this, the holy Apostle had scored a very important goal in uniting the belligerent and Khazraj tribes, thereby leaving no room for contesting his position as the head of the Islāmic State among those who voluntarily and involuntarily followed him.**

The holy Apostle spent ten years in Medina teaching, explaining, and demonstrating to his Sahābas (followers/companions), what Allāh commanded him on Ibādat. He warned his Sahābas against doing any act outside his practice. He told them:

لا الفين احد كم متكا على ا ر يكتّه يا تيهم امرا من امرى مما أ مر ت به او نهيت عنه ، فيقول: لا ا د رى، 30
ما وجدنا فى كتاب الله اتبعناه ، فان السنة جاءت مفسرة للكتاب ، فمن أخذ بالكتاب من غير معرفة بالسنة زل
عن الكتاب كما زل عن السنة

---

30 Shātibi, Allāma Muhaqq Abī Ishāq Ibrāhim bin Mūsa bin Muhammad Lahmi. Al-'Itisām. Manama. Maktabat Tawhīd. 2000.Vol.1:123)

The holy Apostle is here warning his followers to be cautious in accepting the holy Qur'ān alone and rejecting his Sunna/actions. He clearly emphasized that he was the first to be commanded and the first to be prevented and not anyone else. No one should say therefore he does not know, for he was the one with the responsibility to explain what is in the holy Qur'ān. He indeed fulfilled his mission. The Sunna is the direct practical translation of the rituals and Sharī'a in the holy Qur'ān. It is not possible for one to understand the holy Qur'ān without understanding the Sunna, just as it is not possible for one to understand the practical without understanding the theory. The one who does not understand the Sunna does not understand the holy Qur'ān. The holy Apostle is here cautioning us, on what Allāh cautioned us in the holy Qur'ān 6:93, "And who can be more unjust than he who invents a lie against Allāh, or says: 'A revelation has come to me' whereas no revelation has come to him in anything; and who says, 'I will reveal to him in the like of what Allāh has revealed.'"

The Sunan of the holy Apostle are outside the opinion of his followers, because they are not sciences describing the physical world, where experiments are allowed to justify and explain the theory. An opinion in Islām arises from lack of knowledge. The Sunna is not speculative knowledge. The Sunna of the holy Apostle is his manner in obeying, humbling, and submitting to Allāh. We all walk without knowing the meaning of friction, how it relates to our walking, and the amount of heat generated.

In Medina, the holy Apostle's most important exemplary actions (Sunna) were prayers and protecting the city of Medina. Prayer is a very important pillar, for it is what distinguished him with the People of the Book that is the Levi tribe of the Children of Israel. The holy Apostle never regarded what was revealed before him as not an injunction from Allāh. It is not in theory that the distinction lies, because the Levi tribe have their prayer times, but only in action. After the completion of his mosque, when they wanted to establish the call to the prayer, the Sahābas rejected using the horn, because that was the method the Levi tribe used in calling their people to prayer. They also rejected using the bell in the manner the followers of Jesus, the son of Maryam, used. The use of the voice to establish the time of prayer is closer to the Levi tribe's practice of calling their people to prayer than using the bell. This is a very important distinction, for the holy Apostle said, "The difference between him and the People of the Book is in prayer."

He also said, referring to his followers, "Pray in the manner you saw me praying. I will intercede on behalf of the one who prays in the manner I prayed. As to the one who does not do so, Allāh will judge him according to his intention."[31] On the contrary, a follower of Muhammad Rasūlullah who refuses to pray in the manner he prays is likewise different from him. Therefore, the follower of Muhammad from this angle is no different from a Levi Child of Israel.

The followers of Muhammad will never agree, for they will argue saying, "The Jews did not believe in him." Openly no, but they believed in him secretly. Western Christians should take note of the similitude, for there is hardly any prayer congregation in the Muslim world today, according to what I witnessed during my visits to 'Arab countries, as well as recently from their television satellites that are done according to the Sunna of the holy Apostle. This is the same in the non-'Arab speaking Muslim countries. The Levi clan of the Children of Israel have the only legitimate right to discuss the text of Muhammad Rasūlullah on the revelation. Let them ask his followers, referred to in the holy Qur'ān 18:104, to analyze the following words: "Those whose efforts have been wasted

---

[31]   Al-Bāni, Muhammad Nāsiru Deen. Siffatu Salāt Nabiyyi. Damascus. Maktaba Islami. 1987. P. 11. However, this version of hadīth is in an earlier volume.

in his life while they thought that they were acquiring good by their deeds."

Worshipping Allāh ('*Ubūdiyya*)

The relation between mankind (angels and jinn) and his creator right from inception was based on obedience to Allāh alone. This began on that very Friday Allāh created Prophet Adam. This subject is not therefore under the domain of a single civilization, but to all civilizations from that time. This relation is such that no one will escape being asked by the angels on the Day of Resurrection: Who is your Lord?! Why did the angels not ask, 'Who is your Allāh that is the Law-Giver?' Mankind understands Allāh better as his Lord, because his needs are absolutely dependent on Him. Mankind by his very nature is weak and cannot sustain himself without support. Support and interdependency are part of our creation. Giving law is highly restricted. Man recognizes Allāh as his Law-Giver, as he will answer that question saying, "My Lord is Allāh."

The lexical meaning of '*Ubūdiyya* is servitude. The word is derived from the tri-literal root '*Abada* to worship or *Abd*, a slave. The word and its derivatives are mentioned 254 times in the holy Qur'ān, with more than half in the Makkan revelations. According to the interpretation of 'Abdullāh ibn 'Abbas and ibn 'Umar, one should study only this one word to make him understand what it means for one to be a servant of Allāh. This explanation is derived from the holy Qur'ān 6:4: "And never an Āyah (sign [singular]) comes to them from the Ayāt (signs [multiple]) of their Lord (L-rd), but that they have been turning away from it (and not from them)."

The holy Qur'ān, unlike previous Books from Allāh, is the only Book revealed to mankind. In the holy Qur'ān 4:82, Allāh inquires, "Do they not consider the Qur'ān carefully? Had it been from other than Allāh, they would surely have found therein many a contradiction." In other words, was there ever a time, from the Friday Allāh created Adam to just before 610 A.D, that a sign failed to reveal, identify, and convince one of the existence of Allāh? What of the still existing "rainbow"? Is what Allāh revealed to Muhammad not a confirmation of what was in those Books?

Therefore, civilization's calling for assimilation, integration, and tolerance among mankind can only be achieved by turning our obedience to our creator. It is on this basis that the holy Apostle asserted that to reflect on a single sign, proof, or evidence in the holy Qur'ān is more rewarding and beneficial than praying for the whole day and night! It is only after one is fully convinced about Allāh and one positions himself as a servant of Allāh that one can worship Allāh.

The creation of the heavens and the earth is one of the greatest proofs of the existence of Allāh. It is only a fool or one unconcerned with reality that will ever doubt the existence of Allāh. One should not blame such individuals, as for centuries the method adopted by Muhammad Rasūlullah in spreading the last message has been truncated, obliterated, and replaced with rhetoric without practice, despair as against hope, suspicion and doubt as against certainty, darkness as against light. It is cumbersome, if not practically impossible to develop a skill at something that is not practically demonstrated.

The problem people are facing is with the fact that faith, the gateway to salvation, prosperity, peace, and tolerance does not need any practical demonstration from mankind other than realizing and thinking on that very beautiful design of Allāh in the holy Qur'ān 28:71-72. (Allāh ordered Muhammad Rasūlullah to challenge the disbelieving Quraysh.) "Tell me! If Allāh made the night continuous for you till the Day of Resurrection, which ilāh (god) besides Allāh could bring you light? Will you not then hear? Tell me! If Allāh had made the day continuous for you till the Day of Resurrection, which ilāh (god) besides Allāh could bring you night wherein you rest? Will you not then see?" How could someone regarded as unlettered (dubbed by his enemies as an illiterate) compose such argument. Look at the distinctiveness and separation of the applied logic: night with hearing and day with seeing!

Allāh regarded this as His Mercy. There is no machine that does not rest. He further explained the functions of day, as the period we struggle to shape our environment and earn our living and the night as the period we rest. These phenomena are witnessed today, in the Arctic and Antarctic regions. Allāh will call on us to account for this truth as witnesses to His Authority. In the holy Qur'ān 28:75 He says, "And We shall take out from every nation a witness, and We shall say: Bring your proof."[32] Let us believe in Allāh, for on that Day, it will be too late to believe in Him--Then they shall know that the truth is with Allāh (Alone) and the lies (false gods), which they invented, will disappear from them.[33]

Manifestation of Worship

Prophet Abraham was the first messenger of Allāh to demonstrate what is involved in becoming the servant of Allāh. His life history, beginning at the age of three years, according to the Talmud, carried the best explanation and meaning of 'Ubūdiyya: that is how to worship Allāh, Him alone. It involved the use of the mind, the tongue, and the limbs. The narration from Talmud is: That night Terah and his wife, Amathlai, had indeed become the happy parents of a baby boy, who brought a great light and radiance into their home. Terah had hoped it would be a girl, and he would have no terrible decision to make. Now he could not think of giving up this lovely baby, born to him in his old age after such longing.

---

[32] I am your witness and my book is my proof and argument against you.

[33] The first sign is the rainbow apart from the ship of Noah.

He had managed to keep his wife's expectancy a secret. None of his servants knew about the birth of his son. There was a secret passage leading from his palace to a cave in the field. He took the baby to that cave and left it there. As he was returning to the palace, past the servants' quarters, he suddenly heard the cry of a baby. What good fortune! Terah cried. It so happened that one of his servants had given birth to a boy about the same time as his own son was born. Terah took the baby and put him in silk swaddling and handed him to his wife to nurse. Just then the king's messenger arrived.

When Terah with the baby in his arms appeared before Nimrod, Terah declared: "I was just about to bring my son to you, when your messenger came." Nimrod thought it was mighty loyal of Terah to give up his only son, born to him in his old age. Little did he know that it was not Terah's son who was brought to die, but a servant's. For three years little Abraham remained in the cave, where he did not know day from night. Then he came out of the cave and saw the bright sun in the sky, and he thought that it was G-d, who had created the heaven and the earth and him, too. But in the evening the sun went down, and the moon rose in the sky, surrounded by a myriad of stars. "This must be G-d," Abraham decided. But the moon, too, disappeared, and the sun reappeared, and Abraham decided that there must be a G-d, Who rules over the sun and the moon and the stars and the whole world.

And so, from the age of three years and on, Abraham knew that there was only one G-d, and he was resolved to pray to Him and worship Him alone. A life full of many and great adventures began for Abraham.

  i.   *The mind of Prophet Abraham.* Genesis 15:12 describes briefly what is in holy Qur'ān 6:75-83. As argued earlier, belief in Allāh is achieved through contemplating on a single sign, evidence, or proof, which convincingly shows the existence of Allāh.

With Abraham, it was the vastness of the heavens and the earth. It is only the blind that cannot recognize the presence in the heavens of the stars, the moon, and the sun. He considred them as his Lord and his Allāh! The stars can be visualized immediately after sunset. On the western horizon, the appearance of the moon, after conjunction on the first day of the lunar month, is immediately after sunset. This continues until about the tenth day or so when it begins to be seen rising from the east. This continues until the hour of conjunction when it will not be seen rising from the east.

The sun as described by Prophet Abraham rises in splendor. I love watching it rising in splendor as one of the beautiful signs of Allāh. It is indeed greater in size than the stars and the moon. The Sahābas did not ask the holy Apostle which days Abraham saw the stars, moon, and the sun, or was there any hint in the Old Testament and the Talmud. When Prophet Abraham saw each one of them traversing the sky and finally disappearing from sight, he came to the conclusion that they are under the command of the Lord and cannot therefore be his Lord. He now declared in the holy Qur'ān 6:79, "I have turned my face towards Him, Who has created the heavens and the earth Hanīfa (Islāmic Monotheism) and I am not of Mushrikīn."

ii. *The tongue of Prophet Abraham.* When Prophet Abraham saw his people worshipping stones and images (made by them), assigning them the position of Allāh, the clever youth used his common sense and consciousness (an inborn instinct; the ability to discern the truth and discriminate between truth and falsehood). He asked them in holy Qur'ān

21:52: "What are these images to which you are (so assiduously) devoted?" They replied and said in the holy Qurʿān 26:74, "But we found our fathers doing so." That was not possible for they were the immediate offspring of those saved in the ark. Reverend Matthew Henry also believes that their fathers couldn't have been worshipping idols. Prophet Abraham was at one time called Abram, the Hebrew; that is the son and follower of Heber, in whose family the profession of the true religion was kept up in that degenerate age. This Talmudic and Biblical story confirmed the interpretation of Muslim scholars that the father of Prophet Abraham was not an idol worshipper. Now, if someone will quote these relevant passages, the followers of Muhammad will turn and say, "It is the Israelite explanation!" So what?

iii. *The limbs of Prophet Abraham.* Prophet Abraham did not only continue appealing to their intellect, but planned a stratagem for the final proof against their ignorance and abuse of that intrinsic gift from Allāh (quality) that distinguishes man from other animals. Determined, after swearing a fealty with Allāh, he broke all the idols except the biggest of them. Reverend Matthew Henry alludes to this incident and writes, "Note, Religion tends to make men, not cowardly, but truly valiant. The righteous is bold as a lion."[34]

When his people came to worship, they could not believe what they saw. So they asked, as it says in the holy Qurʿān 21:59: "Who had done this to our āliha (gods)? He must indeed be one of the Zālimūn (wrongdoers). "A witness who heard Prophet Abraham's resolve that idols are not worthy of worshipping, told

---

[34] Henry, Reverend Matthew. Henry's Commentary on the Whole Bible. USA.Hendrickson.1998.

them as stated in holy Qur'ān 21:60, "We heard a young man talking against them, who is called Abraham." They confronted Prophet Abraham, and he cleverly made them prove their stupidity in the holy Qur'ān 21:63: "Nay, this one, the biggest of them (idols) did it. Ask them, if they can speak!" Even at that period there was the fundamental human right of speech and expression. Having realized their stupidity, they admitted shamelessly their folly and turning to each other, said in the holy Qur'ān 21:64, "Verily, you are the Zālimūn (polytheists and wrongdoers)."

He now turned on them and paid them in coins in the holy Qur'ān 21:66-67, "Do you then worship besides Allāh things that can neither profit you, nor harm you? Fie upon you and upon that you worship besides Allāh! Have you then no sense?" This argument and proof irritated them, and instead of coming to terms with him and using their faculty of discrimination and judgment, they resorted to violence and said in the holy Qur'ān 21:68: "Burn him and help your āliha (gods) if you will be doing."[35] Who then was intolerant and an extremist among the two parties?

This beautiful story did not appear in the book of Genesis; however, there was an allusion to it. Reverend Matthew Henry says, "By this precept he was tried whether he loved his native soil and dearest friends, and whether he could willingly leave all, to go along with God. His country had become idolatrous, his kindred and father's house were a constant temptation to him, and he could not continue with them without the danger of being infected by them; therefore, get thee out with all speed, escape for thy life, look not behind thee." The Talmud version--closer to the holy Qur'an--says: At the age of fifty

---

[35] See Genesis 15:17-18. Let those talking of terrorism understand its cause and origin. Terrorism cannot be wiped out of the world, as the right of Allāh and that of his last messenger are not recognized.

(in the year 1998) Abraham returned to his father's house in Babylon.

Terah was a high priest of the idol worshippers. He had twelve chief gods, one for each month of the year, and other idols. In fact, there was a workshop in Terah's house, where idols of wood, stone, silver, and gold were made. People came to offer sacrifices to these idols or to buy them, and Terah had a thriving business. Terah appointed Abraham to be the salesman and take charge of the business. How "well" he conducted the business we have already told you.

Abraham's activities, in words and deeds, aroused Nimrod's anger. Both Abraham and his father were ordered to appear before the king. Here the king's stargazers at once recognized Abraham as the one about whom they had warned the king. Terah was taken to task for deceiving the king, and he put the blame on his older son, Haran, who was thirty-two years older than Abraham. Haran had secretly followed Abraham, but he was not quite sure whether he was wise in doing so. He thought that he would come out openly on Abraham's side, if and when Abraham would come out victorious. Nimrod ordered that Abraham be thrown into a burning furnace.

When Abraham came out unharmed, Haran declared himself on Abraham's side and chose to be likewise thrown into the furnace, but he was burnt to death. Abraham, on the other hand, whom G-d had so wonderfully saved from the fire, was acclaimed by all the people; and they were ready to worship him. But Abraham told them to worship G-d, who had saved him from the burning furnace, and that he himself was nothing but a human being. Nimrod was greatly afraid of Abraham. He gave him many precious gifts, among them Eliezer, a member of the king's household, who became Abraham's trusted servant and friend.

iv. *Bearing witness.* This is His absolute right because this was the reason He created mankind and jinn. Worshipping Allāh means asserting the following:

Allāh is the only Law Giver.

Muhammad ibn 'Abdallāh is the messenger of Allāh (the seal of the Prophets and Imām of the Messengers), meaning that one is aware of the truth that Muhammad did not come with a new and independent command of Allāh, but that his message is the total sum of the messages Allāh sent from Adam to Jesus, the son of Maryam. As all the Prophets and Messengers were obeyed by their respective communities, a believer today is bound to follow that command of his Prophet or Messenger if Muhammad Rasūlullah mentions that message at all. Therefore, one must obey Muhammad Rasūlullah in whatever he did according to one's capacity, as he explained.

Muhammad as the seal of the Prophets implies that Allāh will not allow the Sharī'a of Muhammad to disappear, so that He has to send someone with it again to that community. Muhammad is the seal of the Message of Allāh and is sent to mankind or the whole world. There will be no Messenger after him with a Sharī'a. One thus finds in the holy Qur'ān instructions not only related to the Prophets and Messengers of the Children of Israel. The Prophets from Adam to Jacob were not Jews, but we find their stories mentioned in the holy Qur'ān, just as they are in the Holy Bible, the Book of Genesis. In addition, Allāh speaks of the Prophets sent in that period, but they are not mentioned in the Book of Genesis.

To the Ad generation Allāh sent Prophet Hūd with the Pillars of Faith, which is also the Pillar of Islam. This is simply to believe in Allāh by heart and tongue but without the rituals. They do not need to pay anything or contribute from their wealth. He compared his Message with that of his predecessor, Prophet Noah, saying in the holy Qur'ān 11:52, "Ask forgiveness of your Lord and then repent to Him, he will send you (from the sky) abundant rain, and add strength to your strength, so do not turn away as Mujrimīn (criminals, disbelievers in the Oneness of Allāh)." They arrogantly replied in the holy Qur'ān 11:53, blaming Prophet Hūd for failing to explain the meaning of how to worship, "O Hūd! No evidence have you brought us, and we shall not leave our gods for your (mere) saying! And we are not believers in you."

Coming to a conclusion about the Message and sealing it are the problem facing the Muslim world today, after a period of 1421 years. The followers of Muhammad Rasūlullah are yet to understand in practical terms the meaning; Allāh is the One to be worshiped and no one else. It is extremely lamentable and disheartening. They have no grounds for accusing Muhammad Rasūlullah, for Allāh took it upon Himself to explain the meaning of worshipping Him. What Muhammad did was to demonstrate how to put the command into practice. They equally have no grounds for accusing the Sahābas and all the righteous in failing to explain to them the meaning of how to worship Allāh alone.

Shirk (Polytheism)

"Shirk" means the worship of something other than Allāh. Showing your love to one and obeying that one, as a result of the love you have for that one, is one of the greatest sins of the past. It is the highest form of ingratitude to Allāh. If one thought that the thing he loves can be equal to Allāh because it can command or give guidance, Prophet Abraham proved that it is of no value, for it cannot stand, let alone protect itself. Prophet Abraham used that faculty of discrimination bestowed on mankind to understand Allāh. It is expected that one should use the same faculty to demonstrate to others the existence of Allāh and the hopelessness and nonexistence of anything else that assumes to give commands or guidance.

Shirk takes one of the following forms:

    a.   Shirk al-Hawa or the worship of fantasy, fondness, and inclination. Allāh gave examples of this form of worship in many verses of the holy Qur'ān:

See the holy Qur'ān 25:43, "Have you (O Muhammad) seen him who has taken as his ilāh (god) his own vain desire? Would you then be a wakīl (a disposer of his affairs or a watcher) over him?" The one referred to by Allāh is not mentioned, for the address is a general one. It opens the gate of confession, for a deaf person cannot hear the call of Allāh. The address is not an injunction to the insane, the enslaved, or the underage, but to a Mukallif-- one able to discriminate and flee from danger.

Yes, indeed, the holy Apostle was with the Makkan disbelievers in many assemblies in the proximity of the Ka'ba. It was a wonderful thing, and this is expressed by Allāh in the next verse, in the holy Qur'ān 25:44, saying to Muhammad Rasūlullah, "Or do you think that most of them hear and understand? They are only like cattle (including goats and sheep)--nay, they are even farther astray from the Path." How can those who can hear and understand fail to hear and understand the Message sent plainly in his perspicuous language? In the same way that the holy Apostle cannot guide them in their daily lives, likewise he cannot guide them in their lives concerning the Hereafter. This is because they had the knowledge, but with their own freewill chose not to obey.

b. Shirk involving preachers and mankind. 'Addiy ibn Khatim Ṭā'iy, a Christian, was among those who hated Muhammad Rasūlullah most. After the conquest of Makka, he decided to flee to Syria. Khālid ibn Walīd went to destroy the idol of Ṭays at Fulsa. The daughter of 'Addiy and his niece were captured and taken to Makka. When his niece was brought to the holy Apostle, he told her about the magnanimity of her uncle and how kind he was to

41

others in the days of ignorance. She was eventually set free and joined 'Adiyy in Syria.

When she told him what the holy Apostle had said about him, he was overwhelmed and decided to come to Medina to see the holy Apostle. When the holy Apostle saw a gold necklace on his neck, he quoted the holy Qur'ān 9:31, "They (Jews and Christians) took their rabbis and their monks to be their lords besides Allāh (by obeying them in things which they made lawful or unlawful according to their own desires without being ordered by Allāh), and they took as their Lord Messiah, son of Maryam (Mary), while they (Jews and Christians) were commanded (in the Taurat and the Injeel [Gospel]) to worship none but One Ilāh (God La ilāha illa Huwa (none has the right to be worshipped but He)."

'Addiy told the holy Apostle that they do not worship their monks. The holy Apostle asked him whether they make things lawful to them and unlawful to them. 'Adiyy replied in the affirmative. The holy Apostle said, "Then that is worshipping them." It is important we note that in this verse the word 'Lord, that is, Rabb' and not 'Ilāh or Allāh' is used. It is ultimately the desire for wealth that makes one obey the command of someone. When 'Addiy understood his mistake, he resolved to believe in Muhammad.

c. Shirk involving Shaiṭan. This form of worship in no way differs from the above, except that Shaiṭan was involved. Shaiṭan was the Iblis who, in as the servant of Allāh, refused to bow down to Adam while they were in the heavens. His disobedience did not stop at there, but further sank to jealousy, arrogance, egotism, dishonesty, and defiance. When Iblis was cast down from the heaven, he came down with his characteristics to deceive mankind.

Iblis deceived Adam before he was given the Prophet hood, that is, in heaven and not on earth. When he was in heaven, Adam had no knowledge and experience of what it is to disobey Allāh. There was no civilization. Allāh intended the earth to be the dwelling place for mankind and jinn, as well as the place where woeful disobedience will not be forgiven, except when one receives the punishment appropriate for the sin one committed.

Allāh again addresses us saying in the holy Qur'ān 36:60-61, "Did I not command you, O children of Adam, that you should not worship Shaiṭan (Shaiṭan). Verily, he is a plain enemy to you. And that you should worship Me (Alone--Islāmic Monotheism, and set up not rivals, associate-gods with Me). That is the Straight Path." Shaiṭan, in the Hereafter, will confess to his wickedness, envy, and enmity to mankind as it says in the holy Qur'ān 14:22, "Verily, Allāh promised you a promise of truth. And I (devil) too promised you, but I have betrayed you. I had no authority over you except that I called you and you responded to me. So blame me not, but blame yourselves. I cannot help you, nor can you help me. I deny your former act in associating me (Shaiṭan) as a partner with Allāh (by obeying me in the life of the world [for example, saying I am performing this Ibādat on the Madhhab of Sheikh so and so). Verily, there is a painful torment for the Zālimūn."

d. Shirk involving earthly authorities. This is the worship of Ṭaghut or Jibt (superstition), common in the Muslim Umma. It arises as a result of illiteracy and the quest for worldly pleasure. It is a manifestation of cowardice in the Muslim Umma.

e. Shirk involving embellishment.

f. Shirk involving wealth. Some used their wealth
    to support and establish tyrants and the unjust in
    ruling the Umma, refusing to use their wealth to
    help establish the Caliphate. The holy Apostle
    cursed them: "Miserable are those who worship
    wealth, miserable are those who worship fashion,
    for they are pleased only when they are given. They
    will never find solace and peace in their life. Every
    effort they make sinks them down. Blessed are
    those who take their pick axe and go to the forest
    to fetch firewood for their livelihood. They are ever
    patient and striving for good, minding their own
    business."[36]

Since there is not a substance in the world,
but proves that Allāh is One, the worship of Allāh
involves in the first instant, realizing and appreciating
one's limit. We do not own a single thing in this
world. Allāh cautions us to look at our origin, humble
ourselves, submit, pray, seek His guidance, and to
be ever upright in our dealing with one another. In
the holy Qur'ān 22:73, Allāh says, "O mankind! A
similitude has been coined, so listen to it (carefully):
verily, those on whom you call, besides Allāh,
cannot create (even) a fly, even though they combine
together for the purpose. And if a fly snatches away a
thing from them, they will have no power to release
it from the fly. So weak (both) the seeker and the
sought."

---

[36] Ibrāhim Abdul Mun'im. Mughnil Murid. Jāmi'u Li shurūh Kitāb
Tawhīd. Li Shaykh Islām Muhammad ibn Abdulwahab. Makka.
Maktabata Nazar Mustapha Baz. 2000. 218-418.

Chapter 4

THE CALIPHATE

The majority of the Muslim Umma understand Islām to be mainly centered on observing the five obligatory daily prayers, fasting the month of Ramadan, and going on the annual pilgrimage, as well as performing 'Umra, the lesser pilgrimage countless times. They are yet to institute the Zakat. Although there are scattered preachers deemphasizing going for the annual pilgrimage and the 'Umra, it is unfortunate that as of today no one is taking heed because of the absence of a central authority among the Muslim Umma. The establishment of the Caliphate is the cardinal Pillar of Islām, which if not established wipes out all deeds.

The Caliphate is to faith and all activities in Islām what the notochord is to a vertebrate animal. It is what the sun is to life. It is the first challenge of the will, plan, and decree of Allāh-- the Trust that He offered to inorganic matter, which refused to accept, for fear of breaching it. But man accepted it and betrayed it. The world must necessarily fly or swim in its chaotic situation and chasm.

Probably, it was on the fifth day, in the evening after the creation, that Allāh tells us what He told the heavens and the earth and the mountains in the holy Qur'ān 33:72:

انا اعرضنا الآمانة على السموات والأرض والجبال فابين ان يحملها وا شفقن منها وحملها الإنسان انه كا ن ظلوما جهو لا.

(We did offer Al-Amānah to the heavens and the earth and the mountains, but they declined to bear it and were afraid of it. But man bore it. Verily, he was unjust to himself and ignorant of the results.)

Discussion: The verse consists of two parts:

The text includes a caution in accepting Al-Amānat. They understood the consequences of betraying Allāh, and thus they refused. One has no grounds to argue that they refused, because as one knows them today, they have no power of discrimination. Those who do not believe in this discourse assert that they were created before Friday and that they were witnesses that Allāh did not offer that Amānah to the heavens, the earth, and the mountains. Amānah has twenty-five meanings, including guardianship, faithfulness, trust, confidence, uprightness, protection, superintendence, and supervision. It is the opposite of treachery, betrayal, treason, and deception. According to Allāh, the heavens and the earth and the mountains refused to accept it for fear. No one can understand this fear, for as far as we know they do not have the power of discrimination.

However, their refusal and fear could be attributed to the presence of water in them. Allāh described the mountains able to respond to the holy Qur'ān, in the holy Qur'ān 72:74, "Then, after that, your hearts were hardened and became as stones or even worse in hardness. And indeed there are stones, out of which rivers gush forth, and indeed, there are of them (stones) that split asunder so that water flows from them, and indeed, there are of them (stones) that fall down for fear of Allāh. And Allāh is not unaware of what you do."

This is a warning, which is specifically a reminder to the then Levi tribe of the Children of Israel in Medina of what their ancestors had done. The Levi tribe of the Children of Israel were the ones mentioned in the holy Qur'ān 7:159. The verse again addresses the followers of Muhammad Rasūlullah. We must always follow the command of Allāh and not argue. The worst offense is the pretense that one does not understand the command. It is a sign of hypocrisy and denial. Allāh will always be with us in explaining His command, according to our desire and wish. The simplest command was for them to slaughter a cow. But because their intention was to disobey Allāh, they openly showed their readiness to obey Him only if He would forego His command to them.

It says in the holy Qur'an 59:21, "Had We sent down this Qur'ān, on a mountain, you would surely have seen it humbling itself and rent asunder by the fear of Allāh. Such are the parables which We put forward to mankind that they may reflect."

Discussion: We must distinguish between the use of "Had We" and "Had I." The former refers to Irādatul Kawniyya Diniyya, that is, Allāh sent down the holy Qur'ān, on the mountains, but not to humble in the manner we humble ourselves on reciting it. They were commanded to glorify Allāh with Prophet David in the holy Qur'ān 34:10. Allāh did not create the mountain to be his servant in the manner He created us. Allāh created them and had obviously followed His command in a manner not understood by us.

The fear of Allāh means to love Him and obey Him. It was reported that when the holy Apostle Abūbakar Siddīq, along with 'Umar bin Khaṭṭāb, climbed Mount Safah, it shook. He exclaimed, "It is Muhammad, Abūbakar and 'Umar." The shaking of Mount Safah was a sign of humbling itself to the Sunna of the holy Apostle. The followers of Muhammad Rasūlullah in principle humble themselves to the Sunna of the holy Apostle and not to the holy Qur'ān.

Man was offered the Al-Amānat and bore it at a date not specified. That must be after Friday. One could then understand that, at the time the offer was made, man was able to understand the import of the offer and that he could bear it. Fear is not one of the qualities of Allāh, and therefore, it can be argued that fear was not breathed into the soul of mankind. What was then the source of fear? The ability to discriminate is the most probable cause of fear.

It was after man bore the burden that he was described as unjust and ignorant. Man was not born ignorant. Allāh taught Prophet Adam the nature of things before Allāh commanded the angels to bow down to him. Why was the appointment of Muhammad Rasūlullah preceded by commanding him to read? Allāh informed mankind of what happened after His discourse with the heavens, the earth, and the mountains and assured us that it is the Al-Mushrikīn (disbelievers, idolaters, and polytheists) who are ignorant and unjust hypocrites.

After telling us of His desire and intention to offer Al-Amānah to the heavens, earth, and mountains and their refusal to accept it and of our acceptance, He now cautioned us in the holy Qur'ān 8:27, "O you who believe! Betray not Allāh and His Messenger, nor betray knowingly your Amānat." Allāh did not choose the Levi tribes of the Children of Israel to demonstrate how the trust can be betrayed, but chose a respected elderly Sahāba, described as very close to Muhammad Rasūlullah. Abū Lubāba was an ally to the Banu Qurayza clan of the Levi tribe. When they broke their covenant with Muhammad Rasūlullah, by waging war on him and participating in the battle of the Trench, the holy Apostle besieged them for a period of twenty-five nights.

They became exhausted and realizing that they had no way to escape, after refusing to listen to the advice of Ka'b b. Asad, they sent a message to the holy Apostle that he should send Abū Lubaba, their ally, for consultation. The holy Apostle agreed to their request and sent him to their fortresses. When he reached there, they were overwhelmed and came out to greet him with enthusiasm and hope. They said, "O Abū Lubāba, do you think that we should submit to the Muhammad's judgment?" He replied, "Yes," and pointed with his hand to his throat saying, "Otherwise it will be a general carnage."[37] He there and then felt that he had betrayed the holy Apostle, for he could not walk; his

---

[37]   Haykal, Muhammad. The Life of Muhammad (Philadelphia: University of Chicago Press 1976) 311-15.

feet had become glued so to speak to the ground. Abū Lubaba was not sent with the explicit command to pass his finger over his throat signaling slaughter. This was the addition that made him taste the anger of Allāh! A follower of Muhammad is bound to strictly follow his instructions, for Muhammad is responsible to Allāh on the Day of Judgment for our actions. It is wiser for one to blame Muhammad on that day than to be guilty oneself.

Next we turn to a discourse between Allāh and the angels on His intention to establish His authority by creating a vicegerent and placing him on earth. The creation of the angels is not mentioned in the Qur'ān, or in the Holy Bible, although some Muslim commentators have postulated that they were created from blue flame. Since the angels are Allāh's special messengers, representing His Throne, he kept their creation to Himself, for such knowledge is not required by us. It is as if Allāh was saying to the angles: As you have been my special messengers, who do not flicker and flinch at my commands, I am going to create another messenger as my representative, who can do exactly what you have been doing every time I command you, but who will also have the capacity to refuse to obey my command.

Everything exists under the command of Allāh. The breathing of the characteristics of Allāh into Adam and his offspring transformed their will, plan, and decree to comply with the will of Allāh. "When He decrees a matter, He only says to it, 'Be!'[38]--and it is." With reference to us, it is: "Then when you have taken a decision (Azamta),[39] put your trust in Allāh, certainly, Allāh loves those who put their trust (in Him)."[40]

---

[38] Holy Qur'ān 2:117.

[39] "Azamta"means acting on something that one has made up his mind to do. Azama cannot be achieved without taking precaution. ibn Munzir. Lisan Arab. Lisān Arab. Beirut. Dārul Lisānul 'Arab. 1988..4:760-70.

[40] Holy Qur'ān 3:159.

The first Caliph was Prophet Adam, who disobeyed Allāh woefully. The second time the word Caliph was used by Allāh was in the holy Qur'ān 38:26, He says, "O David! Verily! We have placed you as a successor on the earth; so judge you between men in truth (and justice) and follow not your desire--for it will mislead you from the Path of Allāh. Verily, those who wander astray from the Path of Allāh (shall) have a severe torment, because they forgot the Day of Reckoning." This verse throws light on the reason why it was man who was given this responsibility and not the angels. The angels are not resident on earth and do not succeed one another. Gabriel is still alive, as are all the angels.

On the question of succession, Allāh further explains this process in the holy Qur'ān 10:14, "Then We made you successors after them, generations after generations in the land, that We might see how you would work." In other words, the behavior of a generation following a righteous generation will be modeled after its predecessor. There is only one Allāh as emphasized in the Bible. He punishes those who disobey his Messenger and forgives and blesses those who obey His Messenger. His command is absolute. His right must be given to Him. Therefore, it is either for one to be subordinate and loyal or insubordinate and disloyal.

Establishing the Caliphate

A Caliph is the representative of Allāh in the world. He is the one chosen to speak on behalf of Allāh and His angels. That man is the chosen representative of Allāh is made clear in the holy Qur'ān 17:95, "If there were on the earth, angels walking about in peace and security, We should certainly have sent down for them from the heaven an angel as a Messenger."

Establishing the Caliphate is realizing and accepting Allāh as the Creator of the world. Failure to establish the caliphate is equivalent to denying Allāh and usurping His right. Allāh has kept to His promise by sending Prophets and Messengers at every moment people are in distress. Let us remember the challenge of the angels when Allāh informed them as it says in the holy Qur'ān 2:30 that He is to send to the earth a vicegerent, "Will You place therein those who will make mischief therein and shed blood?" It is impossible for mankind to shed blood and make mischief on the earth, because Allāh has breathed into them His Spirit. This is what is termed "*Irādatul Kawniyya Diniyya.*" But under *Irādatul Shar'iyya Diniyya*, one can on his own volition shed blood and make mischief on the earth.

If Allāh did not forbid mankind from shedding blood, no one could avoid doing that. Shedding blood is never done unconsciously, except proven by circumstances beyond the offender's control and the inability of the authority to prevent him from doing so. Our attitude to one another is described by Allāh in the following chapters of the holy Qur'an:

The holy Qur'ān 25:72-73:"And who do not bear witness to falsehood, and if they pass by some evil play or evil talk, they pass by it with dignity."

The holy Qur'ān 28:55:"And when they hear Al-Lagwy (dirty, false, evil vain talk), they withdraw from it and say: "To us our deeds, and to you your deeds. Peace be to you. We seek not (the way of) the ignorant."

The holy Qur'ān 17:37: "And walk not on the earth with conceit and arrogance. Verily, you can neither rend nor penetrate the earth, nor can you attain a stature like the mountains in height."

If there is no security on the streets of mankind, who is going to be held responsible? We shall use two examples to prove that it is the failure of that representative of Allāh chosen by his people to lead them according to the Sharī'a.

In the holy Bible 1 Sam. 8:4, the Children of Israel approached Samuel with the following grievances:

They said, "You are an old man. You set a good example for your sons, but they haven't followed it." Matthew Henry has commented, "It was true that Samuel was old; but if that made him less able to reach the circuit, and sit long on the bench, yet it made him the more wise and experienced, and, upon that account , the fitter to rule. If he was old, had he not grown old in their service? And it was very unkind and ungrateful, nay and unjust, to cast him off when he was old, who had spent his days in doing them good. God has saved his youth from being despicable, yet they make his old age so, which should have been counted worthy of double honor."[41]

Now we want a king to be our leader, just like all the other nations. Choose one for us!" Their reason was stated in 1 Sam. 8:20:

"We want a king to rule us and lead us in battle."[42] According to the holy Bible, Samuel was upset to hear them say that they wanted a king. Nonetheless, he prayed about it. Commenting on their request, Matthew Henry comments:

{This is a} petition for the redress of the grievances, by setting a king over them. . . . Thus far it was well, that they did not rise up in rebellion, against Samuel and set up a king for themselves *vi et armis*—"by force"; but they applied to Samuel, God's prophet, and humbly begged of him to do it. But it appears by what follows that was an evil proposal and ill made, and was displeasing to God. . . . They had a prophet to judge them that had immediate correspondence with the heaven, and therein they were great and happy above any nation, none having God *so nigh unto them* as they had. But this would not serve; they must have a king to judge them with external

---

[41] p. 395-7Matthew Henry's Complete Commentary on the Holy Bible. Are the followers of Muhammad supposed to apply this in their Sharī'a? If they are doing the opposite, are they believers?

[42] Holy Qur'ān 2:246.

pomp and power, *like all the nations.* A poor prophet in a mantle though conversant in the visions of the All-mighty, looked mean in the eyes of those who judged by outward appearance; but a king in a purple robe, with his guards and officers of state, would look great; and such a one they must have. They knew it was in vain to court Samuel to take up himself the title and dignity of a king, but he must appoint them one. They do not say, "give us a king that is wise and good, and will judge better than thy sons," but, "give us a king," anybody that will make a figure.[43]

Thus foolishly did they forsake their own mercies, and under pretense of advancing the dignity of their nation to that of their neighbors, did really thrust themselves down from their own excellency and profane their crown by *casting it to the ground.*

Allāh comforted Prophet Samuel and said that he must not think hard that they have put this slight on him, for they had herein put a slight on God himself. If God interests himself in the indignities that are done us and the contempt that is put on us we may well afford to bear them patiently, nor need we think the worse of ourselves, if for his sake we bear reproach, but rather rejoice and count it an honor.[44] God reigns over the heathen over all the world, but the government of Israel had hitherto been, in a more particular manner than ever any government was, a theocracy, a divine government; their judges had their call and

---

[43]   It is unfortunate that the followers of Muhammad Rasūlullah are yet to understand that on the Day of Judgment the Children of Israel and the Christians they despise will be laughing at them. This is the universal belief of the Muslim Umma. They are hopeless and helpless in choosing a Caliph.

[44]   There are many verses in the holy Qur'ān with the same appeal. For example, 46:35.

commission immediately from God; the affairs of their nation were under his peculiar direction.

God was pleased with their request, but as sometimes he crosses us in love and at other times he gratifies us in wrath, he did so here. God made Samuel humor them in this matter that they might be beaten with their own rod and might feel to their cost the difference between his government and the government of a king.

When they have a king, they will soon have enough of him and will, when it is too late, repent of their choice. He must protest solemnly to them that if they would like a king to rule them, as the eastern kings ruled their subjects, they would find the yoke exceedingly heavy. They looked only at the pomp or magnificence of a king and thought that would make their nation great and considerable among their neighbors, and would strike a terror upon their enemies. However, he must bid them consider how they would like to bear the charges of that pomp and how they would endure that arbitrary power which the neighboring kings assumed.

Prophet Samuel further told them the nature of the king:

Thus he must support his dignity at the expense of what is dearest to them, and thus he will abuse his power as those that have power are apt to do. Moreover, having the militia in his hand, it will be necessary to submit to him. The king must have a great retinue, abundance of servants to wait on him, grooms to look after his chariots and horses, gentlemen to ride about with him, and footmen to run before his chariots. This is the chief grandeur of princes and the imaginary glory of great men, to have a multitude of attendants.

He must keep a great table; he will not be content to dine with his neighbors upon a sacrifice . . . but must have a variety of dainty dishes, forced meats, and sweetmeats, and delicate sauces; and who must prepare these? Why, he will take your daughters, the most ingenious and handy of them, whom you hoped to prefer to houses and tables of their own; and whether you will be willing or not, they must be his confectioners, cooks, bakers, and the like.

He must need to have a standing army, for guards and garrisons; and your sons instead of being elders of your captains must be disposed of at the pleasure of the sovereign.

You may expect that he will have great favorites, whom, having dignified and ennobled, he must enrich and give them estates suitable to their honor. How can he do that, but out of your inheritances? He must have great revenues to maintain his grandeur and power with; whence must he have them but from you . . . ?[45]

The above is the life history of the holy Apostle, matched with the story of Samuel and the commentary of Matthew Henry. Suffice it to mention that Muhammad Rasūlullah was invited to Medina to lead that community, that is, the two Arab tribes and the Levi tribe of the Children of Israel. The condition at that time was so tense that without Divine Intervention, life could have come to a standstill. The Children of Israel used to boast to the Aws and Khazraj tribe that when that Messenger is sent in the long run, they will quickly go to him, for anyone who is with a Messenger, will overwhelm and rule his opponent.[46]

The case of the Quraysh was certainly different. They were never conquered by any world power, were never under the threat of an invasion from any then world power. However, in the

---

[45] Complete Commentary on the Holy Bible, 396-97.
[46] We should stop accusing the Children of Israel of hiding the truth. They have spoken from experience. Is this not enough for the followers of Muhammad to respect the Caliphate?

manner that Allāh sent prophets to destroy the gods worshipped by the Jews, Allāh sent Muhammad to them to destroy their idols. In each case, monotheism, the worshipping of the Allāh of Abraham, Ishmael, Isaac, and Jacob was re-introduced.

Conditions Stipulated for the Selection of a Caliph

The Holy Bible described Saul, whom Allāh selected as a king for the Jews as, "better looking and more than a head taller than anyone else in all Israel." Matthew Henry notes that "No mention is here made of his wisdom or virtue, his learning or piety, or any of the accomplishments of his mind, but . . . he was a tall, proper, handsome man. . . had a good face, a good shape, and a good presence, graceful and well proportioned. Their comment in 1 Samuel 10:27, 'How can someone like Saul rescue us from our enemies?' implied that the one selected must have the qualities and qualifications of the work the community needed."[47]

All prophets and messengers of Allāh performed some miracles proving their supremacy and that they are sent by Allāh. We should note that prophets and messengers were chosen by Allāh **{God}** in the Bible, and His choice is the best choice and complies with the need of the community. The leaders chosen by Muhammad Rasūlullah for a period of thirty years after his death never faulted. The choice of Muhammad is the choice of Allāh.

The request of the Jews to Prophet Samuel is mentioned in the holy Qur'ān 2:246. The qualifications given in the holy Qur'ān are:

At-Taqwa.[48] This is mentioned in the holy Qur'ān, 49:13, "O mankind! We have created you from a male and a female

---

[47] 'Umar ibn Khattab never allowed talking on issues, except that needed by the Umma..

[48] The word means "to keep silent." One has to listen to his master before he obeys him.

and made you into nations and tribes that you may know one another. Verily, the most honorable of you with Allāh is that (believer) who has At-Taqwa. Verily, Allāh is All-Knowing, All-Aware."

Education and physique compared to wealth as demanded by the Jews.

The Sunna of the holy Apostle. The Sunna of the holy Apostle is his method in choosing his leaders. It was based on:

Knowledge of the Sunna. This is because the life of a believer is tied to understanding the Sunna. It is the only system, which, when applied, can save the world from chaos, poverty, and all the sufferings we are facing today. The Caliph is to be supported by the Shūra, comprising experts in Islāmic jurisprudence, on issues dealing with the rights of individuals as demanded by Allāh.

Taking consideration of tribal balance.

Proficiency or competence.

Age.

Muslim scholars have suggested the qualifications to be attained by one selected as the leader of the Muslim Umma. Unfortunately, as they are described in the holy Qur'ān, 2:93--"We have heard and disobeyed"--they have not raised for centuries a Caliph to rule them. Are they better than their predecessors, who disbelieved their prophets? They therefore do not believe, for he said:

من ا ستعمل رجلا على عصابة وفيه ممن هو أرضى لله فقد خانالله و رسوله وا لمؤمنين [49]

This hadīth says that whoever employs someone to a position of trust on the basis of regional or tribal partisanship or false

---

[49]   Zuhra, Muhammad Abū. Tārikh Māzahibu al Islāmiyy fī Siyāsa wal Aqīda wa Tārih Mazāhibu Fiqhiyya. Cairo. Dārul Fikr 'Arabiyy. 89

interpretation of Islām, while there is one in the Muslim Umma more acceptable to Allāh for the post, has indeed betrayed Allāh, His Messenger, and the believers. This is a Medina hadīth, for immediately on arrival after building his mosque, Bīlal bin Rabī'ah, the Abyssinian slave, was made the Mu'azzin, the one to call the believers to prayers. He had the most beautiful and melodic vibrating voice.

The Functions of the Caliph

The most important function of the Caliph is to ensure all are living with their basic needs fulfilled. In today's terminology, nobody is allowed to live below the poverty line! No one is prevented by the Sharī'a from using his own efforts to live a better life-style, as long as he avoids excess and doesn't abuse the rights of others. The Sharī'a demands one to give what is in excess to those in need. This requirement cannot be circumvented, for it is like gravity, water, or light to our way of life.

Man has been given a free hand to shape his life and tame his environment. It is selfishness and ignorance, particularly of the masses, that is responsible for the way we are living today. The euphoria of our youth, if not checked, will further destroy the Caliphate.

The greatest ignorance is in not understanding the full meaning and extent of the Sharī'a. It is not restricted to a particular group of people, a region, a tribe, or what we wrongly define as "religion." There is no religion other than that system of life communicated to us from Allāh, from His Seat of Glory, through the intermediary of angel Gabriel. The so-called secular demands are never independent of the Laws of Allāh. Muhammad began his mission by forcing himself to read. The greatest unpardonable crime of the Muslim Umma is their ignorance of the nature of Allāh.

Other functions of the Caliph include the following:

Leading the five daily obligatory prayers.

Leading the Friday congregation and the two festival prayers.

Preventing misinterpretation of the Sharī'a among the Muslim Umma on trivial issues that are within the rights of individuals, as accorded by the Sunna of the holy Apostle.

Ensuring that the Sharī'a is translated and applied according to the dictates of the time. Call that secularization or liberalism!

Chapter 5

THE SHARĪ‘A

The West and its surrogates generally understand Sharī‘a as having begun only during the time of Muhammad Rasūlullah, meaning nothing other than cutting the hands of a thief, stoning adulterous couples, covering the exposed extremities of the female, marrying four wives, not allowing mixing of opposite sexes, and so forth. This misconception stems from the West's ignorance of the Holy Bible, as well as their association with those who claim to be followers of Muhammad Rasūlullah, but are totally ignorant of the Final Message.

Muhammad did not define Sharī‘a the way it is defined today by the West; nor did he demonstrate the practice of the Sharī‘a in the manner his followers are practicing it. His Sahābas also never defined Sharī‘a other than the way he defined and practiced it. It is unfortunate that neither the West, its surrogates, or the Muslim apologist can tell us the source of their knowledge. One must forgive the West and her surrogates, for they are deceived and bewitched into believing that Muhammad Rasūlullah was not sent to them. If reason and commonsense can prevail and the West, in its quest for knowledge, will study the life of the holy Apostle, they can achieve their dream of governing the whole world.

The holy Qur‘ān is not a book that is to be kept in mosques and read only during prayers or left in the hands of those who cannot synchronize what they do in their laboratories and what they reflect on during their prayers. The holy Qur‘ān is to the world what air, water, light, and blood are to our lives. In fact, it is more than that, for it is the book containing guidelines for our comfort, progress, and the very quintessence of our life.

Sharī'a means "way to a watering place," a "watering hole," or a "drinking place." Logically, those engaged in a certain practical skill are the best at explaining their work. The Quraysh, among whom the final Messenger was raised, were shepherds. Their life in the desert and shepherding made them understood more than anyone the precise meaning, application, and value of a watering hole or drinking place. They were invariably the best to direct a stranger looking for a drinking place to water his thirsty animals. It was not wise for a stranger to disregard or disagree with them about which route to take to the watering place. The object is to get one's animals drinking water. If he does not, then assuredly his animals could perish in the desert. Has water any other source other than from the sky? If there is only one source, can there be any other way to create it?

It must be understood that Sharī'a means the practice of Muhammad Rasūlullah after his migration to Medina. Dr. Roger Garaudy in his article, *The Islamic Alternative*, amplified on this and said, "To apply the Sharī'a means first of all to set up a society-- as is ordained in the Qur'ān--in which the accumulation of wealth for some does not co-exist with the poverty of others, to whom we have not extended our help. Applying the Sharī'a does not mean that one must begin by punishing before a system of education and a political order that will inspire one and all with a sense of dignity and duty."[50]

It is common to describe the Sharī'a as including the holy Qur'ān. By that definition, it is better understood today to mean the Sharī'a revealed to past generations, and not in particular to Muhammad Rasūlullah. For example, the people of Prophet Shu'aibu were commanded to give full measure and not to reduce weight. This same command is repeated in the holy Qur'ān,

---

[50] High preparation committee for the fifth Islamic summit conference Kuwait. Islam and the future. . 1987. Kuwait 109-124.

17:35: "And give full measure when you measure, and weigh with a balance that is straight. That is good (advantageous) and better in the end." I do not know how they weighed and measured at that time. During his lifetime, the holy Apostle used the palm of his hands in measuring grains for Zakat Fitr (the end of the fasting). The Sharī'a calls for distributing grains according to the measure of one's palms. For selling grains, the method is to fill a bowl to the brim and then level the top. "Weighing with a balance that is straight" is applicable mostly in scientific measurement where precision is required. It was in Iraq that the Muslims first introduced the use of a measure.

Classification of Sharī'a

The Sharī'a is classified according to Dr. 'Umar Suleiman Ashqari as:[51]

Ahkām-al-Iqtisādiyya. Allāh created mankind to worship Him Alone and no one else. This is the universal Sharī'a. There is only One Allāh. Believing in Allāh implies believing in His Messengers, angels, the Day of Judgment, and the other articles of Faith.

Ahkām-al-Akhlāqiyya (Moral practices). The first Sharī'a is the prohibition of murder, since Abel murdered Cain. Therefore, the Sharī'a was promulgated as a result of someone's conduct. Every prophet came with a Sharī'a, stemming from the wrong done by his people. In general, one is to be honest and upright, straightforward, loving, innovative and productive, living by and fulfilling promises and developing trustworthiness.

Moral practices are best understood from the speech of Ja'afar ibn Abī Ṭālib to Negus to the King of Ethiopia: "O King, we were an unenlightened people plunged in ignorance. We worshipped idols; we ate dead animals and we committed

---

51 Ashqari, Dr. 'Umar Sulaiman. Khasā'is Sharī'a al-Islāmiyya. Kuwait. Maktaba Fallāh. 1986. 28-30.

abominations; we broke natural ties and we ill-treated our neighbors and our strong devoured the weak. We thus lived until Allāh raised among us an Apostle, of whose noble birth and lineage, truthfulness, honesty and purity we were aware. He invited us to acknowledge the Unity of Allāh and to worship Him, and to renounce the stones and idols we and our forefathers used to venerate. He enjoined us to speak the truth, to redeem our pledges to be kind and considerate to our kin's and neighbors; he forbade us to refrain from every vice, bloodshed, shamelessness, lies and deceit; and asked us neither to encroach upon the substance of the orphans nor to vilify chaste women. He commanded us to pay divine honors to Allāh alone and never associate aught with Him, he ordered us to offer prayers, to pay the poor-due, to observe fast. We acknowledge his truth and we followed him; we followed him in whatever he brought from Allāh; and we worshipped only One Allāh without associating aught with Him. We treated as unlawful what he forbade and accepted what he made lawful for us. Thereon our people were estranged; they persecuted us, tried to seduce us from our faith and forced us to take the idols back for our Allāh; and they pressed us to return to the abominations we used to commit.[52]

Ahkām-al-Amaliyya. This is further divided as:

1. *Al-'Ibādat*. This covers the four Pillars of Islām specific only to the followers of Muhammad Rasūlullah.
2. *Al-Muslaha*. This is described as the Common Good covering mankind without exception. The holy Apostle laid down guidelines on living, allowing that details would be determined by specific civilizations, according to necessity.

---

[52] 'Ali, S. Abul Hasan. Muhammad Rasūlullah. Lucknow. Islāmic Research and Publications. 1979. P. 123

The Place of Sharī'a

The legal claim of the Sharī'a is on the following:

a. The Rights of Allāh, which are classified as
    Belief that He is One and the Rabb of the world.
    Belief in the apostleship of Muhammad Rasūlullah,
    implying belief in all the Apostles of Allāh.
    Obedience to Allāh in executing His positive and
    negative commands either in the Torah or the
    Sunna of the holy Apostle.

b. Worship of Allāh. Its pillar is the establishment of the
    Caliphate.

c. The rights of the soul or body, which are classified as
    The body or soul should in no way be harmed.
    The body should be kept clean. Smiling is half
    of faith.
    Removal of injurious materials from the street is
    half of faith.
    It is prohibited to overeat and strain the gut.
    During prostration and bowing down in prayers,
    the body must rest, that is, the muscle spindles
    must be allowed to recover.

The common right. The holy Apostle said, "Each and every one
of us is a shepherd. We shall be called to account for those under
our guidance."

The rights of other creatures. Domesticated animals and
birds must be given their rights. They should be fed, treated
for their ailments, and given preventive care. They should be
slaughtered with respect and dignity.

The above classification is by no means exhaustive. It is
meant only to serve the purpose of bringing awareness to those
who are confused as to the meaning of Sharī'a.

Chapter 6

JIHĀD

The term "Jihad" was first used around the last stage of the holy Apostle's life in Makka, probably after his injury in Ṭa'if.[53] In the holy Qur'ān, 25:52, Allāh counseled the holy Apostle after telling him that He will not send another Messenger to help him, "So obey not the disbelievers, but strive against them (by preaching) with the utmost endeavor with it (the Qur'ān)."

Now, one should ask how Muhammad Rasūlullah translated this command into action. Since Muhammad Rasūlullah did not engage the Quraysh physically, but only recited what was revealed to him. The Jihād is the holy Qur'ān. The revelation of these verses in the holy Qur'ān, 11 probably came after the events that led to the graying of his hair. Before the revelation of this verse, the holy Apostle and his followers had witnessed the following:

The murder of 'Amr in Yassar and his wife, Sumayya.

The punishment meted out to Bilāl ibn Rabīa.

The karate of the holy Apostle.

The migration to Abyssinia.

The three years banishment of the holy Apostle in the house of Abī Ṭālib.

The Apostle's journey to Ṭa'if and the injury he received.

---

[53] The city Muhammad sought refuge in after the death of his wife Khadija and his uncle Abu Ṭālib. He was stoned and returned disappointed. He was consoled with the Mi 'rāj.

Their hiding in the cave for three days.

The loss of their property in Makka.

Imagine Muhammad addressed as a liar, poet, magician, sorcerer, and seer! Imagine being brought up as an orphan under the care of the impoverished Abī Ṭālib! Imagine his marrying a forty-year old lady!

It was probably immediately after the hijrah that Allāh revealed in the holy Qur'ān 22:78, "And strive hard in Allāh's cause as you ought to strive, (with sincerity and with all your efforts that His Name should be superior)." Referring this instruction to physical engagement, one must then look at the details of the Medina Covenant and apply it strictly. Western Christians, who never see anything good with Muhammad, will never justify the cause of the battle of Badr, which was done at the request of the Muhājirīn in order to seize their property, which was being taken to Syria in the Quraysh caravan.

In the holy Qur'ān 60:1, Allāh says, "If you have come forth to strive (Jihādan) in My Cause and to seek My Good Pleasure, (then take not these disbelievers and polytheists as your friends)."

In the holy Qur'ān 9:24, revealed in the eighth year after the hijrah, Allāh says, "Say: If your forefathers, your sons, your brothers, your wives, your kindred, the wealth that you have gained, the commerce in which you fear a decline, and the dwellings in which you delight are dearer to you than Allāh and His Messenger, and striving hard and fighting for His Cause, then wait until Allāh brings about His Decision (torment)" Striving for the Cause of Allāh (Jihādan) means believing in Allāh and following Muhammad Rasūlullah and not physical engagement.

The Meaning of Jihād

The word "Jihād" appears four times only in the holy Qur'ān. The triliteral roots of the word include "Jahada," meaning difficulty, "Juhada," meaning ability or capacity. On the other hand, the third root of Jihād refers to the Sunna of Muhammad

Rasūlullah; it means the effort one makes in understanding Allāh and following the Sunna of the holy Apostle.

The Sahābas used the word to mean exerting the effort to understand an issue whose judgment is not known to one from the Qur'ān and the Sunna. It is very unfair to apply the meaning of "Jahada" without going back to the life history of Muhammad Rasūlullah in Makka. The arrival of the Levi tribe in Medina threatened the Aws and Khazraj tribes because it was said that "A prophet was to come in the later times with whom they would ally themselves, and kill the heathens just as the people of 'Ad and Iram were massacred."

It is lack of Juhada and Jihāda that is precipitating Jahada (difficulty) in the world. The followers of Muhammad believe that no one knows the correct interpretation and the Sunna of the holy Apostle except an 'Arab and that one is worthy of following if one does not know, or knows but does not apply the Sunna in practice. To Western Christians, no one knows except the tyrants and their surrogate illiterate preachers, but they distort and twist the Sunna of the holy Apostle.

In reality, the meaning of Jihād does not carry the meaning of physical engagement. Western Christians apply the meaning of Jihād to the engagements of the Amalekites, the Philistines, and others with the Children of Israel.

Classification of Jihād

Jihād Nafs. Ibn Qayyim Al-Jawziyya categorized Jihād under this category, which refers to the life of the holy Apostle. It is exemplified by the attitude and behavior of Muhammad ibn Abdullāh before his Apostleship. He was fully conversant with the life-style of the Quraysh and their attitude to Allāh. He preferred to go to the bush and stay in mount Hira, rather than to join them. This is the foremost form of Jihād. One has to purify his soul, mind, and body, before he can understand Allāh. This can only be done through the guidance of Allāh.

The first instruction Muhammad received is found in the holy Qur'ān 96:1-5, "Read! In the Name of your Lord. Who has created (all that exists)." The next command is in the holy Qur'ān 74:4-5, "And purifies your garments! And keep away from Ar-Rujz (the idols). Man is responsible for his deeds and will be called to account for it. All his actions are recorded and kept in a register. On the Day of Judgment Allāh will seal one's mouth and will only allow one's hands and feet to talk.

Western Christians should educate themselves as to what the followers of Muhammad Rasūlullah believe and what they put into practice. There is no value in Islām of any knowledge that is not put into practice. The following, for example, is what the Jihād Nafs cover:

Seeking the truth, this is the Sunna of the holy Apostle. There is no merit in reading the holy Qur'ān without understanding the Sunna of the holy Apostle. There is no merit in understanding the Sunna of the holy Apostle without putting it into practice. There is no merit in learning the Sunna of the holy Apostle, but leaving your neighbor impoverished. When the time for action arrives, put what one knows of the Sunna into practice. The holy Apostle said, "Pray in the manner you saw me praying."

One must not join the crowd. No one should come close to tyrants, lest they inadvertently participate in any form of injustice. It is unfortunate that this is not the call by the Muslims. On the contrary, they preach that it is allowed to join evil society and that out of two evils one can select the least harmful.

The teaching and practice of Muhammad Rasūlullah stresses that there is a choice between evil and good and that one will be rewarded according to the weight of his good deeds and equally to be punished according to the weight of his evil deed. Each evil deed stands becomes part of a unit and cannot be fragmented.[54] Each good deed stands on its own and cannot be fragmented. Prevention is better than a cure.

---

[54] See Matthews' commentary 206 on singular services.

The one who fulfills only three out of the four injunctions described above cannot be classified as a Rabaniyyan (one who can be trusted to lead others).

Jihād Shaiṭan. This is defined as Jihād to ward off anything that will bring doubt or uncertainty or any misgiving in one's Faith. This is best explained in the Message Prophet Moses delivered to the pharaoh in the holy Qur'ān 79:18-19, "Would you purify yourself (from the sin of disbelief by becoming a believer)? And that I guide you to your Lord, so you should fear Him?"

Man is capable of understanding the truth after he receives proof, evidence, and signs from Allāh. One has to give evidence on the Day of Judgment against his failure to be convinced by those signs produced before him by his Prophet. We have many such signs. The failure to make the world peaceful is one of such signs.

Jihād Shaiṭan is meant to ward off anything that can creep into one's mind that would call forth abominable and fanciful things. One has to be patient and never be enticed into doing evil or thinking of evil. Allāh says in the holy Qur'ān 18:28, "And keep yourself (O Muhammad) patiently with those who call on their Lord morning and afternoon, seeking His Face; and let not your eyes overlook them, desiring the pomp and glitter of the life of the world; and obey not him whose heart We have made heedless of Our Remembrance, and who follows his own lusts, and whose affair (deeds) has been lost."

Jihād against disbelievers and hypocrites. This type of Jihād applies to the followers of Muhammad Rasūlullah. Their disbelief implies disbelief in any of the articles of Faith (Īman), that is, in the first Pillar of Islām. Hypocrisy, as explained earlier, began after the migration of the holy Apostle to Medina. Disbelievers and hypocrites have the following characteristics:

When they talk, they lie.
When they make a promise, they break it.

When they are given trust, they do not honor it. Imagine the present Muslims!

Jihād against tyrants and the like. This begins with education.
Conditions to Be Fulfilled before Undertaking Jihād

Separation or running away from an unhealthy, lethal, and putrefying environment may be accomplished by way of migration. The ability given to mankind by Allāh to choose or to refuse is the emblem of Īman. It must be demonstrated physically; if not, the signs and proofs claimed by Allāh as His Tools to be used by mankind in quest of his success, salvation, peace, and progress in this world would be meaningless. Ideas must be put into practice before mankind can benefit from them.

The first to practice migration was Prophet Abraham (AS), the patriarch. He ran away from his people when he saw evidence that they were idol worshippers. He endured the punishment he received from them. Another instance is Prophet Moses chiding Prophet Aaron for not leaving the Children of Israel when he saw them with Samiri making ornaments.

In the holy Qur'ān 2:218, Allāh names three conditions for salvation saying, "Verily, those who have believed, and those who have emigrated (for Allāh's Religion) and have striven hard (Jahadu) in the Way of Allāh, all these hope for Allāh's mercy. Allāh is Oft-Forgiven, Most-Merciful." In the holy Qur'ān 8:72, Allāh further explains the relationship between those who emigrate and those who refuse to do so, saying, " . . . And as to those who believed but did not emigrate, you owe no duty of protection to them until they emigrate; but if they seek your help in religion (mundane way of life), it is your duty to help them except against a people with whom you have a treaty of mutual alliance; and Allāh is the All-Seer of what you do."

Allāh could not have given this instruction if what Western Christians are made to believe and understand about Muhammad—that he taught Muslims to spread his Sunna with the sword--were true. Therefore, Western Christians should stop listening and believing in what tyrants or their false preachers say about the Sunna of Muhammad Rasūlullah.

Besides separation from iniquity, other conditions necessary before Jihad are a strong Caliphate, that is, leadership as defined in the Talmud, and a just environment.

The only way leading to world salvation, then, is to make a hijrah and be with Muhammad Rasūlullah. There is no justification for doubting or delaying the truth, which is as clear as the rising of the sun on a clear blue sky. If Western Christian governments are sincerely looking for a way to establish democracy in Muslim countries, their dream will never materialize while they deal with ignorant, arrogant, and illiterate elites. Western education has so far failed to bring peace and stability in the world. The Sunna of Muhammad Rasūlullah should be studied by all, because he is sent as a bringer of glad tidings to the world, a scavenger of peace. Let us experience it NOW!

Jihād in the Sunna

Out of ignorance of the followers of Muhammad Rasūlullah Western Christians misconstrue the meaning of Jihad as contained in the Sunna. It is the protection of the city of Medina; and according to the covenant, it consists of three parts:

The protection of the city of Medina for his followers. This is similar to the Safe Towns of the Children of Israel.

The protection of the city of Medina for its inhabitants.

The protection of the city of Medina according to 'Arab customs.

Chapter 7

CRISIS WITHIN THE MUSLIM UMMA

It is important to reflect on the appeal of Allāh in the holy Qur'ān 57:16: "Has not the time come for the hearts of those who believe(in the Oneness of Allāh--Monotheism}to be affected by Allāh's Reminder (this Qur'ān and the life of Muhammad), and that which has been revealed of the truth, lest they become as those who received the Scripture (Torah and Injeel) before, and the term was prolonged for them and so their hearts were hardened? And many of them were *Fāsiqūn* (the rebellious, the disobedient to Allāh).

One component of this verse is an address to mankind, irrespective of his time and place, since the final arbitrator of our faith and actions is Allāh. Who does not remember Allāh? Is there an object in the world not showing that there is Allāh? Allāh confirms this, asserting on our behalf in the holy Qur'ān 39:38, "And verily, if you ask them: Who created the heavens and the earth?" Surely they will say: "Allāh (has created them)." Say: "Tell me then, the things that you invoke besides Allāh, if Allāh intended some harm for me, could they remove His harm, or if He (Allāh) intended some mercy for me, could they withhold His Mercy?" Say: "Sufficient for me is Allāh; in Him those who trust (i.e. believers) must put their trust." The mercy of Allāh is here shown to be always available and that He is indeed full of forgiveness, merciful, and ever ready to forgive those who have turned to Him.

The followers of Muhammad Rasūlullah are here advised to reflect on the past and learn from whatever information they have on what happened to the Children of Israel. The body of the pharaoh has been reserved to remind us of this, a monument serving a lesson on their attitude to their prophets. We have Masjid-al-Aqsa common to us. The Children of Israel and those who call themselves Christians should keep an eye on the behavior and attitude of the followers of Muhammad, on how they conduct their lives. This was exemplified by the Levi tribe of the Children of Israel in Medina, who threatened the Aws and Khazraj with extinction when that Prophet eventually arrives. It was that threat that made the Aws and Khazraj tribes of Medina go to the holy Apostle earlier than the Levi clans of the children of Israel. The truth then was revealed that all and sundry know the truth and that the Promise of Allāh should not be doubted.

The word "*Fasiqun*" implies that the discourse is addressed to the future generations of the followers of Muhammad Rasūlullah, drawing their attention again to their lapses and that they are following the footsteps of the People of the Book. This chapter was revealed between the Battle of Uhud and the Truce of Hudaybiya. In practical terms, there is no evidence that the companions of the holy Apostle misbehaved.

Since the conditions for Jihād necessitate hijrah and faith and that there must be a Caliph, the followers of Muhammad are not serious in calling for Jihād. They have no right. Such calls infuriate, provoke, and intimidate the physical world, like saying that Allāh has begotten a child! I am sure the People of the Book know this fully, for I was told that General Moshe Doyen once commented that it is possible for them to be defeated by the Muslims, but they are yet to see the Caliph!

There is no secret in the final message! The followers of Muhammad Rasūlullah have the wrong notion that the People of the Book do not know about Muhammad Rasūlullah. They {the Levi clans of the children of Israel} have experts in the field of the Sira, which is the life history of Muhammad Rasūlullah, except that they {the Levi clans of the children of Israel} do not physically believe in him.[55] Since Western Christians do not doubt the supremacy of the holy Apostle and that no one can break him, there is no justification after reading my exposition of the arrogance and illiteracy of the followers of Muhammad, for them to oppose those calling for the establishment of peace in the world. They should join hands with them and fight it out peacefully, without shedding blood. That was the call of Muhammad Rasūlullah in the holy Qur'ān 3:64, "Say (O Muhammad), 'O people of the Scripture (Jews and Christians): Come to a word that is just between us and you, that we worship none but Allāh (Alone), and that none of us shall take others as lords besides Allāh.' Then, if they turn away, Say: 'Bear witness that we are Muslims.'"

Western Christians should never give up demanding that the followers of Muhammad have, as the representative of Muhammad Rasūlullah, one educated in the Sunna. They were deceived in waging war against Saddam Husain, with disastrous consequences to themselves. My evidence is open to all and should be examined. A sincere follower of Muhammad Rasūlullah, fully aware of the nature of Allāh in the Old Testament and his stand on the Day of Judgment, will never deviate from the manner Muhammad Rasūlullah lived and his calling of the world to peace and salvation.

Muhammad did not rule in isolation. He formed a consultative assembly called the Shura. Today, Western Christians should befriend a follower of Muhammad Rasūlullah with the following qualifications:

a. He should have a comprehensive knowledge of what can bring peace to the world.
b. He must practice what he believes. There is not a single Muslim country that has established the

---

[55] See Suzanne Haneef. What One Should Know about Islam and the Muslims (Chicago:Kazi Publications: 1982).

Caliphate. The failure to establish the Caliphate has resulted in the Muslim countries not performing their Ibādat as exemplified by Muhammad Rasūlullah. On the sixteenth of February, Al-Jazeera television announced that Dr. Yusuf Qardawi, one of the most respected and renowned Islāmic preachers would visit Tahrir Square in Cairo to offer the Friday prayer with his fellow Egyptians. Unfortunately, that Friday I was traveling, and I was unable to follow the news coverage of the event. However, I was able to see a section, where he read a written statement condemning the attack by the Egyptian security forces and requested the opening of the borders between Egypt and Gaza. The first question is: Is he supposed to observe the Friday prayer? Who is he to be the Imām?

The Children of Israel should ask the followers of Muhammad Rasūlullah what prerogative they have over them and whether Allāh will not punish them for the deliberate offences they are committing. Why should Allāh punish the first born children of the Children of Israel for worshipping the golden calf and not punish the followers of Muhammad Rasūlullah for worshipping wealth and power?

c. His Caliphate should be between that of Jesus, the son of Maryam, and those of the Sahabas.

d. He should understand the application of secularism in the Sunna of Muhammad Rasūlullah. The Sunna is so vast that to restrict it is an invitation to extremism, intolerance, and all that we see today.

e. He must be tolerant as demanded by the Shura.

f. He must not only be a champion of doing good deeds, but ensure that they are done by all and sundry, according to exigencies.

Chapter 8

MUHAMMAD RASŪLULLAH
AND THE SAHĀBAS

The Quraysh, the tribe that took over the custodianship of Revelation from the hands of the Children of Israel, were never colonized by any world power, before the beginning of revelation. They had therefore no experience of any form of government, but only that they learned from Prophet Abraham and his son Ishmael. They never had a central government. They lived under loose tribal organizations and alliances. The Ka'ba, with its three-hundred-and-sixty idols, made them very influential in the 'Arabian Peninsula. They served the pilgrims and provided them accommodation. In addition, Makka was standing on the rich trading route. They had contact with the neighboring Byzantium and Roman empires. Thus they knew something about peace, stability, chaos, prosperity, and want.

The beginning of Revelation, in 610 A.D, undoubtedly brought light not only to the Qurayshites, but the whole world. It was meant to be a universal message, for it began with emphasizing and enforcing man to learn and to shun all abominations. It was scientific in its foundation, as stated in the holy Qur'ān 96: "Read in the Name of your Lord Who created (all that exists). He has created man from a clot (a piece of thick, coagulated blood)."

We must address this command: "Read!" What was Muhammad going to read? He was described as unlettered; but if he were to read something, he could read only from the Book of Abraham and the Book was absent at that time. If Allāh did not teach Muhammad the Books revealed to his predecessors, then Muhammad could have stood as an independent Apostle. What he knew would be limited to him alone. In other words, the Quraysh would have believed him about the Ka'ba, the standing of Abraham, the mountains of Safā and Marwa, the well, and so forth without their physical presence. The Jews in Medina would have believed him equally on all that he told them about their ancestors. It is impossible, therefore, to assume that Muhammad was not taught the Torah (Old Testament) and the Injeel (New Testament).

Now, anyone with a sincere heart and a desire to understand the nature of Allāh and His attributes will definitely study and follow the injunctions of Revelation, while those with an insincere heart will also study and comprehend them, but will deliberately refuse to follow the advice of reformation and democracy.[56] For thirteen years, the message dealt with past events, exposing success and failure, peace and conflict, poverty and richness. It revealed that the world definitely had an origin and a creator. It was an open invitation, calling on those who heard the message to sincerely come forward, endorse, and believe in it.

The Quraysh had the Ka'ba reminding them of Prophet Abraham and his son Ishmael, while the Levi tribe, in the far away city of Medina, had the Torah--the written and the oral--for guidance, and the tall palm trees of Fadak Valley. The 'Arab tribes, Aws and Khazraj living in Medina, were influenced by the Torah, but at the same time maintaining their gods. The Quraysh tribe in Makka and their neighboring tribes were not influenced by the Torah. They were polytheists, worshipping their respective gods, according to their tribal beliefs. They were aware of the place of honesty in a civilized society and believed that it is mandatory to listen to an honest man in times of conflict. They

---

[56] They received so-called Western education, without knowing its source from the holy Qur'ān.

77

called Muhammad ibn 'Abdallāh, Al-Amin. They accepted him as their arbitrator during their dispute on who would place the "black stone" on the wall of the Ka'ba in its corner. They were about to spill the blood of cousins, had Allāh not made him enter the Ka'ba at the time of their dispute.

Glory is to Allāh! Was He ever unmindful and forgetful of the needs of his servants? Was the intervention just in time? Did the Quraysh have any reference or knowledge at their disposal, saying that Allāh does not allow bloodshed? The clans of the Levi tribe of the Children of Israel were certainly aware of 1 Kings 12:24, "Don't go to war against the people from Israel, they are your relatives. Go home! I am the Lord. And I made these things happen." Did the Quraysh know this and acted against it? No! The holy Qur'ān 2:84 confirms this prohibition and in 2:85 accuses the Levi tribe of betraying that covenant, saying, "After this (that is, 1 Kings 12:24), it is you who kill one another and drive out a party from their homes, assist (their enemies) against them, in sin and transgression. And if they come to you as captives, you ransom them, although their expulsion was forbidden to you." The Levi tribe knew 1 Kings 12:24 at that time, for if that weren't so, they could have there and then accused Muhammad Rasūlullah of telling lies and concocting revelation. Allāh did not stop them, though Muhammad indirectly stopped them as He reminded them of their Torah. The case of the Quraysh was different, for they had no such rule directly through a prophet. Therefore, the intervention of Muhammad was as a result of the Mercy of Allāh.

There was an apparent "revolution" by 'Umar ibn Khaṭṭāb during the Treaty of Hudaybiya after learning that they had to abort the lesser pilgrimage and return to Medina. He went to Abūbakar Siddīq in rage, exhibiting his chutzpah by saying, "Is he not God's apostle, and are we not Muslims, and are they not polytheists?" Abūbakar agreed with this. 'Umar went on, "Then why should we agree to what is demeaning to our religion?"

Abūbakar pacified him, "Stick to what he says, for I testify that he is God's apostle." Umar said, "And so do I."[57]

That which was demeaning to his faith is certainly demeaning to Allāh, Muhammad Rasūlullah, and all the Sahābas. 'Umar, on behalf of the Sahābas, due to his closeness to the holy Apostle, was the first to react. But Allāh knew more than 'Umar and Muhammad--never to act, but by the command of Allāh. That was not the end of the fury of the Sahābas, for when the holy Apostle shaved his head some of them did the same, while others cut their hair. He said, "May God have mercy on the shavers." They said, "The cutters, too, O, apostle." Three times they had to put this request on until finally he added "and the cutters." When they asked him why he had repeatedly limited the innovation of God's mercy to the shavers, he replied, "Because they did not doubt."[58] In the presence of a leader, his subjects have no authority other than that from him. The above example points out that disbelief would never come from a constituted authority governed by divine Law, but rather the subjects could misinterpret a command, due to personal desires and ambitions. Whenever and wherever such ambitions and desires arise, they should be checked by the authority. The Sunna of the holy Apostle forbade the Muslims to rise against a constituted authority, provided they did not see an open disbelief.

The Sunna of Muhammad Rasūlullah covering the Pillars of Islām is not the same as that covering our daily lives. The Sunna covering the Pillars of Islām has been perfected, for it took into consideration individual capacities, opportunities, and weaknesses. One would, therefore, never expect any uprising. For our daily lives, the Sunna only sets guidelines; Allāh made Muhammad Rasūlullah aware of what would come during his

---

[57] Guillaume, A. The life history of Muhammad. New York, Oxford University Press.1987. 504

[58] Ibid. 505

time and our time. Fundamentally, all issues ought to be compared with such issues during the time of Muhammad Rasūlullah.

A distinction between "means," "expediency," and an "end" must be made. The Sharī'a, on positive values, should not be restricted to the holy Qur'ān, if one finds something in the Old Testament dovetailing an injunction in the Sunna or the holy Qur'ān.[59] The Sunna of the holy Apostle has priority in the life of an individual. Justice must prevail and be made available to an individual before he is punished. Justice begins by education and physical training. For example, when Ma'iz was brought to the holy Apostle accused of fornication, he was not punished without showing proof that he had knowledge of the punishment for fornication. Probably, he did not know what the Torah says.

An uprising over issues dealing with our daily lives is unjustified in the Muslim Umma. An uprising in any civilization is due to that civilization's indifferent attitude to the laws of Allāh. "Revolution," therefore, is wrath from Allāh. This was the case in 70 A.D, when Nebuchadnezzar and Titus respectively razed Jerusalem.

Arab Influence on the Propagation of the Sunna of the Holy Apostle

The general understanding of the Muslim Umma, in view of their illiteracy, semi-education, and arrogance, is that the 'Arabs are behaving in the manner that the Sahābas behaved during the time of the holy Apostle.

There is no Āyat in the holy Qur'ān specifying their superiority over other nations. The holy Apostle explained and demonstrated that an 'Arab is not superior to a non-'Arab, as a white man is not superior to a black man, except by virtue of the Taqwa, that is, the fear and love of Allāh.

---

[59]   For example, on charity and lending.

The Sahābas had the advantage over us in their understanding of the Sunna, because of their proximity to the holy Apostle. This is in conformity with the Decree of Allāh in the holy Qur'ān, 2:110 "You are the best people of people ever raised up for mankind." However, this does not mean that the 'Arabs are disposed (salīqa) today to understand the Sunna as the Sahābas did. The Sunna's rituals can be learned through practice, without necessarily learning the 'Arabic language. The articles of faith and Islamic jurisprudence can only be understood by learning 'Arabic.

It was because they understood the rituals empirically, that Islāmic knowledge deteriorated, resulting in instability in the world. Understanding the Sunna of the holy Apostle is a necessity; for in the long run, one will account for his deeds in the Hereafter. As explained in the holy Qur'ān, on that Day Allāh will address one saying, as stated in the holy Qur'ān 17:14, "Read your book. You yourself are sufficient as a reckoner against you this Day."

Therefore one has to weigh the consequences of absolutely relying on one he assumes to fear Allāh by virtue of his race, without achieving a personal conviction. The holy Apostle clearly said, "There is no obedience on action that is against the Sunna." As there is no compulsion in ad-Dīn, no one is compelled to understand the Arabic language. Language, however, is a conduit for expressing ideas, thoughts, and wisdom. One has to learn the 'Arabic needed to understand the Sunna.

The 'Arabs, have done a lot of work in explaining the Sunna of the holy Apostle, but unfortunately, some have neglected to put it into practice. They might transfer knowledge by way of television programs, some of which are educational and moving.

Chapter 9

EARLY MUSLIM REVOLUTIONS

A fulfilled and blessed "revolution" began when the Children of Israel asked their aged Prophet Samuel to ask God to give them a king who would rescue them from their enemies.[60] But why did they depend on God and not seek help from one of the tribes around them. The permission requested by Hamza ibn 'Abdul Muṭṭallib to fight their Quraysh cousins was not primarily for the oppression they suffered from them, but to prevent the Quraysh from taking their property to Syria to be auctioned. The right for one to defend his property was indirectly given by Allāh, through the demand by Him for Achan to return His stolen property.[61]

According to the Sunna of the holy Apostle, Western Christians are supposed to put into practice what was revealed in their scriptures, and his followers must put into practice what he commanded them. On issues not specified in the holy Qur'ān and the Sunna, Muslims should refer to the Old Testament for a solution, The followers of Muhammad Rasūlullah are expected to appoint or select their leaders according to his Sunna. They will never ask Allāh to appoint them a "king." Equally, they will never ask permission from anyone to execute what is commanded; nor will they ever allow oppressors to be their leaders, for they never had that training from Muhammad Rasūlullah. The ideal life of a follower of

---

[60] See 1 Samuel 10:27.
[61] See Joshua 7.

Muhammad Rasūlullah is that of working hard to earn one's living lawfully. It is not allowed for a believer to complain to his Caliph about any form of hardship, as the Jews complained to Rehoboam.[62] The holy Apostle said, "Complaining is a sign of one's ingratitude to Allāh."

The definition of "Revolution" as an attempt, by a large number of people, to change the government of a country, especially by violent action, has no root in the Holy Bible. In this context, the theory of "revolution" seems to me like a bad dream. By changing the government, I hope it means changing the condition in which the people are living. Violent measures are signs that people have for a long time being seeking a way of changing that condition, which disturbs them. How can the majority change a disturbing situation in a peaceful manner?

This definition must be revisited, in the light of what is going on today; the world powers must agree on what is a just revolution. Disturbing issues that are responsible for nation's backwardness and impoverishment and which lead to crimes against humanity should be something of the past, where the Prophets of Allāh are living. I cannot accept a revolution of violence to remove oppressors, for such oppressors are intruders from a neighboring territory. They must have their own beliefs, customs, and attitude towards justice and humanity. Their ideology could not have sprung out of the blues to be imposed on their neighbors. They would be regarded as unwanted foreigners (the Amalekites and Amorites etc) for according to the Old Testament a foreigner is to be helped and protected.[63]

From time to time, the Children of Israel were invaded by the Philistines, Amorites, and Amalekites whenever they became idolatrous. However, when they listened to their prophets and obeyed the Allāh (God) of Abraham, Isaac, Jacob, and Moses, they got a reprieve. Allāh has never subjected His sincere servants to

---

[62] See 1 Kings 12.
[63] This is the Law in Exodus 22:21.

the rule of tyrants and despots. Prophet Abraham lived in the land of Abimelech, the powerful king of the Philistines. He could have turned the bones of Prophet Abraham into fine powder, had Allāh made him not enter a treaty with Abimelech over the dispute of a well. That was the most precious priceless material at that time.

Matthew Henry observes that, "If our brother trespass against us, we must, with the meekness of wisdom, tell him his fault, that the matter may be fairly accommodated and an end made of it." Likewise, Prophet Moses helped to water the flock of the daughters of the Median priest, Jethro, in spite of his melancholy and distress. Henry observes, "This he did not only in complaisance to the daughters of Reuel (though that did well become him), but because wherever he was, an occasion offered itself. He loved to be doing well. Wherever the Providence of God casts us we should desire and endeavor to be useful, and, when we cannot do the good we would, we must be ready to do the good we can. And he that is faithful in a little shall be entrusted with more."[64]

Fighting between brothers is prohibited in the Old Testament. If one could accept the use of the word "revolution" as defined above by a true believer to justify over-throwing a legitimate institution, this is contestable for there is no place in the Old Testament directly or indirectly where the Children of Israel carried a "revolution" against a constituted authority of Allāh. The killing and assassination of their prophets and messengers, by their rebels, was never understood by them as a form of "revolution."

The first revolution recorded in history against a spiritually and democratically constituted authority was that which resulted in the assassination of the third Caliph, 'Uthman bin Affān. It was planned and executed by a group of disgruntled, semi-educated youths that flooded Medina, during the annual pilgrimage. The holy Apostle already informed 'Uthman bin Affān of his assassination, and told him never to hand over the trust--the

---

[64]   Commentary on the Whole Bible. P. 98.

84

Caliphate--Allāh gave him to anybody. This unfortunate incident should be regarded as complying with the vision of the holy Apostle: an Ishāra hadīth.

Muhammad Rasūlullah never spoke out of his desire, as it says in the holy Qur'ān 53:3, "Nor does he speak of (his own) desire." That incident is a lesson again, confirming the hadīth of the holy Apostle: "People will be occupied with believing a liar, denying what is true, betraying the trustworthy, dealing with deceivers, despicable mediocre delivering Fatwa, on what they do not know, as if there is no one who knows." 'Umar bin Khaṭṭāb warned that, "By the time the young ones take over explaining the Sunna of the holy Apostle, the elderly will resist it. If explaining the Sunna of the holy Apostle is done by the elderly, the young will follow and they will be guided."

'Abdullāh ibn Mas'ud said, "The Umma will prosper and live in peace as long as it is the elderly that teach the young the Sunna of the holy Apostle. When this is reversed, the young, and the most notorious taking control, the Umma will be destroyed." Hasan ibn 'Āli ibn Abī Ṭālib, who witnessed all that happened on that Friday morning Uthman ibn Affān was killed, and all that took place between the riff raffs and his father, said, "An illiterate is like the one going about off the road. An illiterate does more harm to the Umma than good. One should seek and learn the Sunna for the good of his Ibādat." Was Hasan indirectly not saying one should not attend congregation?

The correct form of Ibādat is that done according to the Sunna. People are fond of performing an Ibādat not based on the Sunna, leading them to fight those performing their Ibādat according to the Sunna. If they have the correct knowledge of the Sunna, they will not fight anybody. Mahkul said, "Allowing riff-raff to deliver Fatwa leads to destruction of the Sunna and impoverishment of the Umma."[65] Allowing the low socio-economic class to deliver Fatwa leads to corrupting ad-Dīn."

---

[65]   *Al-'Itāsām.* Vol. 3. P. 132.

There is no doubt that the murder of 'Uthman bin Affān, the battles of the Camel and Siffin, were all caused by semi-educated, illiterate, and ignorant youths, that is, "*ash-shabāb*." They came from Egypt, Alexandria, Syria, Iraq, and Iran. They believed in memorizing the Qur'ān, without relating to it to the Sunna of the holy Apostle. They lamentably understood decisions are binding based only on the holy Qur'ān. 'Āli bin Abī Ṭālib cautioned 'Abdullāh ibn Abbas not to engage them with the holy Qur'ān, but only with the Sunna of the holy Apostle. Those who had a rudimentary knowledge of the Sunna readily understood ibn Abbas. He was able to sway six- thousand ash-shabāb to his side.

"Revolution" is not allowed in Islām, at least in the Old Testament. What is not allowed in the Old Testament will never be allowed in the Sunna of the holy Apostle, at least it would not have been before the banishment of the Levi tribe in Medina. The life of the followers of Muhammad Rasūlullah was controlled and is still standing on the following:

a. "Nasīha" or counseling and advice. The holy Apostle said, "Ad-Dīn is Nasīha." The Sahābas asked: "To whom?" He said, "To Allāh and His Book, His Messenger, and the leaders of the Muslims and the people at large." Nasīha to Allāh and His Book means to stick to the injunctions of Allāh in the Qur'ān. Nasīha to Muhammad Rasūlullah is sending Salāt on him. Nasīha to the Muslim leaders and the common folk is the least, removing an injurious substance from the road. The holy Apostle said, "Three things are in the heart of a believer: Al-Ikhlās that is doing good for the sake of Allāh alone, giving advice and counseling to the Muslim leaders, and standing on what is good for the Muslim Umma.

b. Good wishes. None of you believes until he wishes for his brother what he wishes for himself.

c. Preventive measures. Whoever sees an evil action, let him change it with his hand; and if he is not able to do so, then with his tongue; and if he is not able to do so, then with his heart--and that is the weakest of faith.[66]

If the followers of Muhammad Rasūlullah would live according to those Ahadīth, they could close all avenues of injustice and corruption. Western Christians have an equal responsibility to closely watch the behavior of the followers of Muhammad Rasūlullah the very moment they backslide from any of the injunctions of the holy Apostle, which if not implemented will cause hardship and drive them to poverty. The Sunna of the holy Apostle recognizes the rights of those who are not his followers over the rights of his followers.

The Pattern of 'Arab "Revolutions"

The 'Arabic words close to "revolution" are *"thawra"* and *"qalaba."* Qalaba and its derivative, which mean to turn something in the opposite direction, appear thirty-six times in the holy Qur'ān. They are close in meaning to "revolution." According to the Old Testament, as quoted above, the children of Israel were invaded by the Philistines whenever they turned to idolatry. Everything in the world belongs to Allāh. We must always be grateful to Him, but never out of materialism. Therefore, we are expected to employ *thawra* and *qalaba* according to His Wish.

The world belongs to Allāh, and no event in this world will escape the decree of Allāh. Life under the Sharī'a is distinct from life under the Sharī'a of the unjust. Allāh warns of wars, injustices, and danger in the holy Qur'ān 23:71, "And if the truth had been in accordance with their desires, verily, the heavens and the earth, and whosoever is therein would have been corrupted! Nay, We

---

[66] Baghdadi, Ahmad ibn Rajab Hanbali 'Ali. Jâmi'ul 'Ulûm wal Hikm. Beirut. Dārul Kutb 'Ilmiyy. 1962. P.280.

have brought them their reminder, but they turn away from their reminder." Referring to those who have snatched His right and responsibility Allāh, objects to this in the holy Qur'ān 17:42: "If there had been other ālihah (gods) along with Him as they assert, then they would certainly have sought out a way to the Lord of the Throne (seeking His Pleasures and to be near to Him)."

Then He warned of unrest in the world in the holy Qur'ān 21:22, "Had there been therein (in the heavens and the earth) ālihah (gods) besides Allāh, then verily both would have been ruined. Glorified be Allāh, the Lord of the Throne, (High is He) above all that (evil) they associate with Him." Allāh says in the holy Qur'ān 35:43, "They took to flight because of their arrogance in the land and their plotting of evil. But the evil plot encompasses only him who makes it. Then, can they expect anything (else) but the Sunna (way of dealing) of the peoples of old? So no change will you find in Allāh's Sunna (way of dealing), and no turning off will you find in Allāh's Sunna (way of dealing)." One does not need any further explanation, except to verify this warning with historical events.

After the murder of 'Uthman bin Affān, the Muslim world was thrown into turmoil over the question of succession to the Caliphate. Who should be the Caliph, that is, the leader of the Muslim Umma? Those who thought that the Caliphate should be given to 'Āli bin Abī Ṭālib, because of his relation with the holy Apostle, have grossly misunderstood the Sunna of the holy Apostle. There is no succession to justice under inheritance.

What Allāh ordained to be inherited has been made clear in the holy Qur'ān and further explained by the Sunna of the holy Apostle. The Sahābas received equal treatment from the holy Apostle and were given responsibilities according to their education, proficiency, and 'Arab custom. However, the Trust and the Right of Allāh, that is, establishing the caliphate, became twisted and fell into the hands of ignorant believers. Let us carefully reflect on the holy Qur'ān 30:31-32, "And be not of the Al-Mushrikūn (the polytheists, idolaters, and disbelievers in the Oneness of Allāh). Of those who split up their religion (i.e., who left the true Islāmic Monotheism), and became sects, [i.e. then invented new things in the religion (Bid'ah) and followed their vain desires], each sect rejoicing in that which is with it."

Who can believe that those who caused the upheaval in the selection of the Caliph between 'Āli and Mu'awiya were aware and had full understanding of this verse? Many of them as described earlier were young and never had the chance to study the holy Qur'ān or the opportunity to be taught by the first witnesses. May Allāh forgive them their mistake!

After the assassination of 'Āli bin Abī Ṭālib, the Muslim Umma who resided in Kufa made another mistake. They chose Hasan ibn 'Āli bin Abī Ṭālib as their Caliph. The Muslim Umma living in Syria, on the other hand, chose Mu'awiya bin Abī Sufyan as their Caliph. Hasan marched his forces looking for Mu'awiya, and Mu'awiya marched his forces towards Kufa looking for Hasan. The two forces met at Anbar. A truce was drawn between them, and Hasan gave up his claim to the Caliphate.[67]

Mu'awiya bin Abī Sufyan was born about five years before the hijrah making him older than Hasan. According to the Sunna of the holy Apostle, Mu'awiya was more qualified to become the Caliph. It was reported that when Hasan conceded, Mu'awiya told him that he would succeed him after his death. When Hasan died in 49 A.H, Mu'awiya sought the consent of the people of Syria for his son Yazid to succeed him and they consented. This choice by Mu'āwiya was against the Sunna, for there were Sahābas older than Yazid and better educated on the Sunna.

When Mu'awiya bin Abī Sufyan wrote to the Muslim Umma--'Abdullāh bin Abūbakar, 'Abdullāh bin 'Umar, Husain bin 'Āli, Abdallāh bin Zubayr, and 'Abdullāh bin 'Abbas--in 54 A.H.

---

[67] This is the reason why the Western Christian world should try to understand Muhammad Rasūlullah. What is going on all over the world is a disgrace to intellect and scientific revolution! There is no one to command justice only oppression and tyranny!

seeking their consent, they denied his request. However, when he died in 60 A.H., the Syrians consented to the accession of Yazid to the throne of the Caliphate. Humaid ibn Abdurrahman said, "We went to see Bashir, a Sahāba, on this issue. He said, 'Definitely, Yazid at thirty three years old was not the one according to the Sunna of Muhammad Rasūlullah to ascend to the throne of the Caliphate. But since that was the decision of the majority, we have to live by that.'"[68] Definitely, that was a "revolution" against Allāh, for his Right was denied Him, not at that time caused by poverty, but by illiteracy and arrogance.

Yazid ruled for barely three years eight months. During that period, the Umma witnessed delaying the timing of Salāt, the assassination of Husain ibn Āli, and the battle of Harrah, as well as excesses and vanities. The whole focus of the Umma (probably in Syria and in the provinces that accorded to his ascension to the throne) was directed towards attainment of worldly desires. Indeed, this was the fulfillment of the hadīth of the holy Apostle, "Those who will succeed me after 60 A.H, will not be observing the Salāt in the manner I observed it, and will follow their vain desires and lusts. He will certainly meet with destruction. Then there will be people who recite the holy Qur'ān, but do not cross their necks. They are believers, hypocrites and libertines."[69] Although he died in 56 A.H, Abū Huraira sought refuge from what would happen after 60 A.H, and the leadership of youths.

---

[68] Ibrāhim, Majadi fathi Sayd.Tarikh Islam wal Muslimin fi 'Usri Umayyad. Cairo. Dārul Sahābata lil Turāth Batanta. 1998. P. 60-65.

[69] Shātibi, Allāma Muhaqq Abī Ishāq Ibrāhim bin Mūsa bin Muhammad Lahmi. Al-'Itisām. Manama. Maktabat Tawhīd. 1997. Vol.1:116; Shanqīti, Muhammad Amīn bin Muhammad Mukhtār Jakni. Adwā' Bayān fā Īdāh Qur'ān bil Qur'ān. Vol.2:495-535

The Umayyad Dynasty (41 A.H to 132 A.H)

The Umayyad Dynasty (41 A.H to 132 A.H) is notorious in that there was no peace in the Muslim countries and provinces ruled by the Sunna during this time. According to the observation of Sha Waliyulla Dahlawi, only four caliphs out of the fourteen who ruled in that period were described as ruling according to the Sunna of the holy Apostle.[70] Among them was 'Umar ibn 'Abdul 'Aziz ('Umar II) who reigned from 99-101 A.H. His administrative prowess and his awe of the Supreme Being have been carefully documented, but suffice it to mention his character and financial reforms.

On his character Abūl Hasan Ali Nadwi writes:

Immediately upon his accession, 'Umar dismissed provincial governors known to be cruel or unjust to the people. All the jewellery and valuable presents brought before him on accession to the throne were deposited in the State treasury. He was now a completely changed man; he considered himself a successor of Caliph 'Umar I, son of Khaṭṭāb, rather than Suleiman ibn 'Abdul Malik. Slaves of the royal household were emancipated; the royal court modeled after Persian and Byzantine Royal patterns was now marked by an austere and primitive simplicity. He returned to the State not only his ancestral fief but even the valuable jewellery his wife had received from her father and brothers. He led such a simple and ascetic life as it would have been difficult to find among the monks and recluses much less the kings and emperors. On several occasions he was late for Friday prayers since he had to wait till his only shirt dried up after a wash. Before 'Umar bin 'Abdul 'Aziz ascended to

---

[70] See Sahih Muslim, Kitab al-Imara (Lahore: Islamic Publications Date 1975.)III,1012.

the throne Baitul-Māl, the public treasury, was treated as a personal property of the King from which members of the royal family were granted enormous sums,[71] but now they had to be content with the paltry stipends. Once, when he was walking to his daughters, he notices that the children cupped their mouths while talking to him. On making enquiries he found that since only pulses and onions were available in his house on the day which has been taken by his children, they cupped their mouths lest its smell should offend him. With tears in his eyes, 'Umar said: "My child would you like to have sumptuous food and your father to be consigned to Hell?" He was the ruler of the mightiest empire of his day but he did not have enough money to perform the hajj. He once asked his servant if he had saved anything so that he could go for the hajj. The servant informed him that he had only ten or twelve dinars and that he could not undertake the journey. After a few days, 'Umar II received a sum sufficient to perform the hajj from his personal buildings. The servant congratulated 'Umar II, and said that now he could perform the hajj. 'Umar II, however, replied: "We have been deriving benefit from these buildings since a long time. Now, Muslims have a right to enjoy its fruits!" Then he got the entire proceeds deposited in the public treasury. . . . 'Umar II was careful not for his person alone. He always exhorted the State officials to be extremely cautious in their dealings involving the State property. The Governor of Medina, Abūbakar ibn Hazam had submitted an application to Suleiman ibn 'Abdul Malik demanding candlesticks and a lamp-glass for the official work. By the time the requisition reached the Caliph, Suleiman had died and it was placed before 'Umar II. He wrote: "O Abūbakar, I remember the days

---

[71]   This confirms 1 Sam. 8.

when you wandered during the dark nights of winter without candlesticks and light, and, were you then in a better condition than now? I hope you have now enough candlesticks to spare a few for conducting the business of the State." Similarly, on another request made for the supply of paper for official work, he remarked: "Make the point of your pen finer, write closely and concisely; for, Muslims do not require such detailed reports which are unnecessarily a burden on the state exchequer." . . .

Far-reaching reforms were introduced in the administration of the kingdom. Some of the steps taken were: Weights and measures were standardized, State officials were precluded from entering into any business or trade, unpaid labor was made illegal, pasture land and games-reserve reserved for the royal family or other dignitaries were distributed to the landless cultivators or made a public property, strict measures were taken to stop illegal gratification of state employees who were forbidden to accept gifts, all officers holding responsible posts were directed to adequate facilities to those who wanted to prevent their complaints to them in person, a proclamation was made every year on the occasion of the pilgrimage that anyone who would bring to the notice of the administration any mal-treatment by an State official or prefer a useful suggestion, shall be rewarded 100 to 3000 dinars.

The financial reforms embarked upon by 'Umar ibn 'Abdul 'Aziz, namely remission of numerous taxes and tithes disallowed by the Sharī'a, did not result in pecuniary difficulties or deficits in the state income. On the contrary, people became so much better off that it became difficult to find destitute persons and beggars who would accept the "Zakat" due to the poor.

Yahya ibn Sa'eed relates that 'Umar ibn 'Abdul 'Aziz had appointed him to collect the zakat in Africa. When he got the dues collected, he looked around for the needy and hard up persons, but he could not find a single individual who could be rendered assistance. He adds that 'Umar's economic policy had made everybody a man of substance; therefore, he had no alternative but to purchase a number of slaves and then emancipate them on behalf of the Muslim populace.

Another man from the Quraysh reports that during the extremely short reign of 'Umar bin 'Abdul 'Aziz, people used to remit substantial amounts pertaining to the zakat to the state exchequer for being distributed among the poor, but these had to be returned to them as nobody entitled to receive these charities was to be found. He says that everyone had become so well off during 'Umar's time that nobody remained in straitened circumstances entitled to receive the "poor-due."

Apart from the prosperity of the masses which is invariably a by-product of the Islāmic form of government, the more important change accomplished by the regime of 'Umar ibn 'Abūl 'Aziz was the diversion in inclination, aptitude, and mood of the populace. His contemporaries related that whenever new friends met during the regime of Walīd, they used to converse about buildings and architecture for that was the rage of Walid. Suleiman was fond of women and banquets, and these became the fad of his days. However, during the reign of 'Umar ibn 'Abdul 'Aziz, the prevailing subject for discussion was prayers, supplicatory and benedictory, obligatory and supererogatory. Whenever a few people gathered, they would ask each other about the voluntary prayers one offered for acquiring spiritual benefit, the portion of Qur'ān recited or committed to memory, the fast observed every month, and so forth.

'Umar II's achievement was his effort for moral reformation. This he did by actively participating in preaching and the dissemination of the Sunna and not relying solely on the distorted interpretation usually given by hypocritical scholars and preachers. It was never possible for an Umma to be guided and be prosperous if the leader did not stand in the position of Muhammad Rasūlullah. Muhammad Rasūlullah was not sent as a king or an emperor, but as a servant of Allāh to deliver people from oppression and slavery, which can be achieved only through a participatory educational program.

As Hasan Nadwi writes:

> He sent out quite lengthy letters and directives, which dealt with more about religious and moral reforms than with the so-called administrative affairs. His edicts embodied a spirit of preaching, religious and moral, rather than dispensation of government. In his letters he would compare the social and moral condition of people with that in the days of the Prophet and early Caliphate and elaborate the fiscal and administrative system required to bring about an Islāmic regeneration; impress on the governors and generals the importance of timely performance of their prayers and presiding at these services; exhort public servants to inculcate the awe of God and meticulously follow the regulations of the Sharī'a, charge his officers with the responsibility of spreading the message of Islām in the provinces under them, which he considered to be the sole objective of Divine revelation and the Prophet hood of Muhammad; insist on the enforcement of what is incumbent and on the prevention of that which is forbidden, and warn them of the harmful effects of neglecting this obligation; elaborate the criminal law of Islām and instruct the magistrates to be lenient in awarding punishments; draw attention towards the deviations and innovations, customs and foreign traditions that had found a way into the life of the people . . .

On steps to be taken to defend the faith Umar ibn Abdulazeez wrote to General Mansur ibn Ghalib:

> This is a directive from the bondman of Allāh and commander of the Faithful to Mansur ibn Ghalib.

Whereas the Commander of the Faithful has charged Mansur to wage war against those who might oppose him, the latter is also instructed to inculcate awe of God; since it constitutes the best of provisions, the most effective strategy and the real power. For the sin is even more dangerous than the ruses of the enemy, the Commander of the Faithful bids upon Mansur that instead of taking fright of his enemy, he should fear transgressing the limits of God. We overcome our enemies in the battlefield only because of their vices and sins, for, had it not been so, we would not have the courage to face them. We cannot deploy troops in the same number as our enemies can do nor do we possess the equipment they have got. Thus, if we equate ourselves with our enemies in misdeeds and transgressions, they would undoubtedly gain a victory over us by virtue of their numerical superiority and strength. Behold, if we are not able to gain ascendancy over our enemies on account of our righteousness, we would never be in a position to defeat them through our might. We need not keep an eye upon anything more than the enmity of our own wickedness nor do we have to hold in leash anything more than our own viciousness. You should realize the fact that God almighty has deputed wardens over you who never part company with you and they are aware of whatever you do in your camps and cantonments, secretly or in public. Therefore, do not put yourself to shame by exceeding the limits of God; be kind to others, especially as you have left your hearths and homes for the sake of God. Never consider yourselves superior to your enemies, nor take your victory for granted because of the sinfulness of your foes, for many a people worse than his enemy was granted ascendancy in the past. Therefore, seek the help of God against your own temptations in the same way as you desire the succor of God against your opponent. . .

On International Relations 'Umar ibn Abdul Azeez writes:

> To encamp far away from the habitations which have entered into treaty relations with us, and allow no one from his troops to visit their dwellings, markets, or gatherings? Only those of his men who are firm in faith and trustworthy and who would neither be ill-disclosed nor commit a sin against the people could be allowed to visit such habitations for collection of lawful dues. You are much bound to guarantee their rights as they are enjoined to fulfill the duties devolving on them, i.e., you have to honor your obligations to them so long as they do theirs. You should never gain an advantage over your enemy through persecution of those who have come under your protection, for you have already got a share (in the shape of Jizyah or poll-tax) in their earnings and you neither need to increase it nor they bound to pay more. . . .Now you need to pay attention to the land of polytheists, our enemies, and need not concern yourself with those who have come under our protection. . . .

He ended his letter by cautioning General Mansur that "You ought to keep an eye upon yourself and your actions; be cautious of the acts that unite you with Allāh, on the one hand, and your liegemen, on the other. You are aware that the salvation and safety lies in complete submission to the Almighty and the ultimate goal of all endeavors should be, by the same token, to make preparations for success on the Appointed Day. If you will, you might take a lesson from the happenings around you. Only then I can drive home the truth to you through my preaching. May God have peace on you?" [72]

---

[72]   Saviors of Islamic Spirit. Lucknow. Academy of Islamic Research and Publications. 1997. Vol.1:30-31.

The Children of Israel were given the flag to raise the superiority of Allāh for a period of almost 1450 years by the Covenant Ratified, Fixed, Established and Entailed.[73] However, this was not without conditions. The incursion into their lands by their neighboring enemies and their victory over them, whenever they forgot that the God of Abraham, Isaac, Jacob, and later of Moses and Aaron, confirmed that the Plan, Will and Decree of Allāh and the Covenant must be fulfilled. The reward or net result of standing by the Covenant was peace. It is only after peace is established that a nation begins to prosper. This is explained in the holy Qur'ān 17:6, "Then We gave you a return of victory over them. And We helped you with wealth and children and made you more numerous in man-power." The whole life history of the Children of Israel is summarized in the holy Qur'ān 17:8, "It may be that your Lord may show mercy unto you, but if you return (to sins), We shall return (to our Punishment). And We have made Hell a prison for the disbelievers." In 132 A.H., when the Umayyad failed to establish the Caliphate after a period of about ninety years, their authority was usurped by the tribes of al-Abbas. The causes of their downfall were given as follows:

a. Inqalab Khilāfa al Islāmiyya Ila Mulūk 'Adūd (forcefully changing the Caliphate and the Sunna of the holy Apostle to leadership based on arbitrariness). The Caliphate was established by Muhammad Rasūlullah as carbon print of leadership in the Old Testament. The one to represent the Muslim Umma was chosen based on his knowledge and piety, with age given precedence. The Umayyad changed

---

[73] {This is the appeal of Allāh to the children of Israel (the Levi clans) repeated in many places in the holy Qur'ān. For example see the holy Qur'ān 2:40.}

this system to representation based on ignorance, inheritance, deception, use of force, and wealth.

b. Concentrating on worldly desires and forgetting the rights of the common folk, without even lending ears to what they said and eyes to what they did.

c. Abandoning preaching and transferring it into the hands of incompetent preachers.

d. Sectarianism. The Banu Umayyad became divided into sects, each looking after itself and fighting one another. They did not comprehend that the division of the Children of Israel into twelve tribes was as a blessing. They forgot the lessons in the holy Qur'ān, in which Allāh gives each tribe its watering place, so they quarreled and fell into disputes.

e. Abandoning preaching by the Caliph, this resulted in the emergence of the Khawarij sect.

f. Multiple allegiances in a given time. A reigning Caliph would seek allegiance for his sons.

g. Nepotism. This was widely practiced where governors were appointed according to their family tree and closeness. They thought that this would protect them from "revolution," but it turned against them, as happens today.

h. Overwhelming terrorism. They virtually terrorized their people, especially those with knowledge of the Sunna of the holy Apostle, calling on them to be just and to shun all abominations.

i. Economic stagnation, which led to reduced salaries for the security forces.

The Abbasid Dynasty

The members of the Abbasid Dynasty (750-1258 A.D.) were the offspring of al-Abbas, the cousin of the holy Apostle. They came to power as a result of the failure of the Umayyad tribe of

Quraysh to establish justice and to rule by the Divine Law. This upheaval proved the primary significance of the command that comes from the God of Abraham, Isaac, Jacob, and Moses, that Jesus, the son of Maryam, and Muhammad, the son of Abdallāh, were not sent by Allāh to do away with the Law of Abraham and Moses.

For thirteen years, Muhammad, as a Prophet, taught and reminded the Quraysh and the neighboring Levi tribe of the Children of Israel of the way Allāh dealt with past generations. Muhammad was challenged by the Quraysh and the Levi tribe to change the system, but declined, saying in the holy Qur'ān 10:15, "It is not for me to change it on my own accord; I only follow that which is revealed unto me, I fear the torment of the Great Day (i.e. the Day of Resurrection) if I were to disobey my Lord! If Allāh had so willed, I should not have recited it to you nor would He have made it known in you. Verily, I have stayed amongst you a life time before this. Have you then no sense?"

The Promise of Allāh to His servants is that He will only establish the authority and support one provided that servant will do the following:

enjoin Iqāmat (establish)-as-Salāt, meaning to abide by His system in the same manner as the holy Apostle;

give out the Zakat;

enjoin Al-Ma'ruf (give all equal opportunity to contribute to the betterment of the people);

forbid Al-Munkar (all forms of injustice).

Allāh does not and has never punished his servant at the instant of a crime; He waits until the period of respite expires. This is the Mercy of Allāh, for our abode initially was Paradise and not Hell. However, this period of respite should not be taken lightly and abused; the Children of Israel, for example, who refused over twenty years to march to the Holy Land (Palestine), never got there. Those who saw the Holy Land were all under twenty years of age. After the death of Prophet Moses and the triumphant entry of Joshua into the Holy Land, the Children of

Israel enjoyed peace for a period of thirty years. Joshua, in his farewell speech, said, "Yes, when the Lord makes a promise, he (He) does what he promised. But when he makes a threat, he will also do what he has threatened. The LORD is our GOD. He gave us this wonderful land and made an agreement with us that we would worship only him. But if you worship other gods, it will make the LORD furious. He will start getting rid of you, and soon not one of you will be left in his good land that he has given you." (Josh. 23:15-16)

The Crusades (1097-1250 A.D)

The Crusades were military campaigns undertaken by those who called themselves "Christians" from Europe in the eleventh, twelfth, and thirteenth centuries. They sought to recover the Holy Land, particularly Jerusalem, from the Muslims. From the account given of the Crusades, those so-called Christians were not true followers of the teaching of Jesus, the son of Maryam. Jesus, the son of Maryam, never undertook any military expedition to conquer a land by coercing its inhabitants to follow him. The Holy Wars undertaken by the then Children of Israel were to drive back the intruders who came into their land as a result of their backsliding. Muhammad Rasūlullah did not undertake any military expedition for the sake of worldly gain or position. His were under Divine Commands.

Historians give the number of Crusades as between seven and nine. Allāh warned mankind of the possibility of the Crusades in the holy Qur'ān 47:8, "But those who disbelieve (in the Oneness of Allāh--Islamic Monotheism), for them is destruction, and Allāh will make their deeds vain." If the Crusades were for the sake of establishing justice, they could have checked the excesses and unjust administration of the Abbasid kings.

The Sunna of the holy Apostle is not immune to the decree of Allāh; by this time injustice is the practice among his followers.

Muslim scholars, while always defending their misunderstanding of the Sunna of Allāh, blame the Crusades on those influenced by the Greco-Judaean form of the pure teaching of Jesus, the son of Maryam.

Defeating a sincere believer on a battlefield for the sake of Allāh is something never heard of in world history. Allāh assured the true followers of ad-Dīn in the holy Qur'ān 4:141, "And never will Allāh grant to the disbelievers a way to (triumph) over the believers." In the holy Qur'ān 47:7, Allāh again appeals to mankind, "O you who believe! If you help (in the cause of) Allāh (to establish the Caliphate), He will help you, and make your foothold firm." Whatever misfortune befalls a believer is his own doing, as a result of disobeying Allāh.

The First Crusade began in 1097 A.D (491 A.H), during the reign of the Abbasid king Ab'ul Abbas Ahmad al-Mustazhir, bursting in all its fury and rage in Western Asia. Wikipedia Encyclopedia lists nine Crusades, while Syed Ali Amer mentions eight. The final one ended in 647 A.H., which is equivalent to 1249-1250 A.D. Other historians count <u>seven major Crusades</u>.

According to some Orientalist and Muslim scholars, the Crusade sprang out of fanaticism mixed with the desire to carve out new kingdoms or acquire riches; and "sensuality was allured by the fabulous flavor of Oriental wines, and the magical beauty of Grecian women."[74] This added fuel to an already furious prairie fire.

Justice is common to all religions. The First Crusade (1097–1099), probably the most justified, was a military expedition by Western Christianity to regain the Holy Lands taken in the Muslim conquest of the Levant, ultimately resulting in the recapture of Jerusalem. The Christians were free to travel to Jerusalem for observing their religious rights.

---

[74] Ali, Syed Amir, *A History of the Saracens* (New Delhi: Kitab Bhawan, 1977), 322-387.

Palestine came into the possession of the Turkoman family of Ortok, who acknowledged a lax obedience to the Seljukian sovereign or his Syrian feudatory. Towards the end of the tenth century, there was a large influx of pilgrims from the Latin world to the Holy Land. The large influx of strangers and their furious zeal were equally unintelligible to the rude Turkomans, and the pilgrims were occasionally exposed to ill-treatment and robbery. The tale of ill-treatment, grossly exaggerated as usual, brought to a head the long-term animosity of the Franks. In March and November of 1095 Pope Urban II summoned councils in Placentia and Clermont, respectively, with the primary goal of responding to an appeal from Byzantine Emperor Alexios I Komnenos, who requested that western volunteers come to his aid and help repel the invading Seljuq Turks from Anatolia. An additional goal soon became the principal objective--the Christian re-conquest of the sacred city of Jerusalem and the Holy Land and the freeing of the Eastern Christians from Islamic rule.

Pope Urban II felt that the noble race of Franks needed to come to the aid of their fellow Christians in the East. The infidel Turks were advancing into the heart of Eastern Christendom; Christians were being oppressed and attacked; churches and holy places were being defiled. Jerusalem was groaning under the Saracen yoke. The Holy Sepulcher was in Moslem hands and had been turned into a mosque. Pilgrims were harassed and even prevented from access to the Holy Land. Pope Urban's speech was recorded by historian E.L.Skip Knox:

"The West must march to the defense of the East. All should go: rich and poor alike. The Franks must stop their internal wars and squabbles. Let them go instead against the infidel and fight a righteous war. God himself will lead them, for they will be doing His work. There will be absolution and remission of sins for all who die in the service of Christ. Here they are poor and miserable sinners; there they will be rich and happy. Let none hesitate; they must march next summer. God wills it!"

Another dimension of the First Crusade was the attack on the French Jewish community. Wikipedia describes this incident:

The attacks may have originated in the belief that Jews and Muslims were equally enemies of Christ, and enemies were to be fought or converted to Christianity. Godfrey of Bouillon had extorted money from the Jews of Cologne and Mainz, and many of the Crusaders wondered why they should travel thousands of miles to fight non-believers when there were already non-believers closer to home. The attacks on the Jews were witnessed by Ekkehard of Aura and Albert of Aix; among the Jewish communities, the main contemporary witnesses were the Mainz Anonymous, Eliezer ben Nathan, and Solomon bar Simson. In 1097, after successive defeats, Godfrey de Bouillon took over the command of the Crusades and with 700,000 strong marched towards the plains of Nice. Jerusalem fell to them on 23rd Sha'aban 492, equivalent to 15th July 1099. The success or otherwise of the Crusades have been debated by historians. This is left for those interested to pursue.

An incident not recorded among the Crusades was what the historians described as the Scourge of the Tartars. Sultan 'Ala ud-din Muhammad Khwarism Shah (596-617 A.H) was a powerful Muslim monarch with his domain extending from India to Baghdad, the Sea of Aral to the Persian Gulf. His moral character was unquestionable--pious, just, but at the same time spending his prowess and capabilities in subjugating the Muslim Kingdoms around his dominions.

Chenghiz Khan of Mongolia, who had a vast empire, approached Khwarism to encourage trade between their people. Traders should be allowed from each empire to move freely, buying and selling without any undue restriction. Khwarism

Shah agreed, and soon traders began to move from one empire to the other. But this agreement was short lived. Harold Lamb, reporting on the cause of this break down in his famous book Genghiz Khan.

> But the Mongol's experiment with trade came to an abrupt end. A caravan of several hundred merchants from Karakorum was seized by one, Inaljuk, governor of Otrar, a frontier citadel belonging to the Shah. Inaljuk reported to his master that spies were among the merchants – which may very well have been the case. Muhammad Shah, without considering the matter overmuch, sent to his governor an order to slay the merchants, and all of them, accordingly, were put to death. This, in due time, was reported to Genghiz Khan, who dispatched envoys at once to the Shah to protest. And Muhammad saw fit to slay the chief of the envoys and burn off the beards of the others. When the survivors of his embassy returned to Ghenghiz Khan, the master of the Gobi went apart to a mountain to meditate upon the matter. The slaying of a Mongol envoy could not go unpunished; tradition required revenge for the wrong inflicted. 'There cannot be two suns in the heavens,' the Khan said, 'or two Kha Khans upon the earth.'

Ghenghiz Khan now decided to take revenge; in 616 A.H. he began his military campaign, described by historians as the "scourge of God." Abūl Hasan 'Āli, quoting the author of *Mirsad ul-'Abad*, gave the following harrowing account:

> The year 617 A.H. shall ever remain conspicuous in the annals of the world, for the hordes of heathen Tartans gained ascendancy over the Muslims in that year. The way they ravaged the country, killed the people and plundered and burnt the cities has a parallel neither in

the days of ignorance nor thereafter. . . . It is enough to mention that in Ray, where I was born and lived, in Turkistan and in the lands extending from Rum to Syria more than seven hundred thousand people were either put to sword or made captives. The calamity befalling Islām and its adherents is beyond description and the holocaust is rather too well-known to require any detailed enumeration. God forbid, none of the monarchs and sovereigns of Islām felt the urge to defend the honor of Islām; nor were they alive to their duty of coming to the rescue of their subjects although they were like a shepherd unto their own people, and that they would have to render an account in regard to their safety on the Day of Judgment. It was their duty to have strained every nerve to strengthen Islām and defend the faith as God has ordered: Go forth, light-armed and heavy-armed, and strive with your wealth and your lives in the way of Allāh.[75] They should have sacrificed everything they had – their lives, riches, dominions--for the honor of Islām. This would have given heart to others and fired a frenzy of enthusiasm among the Muslims, which would have contained and turned back the onslaught of the heathens. But now, nothing remains except to seek the refuge of God. Whatever of Islām is still visible is exposed to the danger of being completely effaced leaving no trace of it whatsoever.

The sack of Baghdad in 656 A.H. was described by ibn al-Athir, "The horrors of rapine and slaughter lasted forty days; and, after the carnage was over, the most populous and beautiful city of the world was so devastated that only a few people could be seen here and there. All the streets and markets were strewn with dead bodies; heaps of corpses were to be found like small

---

[75] See the holy Qur'ān 9:41.

mounds from place to place. After the rains the dead bodies began to rot giving out a disagreeable smell of the putrid flesh and then a deadly pestilence ravaged the town, which spread as far as the land of Syria. Innumerable people died as a result of this epidemic. The ravages of a terrible famine and pestilence and the rising prices reigned over the city thereafter."

The bloodthirsty Mongols were not satisfied. They wanted more carnage and devastation. So, they advanced to Haleb and after sacking and reducing it, turned to Damascus, capturing it in 658 A.H., three years before the birth of Ibn Taymiyya. Meanwhile, the Sultan of Egypt, al-Malik as-Muzaffar Saif ud-din Qataz, sensed that the next place to be visited by the Mongols would be Egypt. He did not give them the chance to march, but instead made a quick march and attacked them in Syria. Under the command of Baiber, the forces met at 'Ain Jalut on the 25th of Ramadan, 658 A.H. and dealt the Syrians a deadly blow, slaughtering and capturing a large number of them. Abūl Hasan Ali, quoting Al-Suyuti wrote, "The Muslims were, by the grace of God, victorious and they inflicted a grievous defeat on the tartars. A large number of Tartars were put to the sword. The retreating Tartars were so disheartened that people easily caught hold of them and despoiled them of their possessions."[76]

The greatest victory of Baiber over the Mongols was their unexpected and sudden conversion to Islām. This was credited to the preaching of Islām that ramified and penetrated their hearts. T.W. Arnold, commenting on this incident, has written,

Islām was to rise again from the ashes of its former grandeur and through its preachers win over these savage conquerors to the acceptance to the faith. This was a task for the missionary energies of Islām that was

---

[76] Nadwi, Abul Hasan Ali. Saviors of Islāmic Spirit. Lucknow, Academy of Islamic Research and Publications. 1977. Vol. 1. PP. 292-296.

rendered more difficult from the fact that there were two powerful competitors in the field. The spectacle of Buddhism, Christianity and Islām emulously striving to win the allegiance of the fierce conquerors that set their feet on the necks of adherents of these great missionary religions, is one that is without parallel in the history of the world. For Islām to enter into competition with such powerful rivals as Buddhism and Christianity were at the outset of the period of Mongol rule, must have appeared a well-nigh hopeless undertaking. For the Muslims had suffered more from the storm of the Mongol invasions than the others. Those cities that had hitherto been rallying points of spiritual organizations and learning for Islām in Asia, had been for the most part laid in ashes; the theologians and pious doctors of the faith, either slain or carried away into captivity. [77]

The point to be drawn here is for Western Christians to understand what history has proved Islām to be. If it had been destroyed and forgotten, it could have suffered extinction by now, not only from the hands of the so-called enemies of Islām, but in particular from the hands of those who professed it. Secondly, those who desired to extinguish it, in the long run turned to accept it. Therefore, this book seeks to remind the West about the true light of Islam. The Sunna of the holy Apostle could not suffer extinction when Allāh says in the holy Qur'ān 71:9, "He it is Who has sent His Messenger with guidance and the ad-Dīn of truth to make it victorious over all (other) ad-Dīn even though the Mushrikūn hate (it)."[78]

---

[77] Nadwi, Abul Hasan Ali. Saviors of Islāmic Spirit. Lucknow, Academy of Islamic Research and Publications. 1977. Vol. 1. PP. 292-296

[78] The rendering of this verse appears three times, all during the Medinan revelation and all in relation to the battlefield. If

Chapter 10

TWENTIETH CENTURY 'ARAB "REVOLUTIONS"

I will give a brief history of some Muslim preachers, whom Western Christians are made to believe were extremists and Jihādists. They were, in fact, saviors of Islām.

Abū Husain Muhammad bin 'Abdulwahab bin Suleiman bin 'Aliyu bin Mushasrraf Āli Ma'dhād Wahībi (1115-1206A.H.)

The year 1115 A.H., equivalent to 1694 A.D., witnessed the birth of Abū Husain Muhammad bin Abdulwahab bin Suleiman bin Aliyu bin Musharraf Āli Ma'dhād Wahībi, in 'Uyayna, in the vicinity of Yamāma in the 'Arabian Peninsula. He was from the tribe of Banū Hanzala bin Mālata Tamīmī. In Yamāma lived 'Abdurrahman, alleged by Abū Jahl to be the teacher of Muhammad Rasūlullah. It was the city that witnessed the first uprising in Islām after the burial of the holy Apostle. The number of Sahābas who settled there is uncertain, but they have no excuse to plead ignorance to Allāh on the Day of Judgment. May Allāh forgive us!

Abdulwahab's Ijtihad was a result of inadequate knowledge of the principles of Islām, particularly that resting on the first pillar--Īman and Islām. His work is an explanation of the faith

---

the Muslim Umma could survive after a particular battle and participate in another battle, then the question of vanquishing it should be revisited. Chapter Holy Qur'ān 8:28 ends with "And All-Sufficient Allah is as a Witness."

and action of patriarch Prophet Abraham. It is thus a piece of spiritual literature that should be adhered to by all. It is wrong to limit its use to only a section of mankind. There are about twenty-four authors today on this subject; none of them differs, except in understanding based on one's profession. His original work has been now upgraded into eleven volumes by 'Abdul Mun'īm Ibrāhim.

According to Jābin Ghanām and Ibn Bashir, practical evidence on the Sunna of the holy Apostle had disappeared in the mosques.[79] There was nothing but innovations, ignorance, sectarianism, bigotry, and religious intolerance. People were worshipping people, graveyards, trees, rocks, and caverns. The 'Arabs began to live as if Muhammad Rasūlullah was yet to be sent. The most atrocious thing was the apparent indifference of the people--the preachers, priests, students, deputies--as if the revelation was not in their mother tongue. Even if that region was ever governed by a Caliph, those who took over the custodianship of the Muslim Umma probably were resistant to the Sunna of Muhammad Rasūlullah. The people became not only ignorant of the Sunna, but were equally averse to hearing it. In Islām, one who rejects the Sunna and introduces something else, in spite of being cautioned, is a worse offender than one who believes in the trinity.

The Aqīda (conviction) of Abdulwahab

When he was asked his thinking and attitude towards the teaching of Muhammad Rasūlullah, he replied as follows:

One should believe in the articles of faith as explained by Muhammad Rasūlullah.

One should believe in the attributes and qualities of Allāh as described by Muhammad Rasūlullah.

---

[79] Sadlani, Dr. Sālih Ghānim. Ṣalāt Jama'a. (Riyadh: Dārul Balnasiyya, 1995.9-12).

Allāh has no partner.

He is All-Hearing and All-Seeing.

One must not reject the descriptions of Allāh as put forth by the holy Apostle.

No one should change a word from its intended meaning or conceal it.

No one should enquire about the form or shape of Allāh.

Allāh should be sanctified.

The holy Qur'ān is the revealed Word (Speech) of Allāh to Muhammad Rasūlullah, which originated from Him and will in the end return to Him.

No one should question Allāh. He does what He likes. Nothing will exist except by His Irāda (Will) and nothing will ever escape His Mashī'a (Desire).

Nothing in the world will ever escape his Taqdir (Plan).

Nothing can set in except by His organization.

No one can escape from what He has ordained for him.

No one can escape from what is ordained in the Scroll.

Everything that the holy Apostle said about life after death will be seen.

The soul will be restored to the body after death for accountability--enjoyment or punishment.

Muhammad Rasūlullah is full of awe concerning the Day of Judgment; the water on that day will be whiter than milk and sweeter than honey. There is an abundance of cups--more than the number of stars. Whoever drinks the water will never feel thirsty.

The Sirat will be placed on the edge of Hell-fire, and people will walk over it according to their deeds.

Muhammad Rasūlullah will be the first to intercede except on behalf of those who disregarded his Sunna.

Paradise and Hell fire are two creations of Allāh.

The believers will see Allāh in the manner they see the moon.

Muhammad Rasūlullah is the Imām of the Messengers and seal of the Prophets.

Abūbakar Siddīq is the most respected and honored among his disciples, followed by 'Umar ibn Khaṭṭāb, Uthman bin Affān, 'Ali ibn Abi Ṭālib, the ten Sahābas promised paradise, and the participants of Badr and the Hudaybiya treaty.

The Sahābas are also honored.

The wives of the holy Apostle are the mothers of the believers and are free from all want.

People differ according to their faith, but none will ever give command.

It is only those described by Allāh and his Apostle who are destined to enter paradise or Hell fire.

No one is allowed to call another a Kafir, except for those allowed by the holy Apostle. One should hope for those who do good deeds and fear for those who do evil deeds.

Jihād is without limit under the command of a Caliph or one not a Caliph.[80]

One is allowed to pray behind them.

Jihād is permissible up to the moment Dajjal will be killed.

The cardinal principles of the call of Abdulwahab are:

The Din is that described by Allāh in the holy Qur'ān 3:85, "And whosoever seeks ad-Dīn (a religion) other than Islām, it will never be accepted of him, and in the hereafter he will be one of the losers."

We call people to profess the Unity of Allāh according to what Allāh revealed to Muhammad Rasūlullah in the holy Qur'ān12:108, "Say O Muhammad: This is my way; I invite unto Allāh with sure knowledge, I and whosoever follows me.

---

[80] I used the word "Khalīfa" to mean Imām birran and "not a Khalīfa" to mean Imām fājiran. If one commits an offence and is punished under the Sharī'a, he is free and should command. However, the situation is different today. People commit all crimes and are not punished. So they cannot lead one who is knowledgeable and free from vices. The Sharī'a is clear on vices.

And Glorified and Exalted be Allāh (above all that they associate partners with Him). And I am not of the Mushrikūn."

We call people to avoid associating Allāh with something, He did not approve. He says in the holy Qur'ān5:72 "Verily, whosoever sets up partners (in worship) with Allāh, then Allāh has forbidden Paradise to him, and the Fire will be his abode."

Ijtihad is to understand the Sunna, based on proof and evidence.

We shall abide by the Book of Allāh and the Sunna of the holy Apostle and the Sahābas and their pupils.

We shall not say anything that contradicts the Ahadīth of the holy Apostle, or something the intellect will reject.

We shall fight those who worship idols in the manner the holy Apostle dealt with them.

We shall fight those who refused to pray and give out the poor dues, in the manner done by Abūbakar Siddīq.

A disbeliever is one who disbelieves in an article of Faith or Islam.

We shall not slay anyone except the one who takes life, apostasy after having full conviction.

We shall establish Salāt, giving out the poor due and all that Allāh and his Apostle commanded.

We shall not allow usury, consumption of alcohol and all that is abominable to mankind.

The Beginning of 'Abdulwahab's Call on the Sunna

The exact period is not mentioned, but it could be around 1160 A.H. Abdulwahab began from his hometown, Haryamla, and then moved to Uyayna. He met their king, 'Uthman bin Mu'amar, who gave him a warm reception. But the king could not withstand the establishment of the Sunna for fear of reprisals from other kings. Therefore, 'Abdulwahab left and headed further north to Dar'iyya, and was received gracefully by the king, Muhammad ibn Mas'ud. 'Abdulwahab explained to him the aim of his call on the Oneness of Allāh. His mission was not born out of pride, arrogance, or desire for worldly gains, but purely because no one was courageous and bold enough to come out and face the challenge that the messengers of Allāh had faced--evil must be uprooted and the poor salvaged.

The Significance of the Call of 'Abdulwahab

Man was not only created to be subservient and the slave of Allāh, but for a more important and distinctive position: to function as the deputy of Allāh in the world. If Allāh were to rule directly, he would not have created mankind as a vicegerency. In fact, the world will never be as we know it today. The physical presence of Allāh in the world is represented by inanimate objects as well, compelling mankind to believe in Him. They are there for our security and benefit and are completely under the command of Allāh. This benefit takes precedence over that of enslavement.[81]

Man must be just and tolerant and show mercy not only to his fellow beings, but also to the lower primates. This can be inferred from the breathing of the Spirit of Allāh into man. He has thus to some extent the qualities of Allāh. The power of will, that is, the ability to choose and refuse, which has been bestowed on mankind, makes him account for what is good and what is bad. Man will thus be rewarded or punished in this world and in the Hereafter.

Man must therefore steer his destiny. As a deputy of Allāh, he is expected to use his power of initiative, always cognizant of the Plan, Will, and Decree of Allāh. A deputy has no independent will, for his will is always that of his master. His action should always be directed to the pleasure of his master. The choice given to man in some circumstances is due to the relativity of time and the mercy of Allāh on what He blessed us with.

---

[81] They were created first.

Man undertook a covenant with Allāh according to the holy Qur'ān 7:172-173. Explaining this covenant, Ubay ibn Ka'b said the following:

> Allāh gathered the whole of mankind and arranged them into separate groups according to their kinds or periods and gave them human shape and power of speech. Then He took a Covenant from them and made them witness concerning themselves and asked, 'Am I not your Lord?'[82] They answered, 'Most certainly, You alone are our lord.' Then Allāh said, 'I ask the earth and the heavens and your father Adam to bear witness to this effect lest you should say on the Day of Resurrection that you had no knowledge of this. So note it well that none other than I is worthy of worship and that there is no other Lord than I. You should not set up any partner with Me. I will send to you My Messengers, who will remind you of this covenant that you are making with Me; I will also send My Book to you.' At this the whole of mankind replied, 'We bear witness to this: You alone are our Lord and our deity: we have no other lord or deity than You.'

In the holy Qur'ān 17:22-38, Allāh mentioned the duties of man and what is expected of him as a servant of Allāh. "Speaking the truth" invariably refers to that knowledge Allāh gave to Prophet Adam in the holy Qur'ān 2:71. Man is yet to create his own planet or something equivalent to the weight of a mustard seed or as heavy as the covering of a date seed. Man can copy the product of Allāh but cannot initiate that product.

When Allāh commanded Prophet Noah to build his ship in the holy Qur'ān 11:37, "And construct the ship under Our Eyes and with Our Revelation," Adam told Allāh that he does not know how to construct a ship. Allāh then told him to kill a

---

[82] "Lord" means our sustainer, guardian, master, and administrator.

bird and construct it in the shape of the bird's breast. Prophet Noah most likely did not know why he was commanded by Allāh to construct a ship, but he did so. Then Allāh commanded him to embark on it with only those who believed in his message. He obeyed the command. Then suddenly the heavens and earth opened up and water began to pour down. Prophet Noah alone, in the absence of any contesting world power was saved by Allāh; the disbelievers drowned. Prophet Noah and those who believed in him were thus the servants of Allāh in the sense that a servant obeys the command of his master.

On the other hand, in the holy Qur'ān 33:72-73, Allāh mentioned the position of man as his deputy (vicegerent) implying trust or moral responsibility. He says, "Truly, We did offer Al-Amānah (the trust or moral responsibility or honesty and all duties which Allāh has ordained) to the heavens and the earth, and the mountains, but they declined to bear it and were afraid of it {afraid of Allāh's torment}. But man bore it." Man is here depicted as a representative of Allāh. Was the choice of Allāh justified? Is it suitable to the creation of man and all that Allāh has appropriately given to man?

Matthew Henry's commentary on the covenant with Prophet Noah in Genesis 6:18 says, God (Allāh) makes Noah the man of his (His) covenant. The course of providence: that the course of nature shall be continued to the end of time, notwithstanding the interruption, which the flood would give. This promise was made to Noah and his sons. They were as trustees for all this part of the creation, and a great honor was thereby put upon him and his. The covenant of grace, that God would be to him a God and that out of his seed God makes a covenant, he establishes it, makes it sure, he makes it good; his are everlasting covenants. The covenant of grace has in it the recompense of singular services, and the fountain and foundation of all distinguishing favors; we need desire no more, either to make up our losses for God or to make up happiness for us in God, than to have his covenant establish with us. Indeed there is similarity in substance and import in these mentioned covenants. The book of Genesis also mentioned another covenant Allāh undertook with Prophet Abraham.[83]

By providence, 'Abdul Wahab never got the seat of vicegerent. He was not a Saudi, but a Yemenite. While one could welcome his association with Muhammad Sa'ud, one should never attribute to him whatever Muhammad Sa'ud did and said. There is freedom of speech in Islām, because it is the most democratic institution in the world! The reference points of a believer are the holy Qur'ān and the Sunna of Muhammad Rasūlullah and not anyone else.

Hasan al-Banna (1906-1946)

Al-Banna was born in the town of Mahmadiya in Egypt from a religious family. He was associated with the formation of the Egyptian Muslim Brotherhood in 1928. He was assassinated in the mid-1940's, at the behest of the CIA according to some historians. He was believed to be a threat to world peace, progress, and prosperity because he was calling for Muslim unity and the establishment of the Caliphate.

Hasan Banna wrote extensively, but out of his seven collections, I am able to access only *Fi Afaqi at-Ta'alim* (*The Horizon or the Depth of Education*). It is a long book consisting of nine chapters. I very much doubt that those who believe that Hasan Banna was a threat to world peace have ever read all his books or even just this one. If they have read him and come to the conclusion that he was a threat to world peace, they are Muqalladun, that is, they just read without relating what they read to the basic teaching

---

[83] Henry, p.44

of Muhammad Rasūlullah or the reality on the ground.[84] I will briefly summarize what he wrote in Chapter 5 on how the Muslim Brotherhood can achieve their aim and objective.

In spite of the diversity of human beings in their abilities, tendencies, foresight, and other qualities, they should be treated as equal and given the opportunity to grow through appropriate training in the way to succeed and how to control their environment. One should not allow himself to be influenced to adopt a way of life contrary to the Sunna of the holy Apostle. In that circumstance, the behavior has to be changed. Attention should also be directed to training females and the young.

The young should not be left to become indolent, but trained to face the challenges of their time and the future. Because of their potential in assimilating and retaining knowledge, they should be exposed to the fundamental teaching of Islām--Faith--so as to grow with the strength necessary to build a healthful, egalitarian Muslim Umma, free of bigotries, indifference, intolerance, hatred, and deceit. They should also learn the following:

To establish a happy home.

To fraternize, which Islām encourages and commands, so as not to leave a brother impoverished.

To pay attention to female education and to establish ways of empowering women.

To marry from a well-behaved family.

To be in close association with one's nuclear family.

To open up opportunities for relationships to help each other in times of difficulty.

To guard against sectarianism and forbid anything that will breed misunderstanding.

---

[84] Many Muslim scholars are fond of misinterpreting the meaning of the Qur 'an, forgetting the life of Muhammad. For example, in the holy Qur'ān 8:60, how could Muhammad dare go forth to Tabuk?

To provide recreational facilities for women.

To encourage females to teach each other and to come out with their educational curriculum.

To treat women with respect and dignity and keep them engaged. Widows should be looked after.

The Caliph the Caliphate and the Umma are one.

The overall ideology and thinking of Hasan Banna is his understanding of Islām as a Message from Allāh, which regards mankind as equal, irrespective of their color, belief, place of residence, or origin or whether they believe in practicing the rituals. This is what Western Christians advocate, although they have so far failed to establish such tolerance. They are very discriminatory and highly suspicious; they have double standards; and they are tricksters, pretending to practice chastity and justice.

Western Christian failure to understand the message of Muhammad Rasūlullah, in its universal application, is because they do not believe in the Torah and the holy Bible, or do not understand them. Nineveh was not in Jerusalem; but when Allāh decided to send a warning to the inhabitants of that city, he sent them Prophet Jonah. When Jonah arrived, he told them of the approach of their doomsday. Everyone in the city in all honesty and sincerity decided to abandon his evil past. All the people tried to mend their ways. Possessions unjustly acquired were returned to their rightful owners and false judgments were revised. G-d saw that they were sincere in their repentance and accepted it. Nineveh was saved.

If a city can only repent after they receive the Message of Allāh, the Western Christian world should look for someone like Prophet Jonah to join hands with an Al-'Ālim (an educated one) from the followers of Muhammad Rasūlullah, so that they can rid the world of its evil. I am challenging Western Christians to understand that from 610-632 A.D. nobody disbelieved in Muhammad. Your friends are fooling you!

Abdul Qādir Audah claimed that eighty percent of the Muslim Umma are illiterate. The remaining twenty percent, made of the elites, are no better than the eighty percent. I must make it clear that the present Muslim Brotherhood of Egypt, as well as other organizations, have nothing to offer to the Egyptians in helping them to attain their desire for freedom, progress, and prosperity.

In a BBC *Hard Talk* program, Dr. Issam el Arian (or Essam El-Erian) made this clear to Stephen Sucker. He confessed that the intellectuals, liberals, and secularists are not to be trusted, because they are a minor group, always complaining. Dr. Arian was proud to tell the true believers that eighty-five percent of their members are youths and women. This confession immediately made me remember the moment Jesus son of Maryam was followed from Galilee to Jerusalem the place of cruxification, a distance of eighty to a hundred miles by women. His twelve male disciples have evaporated in the air. Their hearts failed them, they durst not appear, for fear of coming under the same condemnation.

It was pathetic that Mr. Sucker, unaware of the similarity of the holy Quran and the Old Testament, did not ask Dr. Arian, whom Allāh will listen to, to speak to Allāh on behalf of the followers of Muhammad Rasūlullah. The Practice of Allāh is to listen to prayers spoken with a pure heart from his community; Allāh has not changed that with Muhammad and his followers. The followers of Muhammad Rasūlullah must be made to confess their illiteracy before the world can enjoy peace and prosperity. If Egyptian elites, except for those in the Muslim Brotherhood, are not to be trusted, then who is to be trusted to stand alone and speak on behalf of Muhammad Rasūlullah? Are the elites of the Muslim Brotherhood trustworthy?

I will briefly summarize what he wrote in Chapter 5 on how the Muslim Brotherhood can achieve their aim and objective:

I am not saying that the Muslim brotherhood are trustworthy. What is relevant is: Have they understood the Sunna of Muhammad Rasūlullah thoroughly in understanding that Muhammad did indeed simplified and established the Ten Commandments. Can the Muslim Brotherhood, the Salafis etc, erase the falsehood that a Christian is not a Muslim? Will the Christians also understand that they are equally Muslims followers of Muhammad Rasūlullah in working on a common goal for the good of all in this earthly world? Has the time not come for all to understand that it is impossible to live in peace putting aside the guidelines set by Muhammad Rasūlullah for that? This is the litmus test for the Muslims Brotherhood and the rest of those calling themselves followers of Muhammad Rasūlullah. *Michael Kennedy and Shiva Balaghi* co-authored an article asking "what to do now and who can lead Egypt?" They concluded saying:-

1.   Replacing Mubārak without instituting real political, social, and economic reform will only punt the ball and leave the Egyptian playing field open to malfeasance.
2.   What Egyptians and the international community must do is set a table with room for many men and women who can sit and talk in private about building an alternative future for Egypt.

They postulated that Poland circa 1989 presents us with a road map for successful if gradual political transition. The postulate is:

From February 6 to April 4, 1989 the Polish government organized a series of round table discussions with the Solidarity Movement and other opposition groups. The street protests moved into roundtable negotiations. The Polish Round Table made enemies into collaborators and showed the way towards radical but non-violent change. The secret meetings were chaired by the head of Solidarity, Lech Walesa, and the Minister of Internal Affairs, Czeslaw Kiszczak. The Polish government hoped the talks would allow them to co-opt the opposition; instead the talks transformed Polish society, leading to the end of Soviet-style communism in Poland.

In the rush to build a new society on the ruins of communism, the imagery of collapse fit very well those who would design, or impose, institutions anew. With communists vanquished, questions of how their exit was made possible seemed best relegated to the historians, once sufficient time could intervene to allow neutral portraits to be painted. However, as more time intervened, it became clear that communist rule produced a pattern of social relations that made the communist-ruled past an integral part of understanding and creating a democratic future. Although that made analytical sense, it still left a powerful political distaste for many, especially when communists could be perceived to have profited from their own exit. The Round Table, it has been said, was a deal that privileged its attendees. There was, however, another way to see this Round Table, but it required stepping outside the stream of popular Polish history into a world of contingency and comparison. It required thinking about the Round Table as an instance of peaceful, but radical change.

When we think about radical change, we normally think about violence. For some of the negotiators at the Round Table, violence was a possibility they sought to avoid. Indeed, the struggle to avoid violence could be read as a leitmotif of recollection, but rarely a major theme of analysis. Once violence becomes a possibility in the narrative of communism's collapse, however, its relationship to other features of social transformation becomes critical and manifold.

In 1988, nobody in Poland wanted to negotiate with the other side. Communists ruled the state, and could count on force to prevail. However, they also saw that Poles killing Poles was no way to create a sustainable peace. There was no way for authoritarians to live with themselves, and their families, if they committed crimes of violence against their own people. Authoritarians needed a way out.

And Solidarity needed a way out. Those committed to democratic and peaceful change wanted to make a revolution against revolution – wanted to create a lawful state through legal means within a condition that disrespected basic human rights, civil rights, political rights. By the summer of 1988, it became increasingly impossible to manage the protest movement as young men got sick of their elders' compromises. Both Solidarity's elite and communist authorities realized that unless they negotiated a compromise, violence could be the only winner.[85]

Definitely, the Poland Circa has failed. The Western World should understand accept without any delay as an alternative to it, the Madinan Covenant entered by Muhammad Rasūlullah and the citizens of Medina including the Levi clans of the children of Israel. Indeed an American University of Cairo law professor Amr Shalakany has opinioned this saying, "An Egyptian round table might help more heroes emerge, the kind like Lech Walesa who showed he could do more than organize protesters. An Egyptian round table might not bring about immediate justice, but it can help reconcile calls for freedom with practical concerns and help bring about radical but peaceful change. We stand with the Egyptian people who are today in the midst of "a sweet revolution" and support them in their quest for a pathway to justice, peace, and freedom."[86]

The Egyptian "Revolution"

For centuries, the 'Arabs were continuously revolting against their governments. There was hardly a province that did not at one time rise against a tyrant and an unjust ruler. Before the 1919 Egyptian "revolution," Egypt was filled with Islāmic

---

[85] An article written by *Michael Kennedy and Shiva Balaghi in a BBCnews.uk.co. bulletin.*

[86] An article written by Omnia El Shakry: Jadaliyya.February 2011.). This is indeed a folly, for there is never recorded from 632 A.D a positive and much desired revolution that swept the word as that happened between 623-632 A.D.

scholars of world repute. Among them was Muhammad Abduh (1849-1905). When Britain invaded Egypt in 1882, he rose against their invasion and subsequently got the hammer through banishment to Syria. He was the Editor, of the government gazette, called *Waqai Al-Misriyya*. He returned to Egypt in 1888 and was appointed a judge. The Prime Minister of Egypt at that time was Pasha. According to the Sunna of the holy Apostle, Pasha could be appointed the Prime Minister (Caliph), if he had the best understanding of the Sunna of the holy Apostle and was pious and elderly. At that time Muhammad Abduh was thirty-nine years old.

The 1919 Egyptian revolution, which freed Egypt from the colonial mentality of the Britons, was caused most likely by the despotic administration of Pasha. An editor of *Jadiliyya*, Omnia el Shakry, writing on the internet believes the revolution to have been caused by the competition for political power that ensued between the effendiyya (middle class nationalists) and the colonial regime.[87] But was the 1919 rebellion a unified uprising in which peasants, workers, and politicians coalesced in support of a nascent nationalism when the British failed to give Egypt its promised independence? What role did the Muslim Umma play in selecting a leader according to the teaching of Prophet Moses and the Sunna of Muhammad Rasūlullah?

In 1952, Gamel Abdul Nasser lead a military coup by the Free Officer's Movement, which later became known as the July Twenty-third Revolution. The revolution toppled the rule of King Farouk with the ascendance of Muhammad Naquib to the Presidency. The reign of King Farouk had been full of notoriety and vice. Yet, the Muslim Umma saw evil circulating within the very tip of their nostrils, and for reasons best known to themselves, could not remove it. Their scholars may not have been aware of the hadīth of the holy Apostle: "When my Umma get contended with the rule of tyrants, and immoral rulers, and

---

[87]   An article written by Omnia El Shakry: Jadaliyya. February 2011.

see all form of abominations in their midst and yet fail to remove them, Allāh will visit them with torments and hardship. They will never be able to come out of it, until they change to doing what is good. All their deeds will be null and void."

According to the interpretation of some Muslim scholars, it is allowed by the Sunna to follow a tyrant who seizes power by the use of force. On the other hand, Umar bin Khaṭṭāb explained such a leader should not be obeyed. What did the rule of Gamel Abdel Nasser bring to the Egyptian masses? Summing up the success of Nasser, El-Shakry writes:

> Nasserism thus represented the formation of a state capitalist class, the liquidation of its main ideological rivals, and the suppression of popular mobilization from below even as it was coupled with a powerful social welfare ideology and a charismatic anti-imperialist rhetoric (immensely strengthened by Egypt's mobilization in the face of a tri-partite foreign aggression and nationalization of the Suez Canal). This social welfare model can be seen as a Faustian bargain in which "the people" exchanged democratic political liberties and a more radical restructuring of the social order for social welfare programs that deflected attention away from the restructuring of class relations, by emphasizing the piecemeal and palliative reforms for the laboring classes. In other words, it was *a passive* "revolution."[88]

'Abdel Nasser died of a heart attack and was succeeded by Anwar Sadat in 1970. Anwar Sadat, one of the participants in the 1952 uprising, took over the government. On October 6, 1981, Anwar Sadat was assassinated by a Jihād movement. It was the signing of a treaty with Israel (done not according to the Sunna of Muhammad Rasūlullah) that prompted his assassination. It was

---

[88]   Jadaliyya. February 2011

alleged that the Egyptian blind cleric, 'Umar ibn 'Abdurrahman, instigated the assassination as a result of his Fatwa (Islāmic legal ruling). I was able to read the English version of his Fatwa. All my efforts at getting the 'Arabic text to get to the true meaning of the fatwa failed. In the English translation (without taking regard of 'Arabic grammar and rhetoric), he warned the followers of Muhammad Rasūlullah against following tyrants and ignorant rulers. For each argument, he gives relevant Qur'ānic passages, hadīth backed by history (practical evidence).

This was not taken lightly by the Western Christian civilized world, because they interpreted it to mean waging war against the State of Israel. 'Umar ibn 'Abdurrahman is probably still lingering in one of the prisons in the USA. No Arab country has waged any protest against this imprison, even though there is no evidence from his fatwa that he wanted Anwar Sadat to be killed.

In the Sunna of the holy apostle, it is the perpetrator of a crime who is to be punished, after taking all due precautions to exclude provocation, intimidation, and oppression of the perpetrator. Going against the peaceful existence of the Israel State in the language and terminology of the Western Christian world is upholding the Torah and the Sunna of Muhammad Rasūlullah. That is, they expected a symbolic Muslim to help them and never a real Muslim, whose words are equal to his deeds, getting a blessing from the Lord (L-rd).

The revolution taking place in the 'Arab Muslim countries was triggered by oppression and injustice as is the case in all revolutions. If Allāh intended poverty to be the source of religion, associating it and oppression with obedience to Allāh, a scenario that would have made the whole world quake in rejection, man would not be nourished inside his mother's womb. During my medical student days, I conducted a nutritional study among the much deprived, illiterate, and rural society. I was astonished to find their hemoglobin concentration matched that of the upper and middle urban social class. Yet these lower classes of people were content to live on what was unjustifiably imposed on them, believing ignorantly that Allāh had a hand in it. This is an incorrect interpretation of their scriptures from ignorant preachers and leaders.

It was not the level of their conscience or unawareness of their environment that made them fall into the trap of determinism, but rather, the effect of colonialism and indirect rule. This is the reason behind the backwardness of the Muslim countries. Today, the Muslim countries are still colonized at an unprecedented level, for their economy is dictated and controlled by Western Christian powers. It is an economy aimed at strangulating their mercantile throat, creating fear and hatred in the society. Anyone who has ever stayed for a day in the so-called Western Christian cities will see this reality. They have the pretext of helping the poor, but never in the depth and measure as commanded in the Torah.

The first step to a revolution is the ability to synthesize facts and events. The advice Jethro gave to Prophet Moses was the first mutual consultation in the history of ad-Dīn (religion) that was aimed at strengthening brotherhood and finding ways out of darkness. By the time a leader receives difficult issues that cannot be solved by the community his duty is to pass the problem to the Lord. But according to the Torah, such requests, even if passed, are of value only if they are not passed through a righteous leader. Such requests should not be done with impunity to intimidate or provoke the Lord.

Had the case between the pharaoh and Prophet Moses been understood and believed by the Jews, the world could have long since enjoyed peace and prosperity. Revolution needs both arms: all must stand up and join. Our additional requests to Allāh must be as a result of our gratefulness to Him; otherwise, we shall be in a worse situation than before. Allāh will certainly ask us, upon hearing our requests, what efforts we have made that have failed. According to the Book of Genesis, we are not born as leviathans. One should not seek a way other than the straightway, lest he fall into fetishism.

In the holy Qur'ān 2:205 Allāh says, "And when he turns away, his effort in the land is to make mischief therein and to destroy the crops and the cattle, and Allāh likes not mischief." "Turning away" has the following meanings:

Not assuming responsibility. No one should seek position through deception, for the one who seeks position through deception will never be of any good to his society. It is unfortunate that the followers of Muhammad Rasūlullah, in this fundamental issue of the Caliphate, have failed the world. It is most unfortunate that the Jews have kept silent on this, as if they have forgotten their history and what their ancestors, the Levi tribes, enjoyed at the hand of Muhammad Rasūlullah and his rightly-guided Caliphs.

To misguide and fall into indignation. One pretends not to hear the recitation of Muhammad Rasūlullah, thereby remaining ignorant, or one hears the recitation but either cannot understand it or is prevented by someone, in this case the West, to follow its injunctions.

A revolution that is spearheaded by the young, by females, and the riff-raff is bound to fail, because such a revolution is not intended to improve the lot of the society, but rather to further impoverish it. In this type of revolution, one hardly finds a leader, to steer it to a conclusion. It is a revolution with a blackened spirit and amputated limbs. No one will doubt this, for if the revolution taking place in the 'Arab countries were a positive one, it could have achieved its objective by now. However, one cannot expect any positive result from this revolution devoid of faith and positive commitment.

It is most annoying and lamentable that the whole world is rejoicing and applauding a revolution that has no historical root. How many demonstrations at universities (student revolutions), filled with youthful exuberance, have ever yielded any positive result? What do they control and what do they know? If those armed with the prerequisite knowledge and practical experience have failed a nation, how can that nation grow again under the hands of the youths? However deeply the revolution attempts to uproot and disorganize the structure that precipitated it, achieving success is like chasing one's shadow.

Causes of Arab Revolution

The world has given its arrogant reasons for the causes of the current revolution, tantamount to daring Allāh to send a prophet to contradict Muhammad Rasūlullah. Let us sincerely reflect on the holy Qur'ān 13:14, "To Him is the Word of Truth. And those whom they (polytheists and disbelievers) invoke, answer them no more than one who stretches forth his hand (at the edge of a deep well) for water to reach his mouth, but it reaches him not; and the invocation (all rituals) of the disbelievers is nothing but error (i.e. of no use)."

The causes of revolution are many, but suffice it to enumerate a few:

Illiteracy. The Muslim world is illiterate and cannot demand or uphold their rights. It cannot get its right without giving Allāh his right.

Corruption. The main cause of corruption is the hardening of the minds and hearts of the Muslim Umma. This hardening is nothing other than ignorance of the Sunna of the holy Apostle, and not of the holy Qur'ān. If corruption is an abomination hated by the Muslims, it can only be eliminated from the Umma by its correct antidote–piety and fear of Allāh. No one can fear Allāh without a firm belief that one will need to render an account in the Hereafter of what he possesses and what he gave out. It is only that which is pure and given out for the sake of Allāh that will deliver one from the torments of that day.

No one can fear Allāh without knowing the Sunna of Muhammad Rasūlullah. No one can fear Allāh without having a leader who is the representative of Muhammad Rasūlullah. If the followers of Muhammad Rasūlullah believe that they will prosper and progress in this world without establishing the Caliphate, they are indubitably saying that their prayer is accepted without external purification of the body. The crime of Iblis was his deliberate refusal to bow down to Adam, as the representative of Allāh. Heaven was never a place meant for worship. Therefore, the bowing down requested by Allāh was not that involving the rituals. The act of bowing down to someone denotes humility. It is a form of Ibādat that is akin to love and obedience.

Lack of democracy. By "democracy," the ancient world meant that system of leading people to prosperity, peace, and progress in this world only, with nothing similar to it in the Hereafter. World history has never shown how that was achieved. The way of life of the Philistines, Canaanites, Amalekites, Amorites, and those tribes living around the territories of the then Children of Israel, is not given in the Bible. Their frequent incursions into the lands of the then Children of Israel was not as a result of their being tyrants and unjust; rather, according to the Bible, they were punishment of the Children of Israel for their disbelief.

Democracy as the choice of man to be governed according to the way he thinks is best for him is described in the Bible as an unattainable feat. The holy Qur'ān 16:76 rejects such assertions, thoughts, and beliefs of mankind: "Allāh puts forward (another) example of two men, one of them dumb, who has no power over anything (disbeliever), and he is a burden on his master; whichever way he directs him, he brings no good. Is such a man equal to one who commands justice, and he is himself on the Straight Path?"

If, by "democracy," we mean a system of governing people, by the people, of the people, for the people, as the Greeks defined it, we all know that the Greeks never had that experience, for they never had a Prophet from their tribe. The reign of Alexander the Great has no breath or fragrance of democracy. It is unfortunate that the 'Arabs, especially the Egyptians, have forgotten their history, and all that Allāh did for them in the time of Prophet Joseph. How could they, once world leaders, be subjugated today?

Lack of Freedom of Speech. If Allāh never wanted mankind to have freedom of speech, He would not have taught Adam "the nature of things" and then request of the angels in the holy Qur'ān 2:31, "Tell Me, the name of these if you are truthful." Why did Prophet Abraham advise his people to ask the biggest idol who broke their idols? Why did Prophet Moses beseech Allāh to remove the impediment of his speech? The greatest freedom of speech is the ability of one to explain his objective in clear and plain language, which leaves no doubt or uncertainty, in the presence of the mightiest of the mighty. The task of achieving his aim is now entirely in his hands. It was reported that when Muhammad Rasūlullah returned from the Tabuk expedition, he told the Sahābas, "We have come back from a minor Jihād, going into a major one." The Sahābas asked about that major Jihād. He replied, "Telling the truth in the presence of a tyrant."

Selfishness. As a result of our ignorance, we look down upon others with contempt, impunity, hatred, and suspicion. This leads to inconsideration and fear. We are all equal in the sight of Allāh. Allāh did not create time to be filled with hatred. Selfishness makes one inconsiderate and arrogant. The selfish person refuses to listen to the advice of individuals and that of the constituted authority, whereas the basic and common teaching of the scriptures is based on the fear of Allāh and belief in the prophet sent at that time.

Selfishness breeds the following:

a. Indifference to Muhammad Rasūlullah and the holy Qur'ān. Those who are selfish do not at all live with the Prophets or they would not allow "nationalism" to bury the concept of an "Umma." Dr. Roger Garaudy observes that, "Nationalism turns the unconditional defense of one's race, territory, market, historical or cultural mythology into an end in itself. It tends towards the disintegration of humanity through colonial domination, wars, and latterly 'the balance of terror.'"[89] The Arabs are proud to be known as a "Nationalist" party and not an "Umma." According to Beitler and Jebb, in their *Egypt as a Failing State*, "Egyptian nationalism has a seven thousand year long history." [90]

Egyptians have alienated themselves from the true spirit of Islām.The Muslim world is looking at them hoping for a way to the Straight Path, because the final message was revealed in their language; however, the essence of salvation, progress, and peace is not in the language, but in the substance in that language. The substance required by the world to be stable is common in all languages, for it was taught to Prophet Adam (AS).

b. Capitalism. The relation between wealth and mankind is so clear in the scriptures that had mankind believed in Allāh and applied what Allāh believed is best for them, there would be a surplus of wealth in the world, as mimicked during the time of 'Umar ibn 'Abdul 'Aziz. To Allāh belongs all that is in the heavens and earth.

The love of his people, even at that time, for a leader is greater than the love of wealth. King Melchizedek of Salem was a priest of God Most High and King of Sodom. When Abram gave the King a tenth of what he possessed, the King told him,

---

[89] Islām and the Future. PP. 109-124. This is from the proceedings of a conference organized by the Emir of Kuwait in 1987.

[90] INSS Occasional Paper 51. July 2003.

"All I want are my people. You can keep everything else."[91] The fact that the holy Qur'ān tells us that Allāh bestows wealth on whom He likes, and withholds it, does not mean that the one he bestows wealth on is not in any way better than the one He withholds wealth from.[92] Those on whom Allāh has bestowed wealth, who then withhold it from others, will be the most wretched ones in the Hereafter. He clearly threatens this group of people in the holy Qur'ān 2:180, "And let not those who covetously withhold of that which Allāh has bestowed on them of His Bounty (Wealth) think that it is good for them. Nay, it will be worse for them; the things which they covetously withheld shall be tied to their deeds like a collar on the day of Resurrection. And to Allāh belong the heritage of the heavens and the earth; and Allāh is Well-Acquainted with all that you do."

In the Bible, Allāh gave the then Children of Israel the following Sharī'a:

a. "Do not charge interest when you lend money to any of my people who are in need. Before sunset you must return any coat taken as security for a loan, because that is the only cover the poor have when they sleep at night. I am a merciful God, and when they call out to me, I will come to help them. (Exod. 22:25)

b. "Don't fail to give me the offerings of grain and wine that belong to me. Dedicate your first-born and the first-born of your cattle and sheep. Let the animals stay with their mothers for seven days, then the eighth day give them to me, your God." (Exod. 22:29)

---

91 See the Holy Bible, Genesis 14:17-21.
92 See the holy Qur'ān 34:36.

Summing up the teachings of Prophet Moses, the Prophet Jesus, son of Maryam, said to the rich young man, "If you want to be perfect, go sell everything you own! Give the money to the poor, and you will have riches in heaven. Then come and be my follower. . . . It is terribly hard for the rich people to get into the kingdom of heaven! In fact, it's easier for a camel to go through the eye of a needle than for a rich person to get into God's kingdom." Matthew 19:23.

In Matt.19:29-30, Jesus, the son of Maryam, said, "All who have given up home or brothers and sisters or father and mother or children or land for me will be given a hundred times as much. They will also have eternal life. But many who are now first will be last, and many who are last will be first." The true teaching of Prophet Jesus, the son of Maryam, has nothing to do with capitalism, and therefore it has no root whatsoever in what some people call Christianity. Prophet Jesus, the son of Maryam, was reported to be the meekest of all the Prophets of Allāh. Why should the Western Christian world then build its life, both in this world and the Hereafter, on sand and salt?

When Muhammad Rasūlullah came, he did not in any way alter the Torah or the Injeel, but straightaway applied the rule of brotherhood and everyday justice to the newly constituted Muslim Umma in Medina. He established "brotherhood" among the Muslim Umma. The wealthy Aws and Khazraj tribes were ready to share their wealth with the equally rich Makkan emigrants, compelled to abandon their richness, for the need of the people of Medina. Allāh confirms this in the holy Qur'ān 9:24, "Say: if your fathers, your sons, your brothers, your wives, your kindred, the wealth that you have gained, the commerce in which you fear a decline, and the dwellings in which you delight are dearer to you than Allāh and His Messenger, and striving hard and fighting in His Cause, then wait until Allāh brings about His Decision (torment). And Allāh guides not the people who are Al-Fasiqun (the rebellious, disobedient to Allāh)." The teaching of the holy Apostle on social welfare was never separate from or contrary to what his predecessors taught, preached, and practiced.

Muhammad Yunus, the winner of the 2006 Nobel Peace Prize, has proved that the causes of poverty and impoverishment aren't from Allāh, but from us. A British Broadcasting Corporation report of March 2, 2011, says, "Muhammad Yunus is often referred to as 'the world's banker to the poor.'"

His life's work has been to prove that the poor are credit-worthy, and he received the Nobel Prize in 2006. His revolutionary micro-credit system is estimated to have extended credit to more than seven million of the world's poor, most of them in Bangladesh, one of the poorest nations in the world. The vast majority of the beneficiaries are women.

Prof. Yunus says that he came up with the idea in 1976 while a professor of economics at Chittagong University in southern Bangladesh. The first loans he issued had a value of $27 (£14.50). Their recipients were 42 women from the village of Jobra, near the university. Until then, the women had relied on local moneylenders, who charged high interest rates. The conventional banking system had been reluctant to give credit to those who were too poor to provide any form of guarantee. The success of Prof. Yunus's scheme exceeded all expectations and has been copied in developing countries around the world.

His micro-finance initiative reached out to people shunned by conventional banking systems-- people so poor they have no collateral to guarantee a loan, should they be unable to repay it. Prof. Yunus has tried to transform the vicious circle of "low income, low saving, low investment" into a virtuous circle of "low income, injection of credit, investment, more income, more savings, more investment more income." It was so successful that even beggars have been able to borrow money under his scheme. In 2000, Hillary Clinton famously remarked that Mr. Yunus had helped the Clintons introduce micro-credit schemes to some of the poorest communities in Arkansas.[93]

---

[93] http://www.sudanvisiondaily.com//modules.php?name=News&file=article&sid=16011

Unemployment should not be attributed only to corruption, which contributes an insignificant percentage. The main cause of employment is capitalism and greed, to make money quickly, for machines can work for twenty-four hours non-stop. Young people should better understand that they will soon be redundant because technology, will greatly reduce man-hours.

The Arabs View on "Revolution"

According to Omnia Al Shakry, the 1919 (Egyptian) Revolution had two aspects: the short, violent period in March, 1919, which involved large-scale mobilization by the peasantry in rural areas and which was suppressed by British military action, and the protracted phase beginning in April, 1919, which was less violent and more urban, with the large-scale participation of students, workers, lawyers, and other professionals. Al Shakry concludes: "Whatever perspective we adopt, it is clear that the 1919 'revolution' meant different things to different segments of the population. But, at least from the perspective of the emergent dominant national ruling elements, it did not aim at the radical transformation of the social structure or class relations, but rather at the assertion of territorial nationalism in the face of British colonialism. In other words, it was *a nationalist 'revolution.'*"

From the onset of the Tunisian revolution, in which a twenty-seven-year-old graduate student Muhammad Bouazizi, took his life out of deprivation, frustration, and want, to the last one, however long that will take, the true cause of their 'revolutions' will never be comprehended and accepted by the Arabs. They can only succeed and get the benefits of revolution if they are assisted not from an alien source, but from the very source they recognize, but reject.

For almost a century, the amplitude of vibration has maintained a certain crescendo, but without giving any way for improvement. The fact is that the 2011 revolution, which began according to analysts in Alexandria on December 18, 2010, was triggered by poverty and election rigging. It turned into an insoluble precipitation on January 25, 2011, dubbed "the day of anger," and terminated on Friday, February 11, 2011. Al Shakry summed up the precipitation as: "the product of an unprecedented historical assemblage of complex forces and contradictions."

As Mohammed Bamyeh noted in "The Egyptian Revolution': First Impressions from the Field,"

> . . . The revolt has been characterized by a large degree of spontaneity, marginality, a call for civic government, and an elevation of political grievances (unconsciously calling for establishment of the Caliphate) above economic grievances. Thus, we have seen the participation of a wide range of groups with differing ideological orientations but nonetheless coherent and articulate in their demand for an end to the *ancient regime*. These have included strong elements of trade unions and other labor organizers, such as the April 6 movement (named after its call for a General Strike in support of the workers in Mahalla). Indeed, since 2008 there has been a tremendous upsurge in labor and union organizing. But labor movements do not exhaust the types of players involved—including, of course, the new social movements (whether leftist, feminist, legal-judicial, NGO based, or social-media galvanized organizations) discussed in Paul Amar's "Why Mubārak is Out," as well as the Muslim Brotherhood who have publicly declared their commitment to a civil and pluralist government.[94]

---

[94] http://www.jadaliyya.com/pages/index/561/the-egyptian-revolution_first-impressions-from-the-field-Jadaliyya.

According to other commentators and opinion seekers, revolutions are not on ideological and religious grounds, but for purposes unidentified by him. As usual, the commentary is filled with undefined jargon--Islāmists, Moderates, Liberal 'Arab Nationalists, and Secularists. People are described as having the right to protest and Egyptians as having credible demands. It is surprising that an 'Arab could use the word "Secular" in describing his way of life or aspirations since the word also means "illiteracy."

The revolution across North Africa and the Middle-East has the in contestable dimension of being in predominantly Muslim countries. It has impeccably demonstrated that Muhammad Rasūlullh's role as the Messenger of Allāh and as a leader to mankind proclaiming his religion above all other religions was either ignored or if present ineffective. There was not a single religious sect that sprang from Prophet Abraham that did not participate in the uprising. According to a BBC reporter on 1/02/11, all religious organizations, including the Jews, participated.

No one is sure whether the Jewish tribe in Egypt participated because they are also oppressed or did so because they have no alternative but to participate due to their insignificant number. If the Jews in Egypt and the rest of the 'Arab countries participated in the revolution, what then are they after? They must wish to be treated as Muhammad Rasūlullah and his Sahābas treated their ancestors, for they know very well that when Helkiah accidentally discovered the Torah, he followed what was ordained. They lived in peace and prosperity.

Those days indeed did remind the believer of the words of Allāh in the holy Qur'ān, 17:41, "If there had been other ilāh (gods) along with Him as they assert, then they would certainly have sought out a way to the Lord of the Throne (seeking His Pleasures and to be near to Him)." In other words, the demonstrators will go to get what they want to that being who, is going to provide them what they need and desire.

Western Christians were aghast at the spontaneous eruption of the uprising, although they believed at the bottom of their hearts what the demonstrators love and are ready to comply with will never be achieved. The West will ever welcome the genuine establishment of the Caliphate, for they never concurred that they are fighting Islām, that is, the Sunna of Muhammad Rasūlullah. According to the teaching of Muhammad Rasūlullah, they will never dare fight Islām, for it means fighting Abraham, Isaac, and Jacob, as well as all the Prophets and Messengers before Muhammad Rasūlullah.

Western Christians have never disagreed that establishing the Caliphate in its original model could bring peace, stability, and progress in the world. Yet, they preferred to sit on the fence, neither here nor there, casting doubt and shadow on what they say and do, as if they are averse to its implementation. Socialism and equality, although preached by them, are only for the benefit of fooling those who are yet to know the benefits of independence. Thus, the Finance Ministers immediately announced assistance programs, and some billionaires also pledged certain amounts of their wealth to help the poor. These gestures were too little too late.

The greatest fear of the Western Christian world in this revolution, involves the fate of the Jewish State of Israel, because they believe that President Mubārak did a lot to protect them, bringing peace and mutual understanding in the Middle-East. Yes, indeed he did, but superficially, without a base for growth and development. Building peace must be done on an everlasting and solid foundation, as accomplished by Prophet Abraham (AS). There cannot be peace the moment the rights of people are usurped, which distinguish man from an animal.

It is not peace when the Jewish and Egyptians leaders hug each other, while the Israelites fight the Lebanese, the Palestinians fight one another, and unjust rulers kill their people without any measure. Muhammad Rasūlullah established his State by signing peace accords and treaties, covering an area of one million square miles. It was not a conversion exercise under the New Message, but a treaty of peace under the Guidance of Allāh, for oppression and tyranny are not part of the Spirit of Allāh. It is not the core 'religion' that is responsible for the chaos we see today, but the Western Christian capitalistic world's hatred of the Biblical portion Allāh included in the holy Qur'ān—that the essence of knowledge lies not on industrial might and heavy arsenals, but on those core morale values that bind humanity together.

Our lives and survival are inseparable, like the way the body works. Walking ahead and straightforward does not mean that one does not know what is behind him or by his side. Survival of the fittest is not part of our inborn dispensation. We must love each other and lift up each other every time the weak are about to fall. The Western Christian world believes that intimidating and threatening people with heavy arsenals is the only way to rise above their wants. This ideology has today proved to be not only wrong but unattainable.

Allāh could have substituted in our place others who would do what He exactly commands them. We forget that He has been merciful. However, despite the long period given to successive world powers, whenever their time of extinction comes, it will be as if they have existed for only a single hour. There is no power superior to the Promise of Allāh despite past generations' challenge and indifference to it. The case of the embalmed body of the pharaoh is an indelible warning to the Western Christian world.

Only one nation will be proud of that Promise of Allāh, and that nation is none other than the nation of the Children of Israel. I am praying and sincerely hoping that they will one day recall the favors Allāh did for their ancestors. Even so, it is not this physical evidence that makes them what they are they are today, for gratitude to Allāh entails one to obey Him. Indeed, whatever came after that period has been linked to obedience and as such cannot be effaced from world record. Any move and attempt by one to undo what Allāh has done for them is concomitant to leaning to what the pharaoh said to Haman, in the holy Qur'ān 40:36-37, "O Haman! Build me a tower that I may arrive at the ways--the ways of the heavens and I may look upon the ilāh (Allāh) of Moses (Moses): But verily, I think him to be a liar."

The tiny, indelible Jewish State must be respected and safeguarded according to the Taqdir of Allāh. How could a name mentioned three times in Medina immediately after the hijrah, each time preceded with a compassionate appeal, turn later on to be chastised and disgraced by Allāh? The Children of Israel mentioned in Medina were those who lived during the time of Prophet Moses (AS) under Taqdir-al-Kawniyya Diniyya, when Allāh decreed on them not to obey Him, as a practical lesson for future generations. They were punished by Allāh and forgiven in the manner the veterans of the battle of Uhud were punished by Allāh and forgiven. The Jews should be proud of that; and as a memorial of the Mercy of Allāh on their forefathers, they should strive hard to obey Allāh.

This is what is not happening today, simply because they have thrown themselves in the background, as if they have no blood relation with Prophet David (AS) David. They were the champions of the Message, and as such they should not feel shy or become disenchanted whenever there is a need for them to come out to speak or lead again.

No one can dictate to Allāh, and no one can estimate the Will of Allāh. The holy Qur'ān is an invitation to mankind, not restricted to time, place, race, or to past offenses done without resolve to repent and amend. The one who believes in the holy Qur'ān and then misbehaves and the one who refuses to invite others to it, according to the exigencies and exegesis of his time, is a worse offender in the sight of Allāh. This clear Message is in the holy Qur'ān 16:94, "And make not your oaths a means of deception among yourselves, lest a foot should slip after being firmly planted, and you may have to taste the evil (punishment in this world) of having hindered (men) from the Path of Allāh (i.e. belief in the Oneness of Allāh and His Messenger Muhammad ibn Abdallāh) and yours will be a great torment (i.e. the Fire of Hell in the Hereafter)."

The Jewish State of Israel should come to terms with the true and sincere followers of Muhammad Rasūlullah, for anyone studying the scriptures must conclude that the Jews indeed believe in the Oneness of Allāh. I am a living witness to this. The communication gap between the two must be closed now, for there is nothing that can bring peace, stability, and progress in the world other than doing so. The agreement has to be open, demanding that the Jews read the holy Qur'ān in the manner I read the Torah, the Talmud, and the rest of the books on Jewish history. The belief that the holy Qur'ān is not to be touched by non-Muslims is a far-fetched idea attributed to Muhammad Rasūlullah. If Muhammad Rasūlullah had said so, there is no way he could have claimed that he was sent to mankind. The mercy and forgiveness of Allāh would then be limited only to a few.

The followers of Muhammad Rasūlullah have not weighed the position of the one who professed the "Kalimat Shahadatyn," but have gone on committing the major sins. The Jews are taking advantage of this and engage the so-called followers of Muhammad in the battle, for they know that they will win in the long run. On the other hand, the Jews again have forgotten that force was never an instrument in defeating their enemies, but only the fear of Allāh, the (G-d) of Abraham, Ishmael, Isaac, and Jacob.

The contending parties should take a lesson from the help Allāh (G-d) gave to Samuel when he was attacked by the Philistines. According to Jewish history, Samuel longed to restore unity, peace, and safety to his nation; but he felt that this was impossible as long as idolatry prevailed. Therefore, he called the people of Israel together and exhorted them to put away their strange gods and return to G-d with their whole hearts. The multitude listened to his earnest appeal; and in response to it, they removed the images of Baal and Astarte and served the L-rd alone. Then Samuel summoned them to Mizpah for a great public sacrifice and a day of prayer. The Philistines, hearing of this peaceful assembly, resolved to attack them at once, and the affrighted Israelites bade Samuel pray for them.

The Jews saw the Philistines approaching and cried out to Samuel to pray to G-d to save them. The prophet offered up a burnt sacrifice to the L-rd and invoked His aid for the people. As the smoke was rising from the altar, the Philistines approached in battle array; but a terrific storm burst over their heads and discomfited their army. They were put to flight, and the Israelites pursued them to the southern frontier of the land and utterly routed them. The Hebrews now easily reconquered all the towns that the Philistines had previously taken. Indeed, the Philistines were thoroughly subdued and weakened and did not dare to attack the Hebrews again during the lifetime of Samuel. This incident was repeated during the battle of the trench, when Allāh sent storm, wind, and thunder to uproot the tents of the confederating forces, forcing them to retreat.

The fear of the tiny Jewish State is real, virtually sitting in limbo, since the majority of them do not know the life history of the holy Apostle in Medina. But they know their ancestral past and the threats from the ignorant followers of Muhammad Rasūlullah to wipe them from the globe. I never understand that threat in a literal context, but rather in a solemn context, the Jews accepting the holy Qur'ān, as a continuation of the Torah. This is the only way to eliminate the discord, hatred, and belligerence between them and the Muslim 'Arabs. As I said earlier, it is not possible that an incident mentioned in Medina after the Hijrah can cease to exist in the world.

If Allāh had wanted the Jews to suffer or be effaced from the globe, that could have been done in 6 A.H, according to the Torah. The holy Apostle moved the Levi tribe living south-east of his mosque, sequentially to Fadak, then to Khaybar, and then finally to Syria, to free them to practice their religion. It is most unfortunate that those who want to sow the seeds of discord and hatred have accused the holy Apostle of maltreating them. There is no need to defend him against this false accusation; anything wished or intended by the holy Apostle would have materialized there and then. I want to assure the tiny Jewish State that what was *not* done during the time of Muhammad will *not* be done today as well. The Sahābas said:

فما لم يكن يومئذ د ينا فلا يكون اليوم د ينا

The Sahābas are here warning others to guard against taking steps and measures to solve their problems outside the Sunna of the holy Apostle. Success and victory are only possible in sticking to the guidelines given by the holy Apostle. History books are available to prove me right or wrong.

The United States of America has so far failed to protect the Jews from their "cousin enemies." The so-called protection offered to them by the USA is nothing other than sowing further seed of discord, hatred, threats, and intimidations. It is impossible for the United States of America to help Jews in this matter, for the origin of the United States of America is indeterminate.

From my discussions with "Mr. John" from Scotland over the internet, I have learned that around the middle of the seventeenth century, the Puritan Party from Britain, following their failure to practice the Commandments in the New Testament, migrated to the USA, with the hope that they could establish a Christian State. But they failed! Therefore, according to his thinking it is possible that the Muslim Umma calling for the establishment of the Sharī'a, might suffer the same fate. I exclaimed to him that, in the Sunna of the holy Apostle, that is not possible for specific guidelines have been set up by the holy Apostle on how to establish the Sharī'a. On the other hand, I now believe that his claim is bound to be so, since in the present dispensation, Islām is "People without ad-Dīn."

Again, we should review the past, for this was the call of the holy Apostle. We need a change in strategy and a new road map.

This strategy and new road map can be drawn only between the Jews and the sincere, educated, and unprejudiced followers of Muhammad Rasūlullah. Therefore, there must be a revolution in the Middle East and in the rest of the Muslim world. In this revolution, there is every hope of success, if the Jews will faithfully, willingly, and voluntarily participate in it.

The Jews lived in Egypt, established justice, and made life better. They lived in Medina, awaiting the arrival of that Messiah, according to historians. Wherever the Jews lived, they were the masters of the scriptures and directed the affairs of that civilization, according to what was believed by them to be from the scripture. The holy Qur'ān, comprising about ninety percent of the Torah, the Talmud, and other Jewish history, could not therefore give the Jews guidance that is unknown to them. The life of Muhammad Rasūlullah in Medina was never in conflict with what the Levi tribe knew. They always confirmed to him that what he did is also from the Torah. The Sharī'a on crime is their doing.

The Influence of the Final Message on the Egyptians

Neither the Holy Bible nor the last Message revealed through Muhammad Rasūlullah ever mentions a Prophet arisen from the Egyptians to warn them. Nonetheless, their geographical position and the gift of Allāh to them--the fertile Nile Delta, their neighborhood to the Mediterranean Sea, made them a civilized and prosperous country. By such implication, they had indirectly received the Message of Allāh: the Message in favor of the liberation of mankind as deemed by their needs. It was never a general Message, for it was never said to have been perfected, except on 8th Zul-hajj 10 A.H., equivalent to Friday, March 6, 632 A.D.[95] Therefore, what was communicated to them, for

---

[95]   See the holy Qur'ān 5:5. Ali, S. Abul Hasan. P.277

example, by Zul-Qarnain should serve as guidance and a way of life, until such a time that another messenger is sent to them.

The year 610 A.D. was a remarkable and memorable year in world history for that was the year the People of the Book celebrated the birth of Muhammad ibn 'Abdullāh bin Abdul Muṭallib. His birth signaled the dawn of civilization, fundamental freedom of worship and association, and a return to monotheism as preached and propagated by his predecessors. The Egyptians received the Message of Prophet Isa, the son of Maryam, in an adulterated form, getting the news of the Final Message after the Hudaybiya Treaty. This was the year the holy Apostle sent ambassadors to the nearby kingdoms. His letter to the Prefect, as well as to the Patriarch of Alexandria, who was acting as the Governor of Egypt on behalf of the Byzantine Emperor reads: "In the name of Allāh, the beneficent, the Merciful. From Muhammad the Messenger of Allāh, to Muqauqis, the Chief of the Copts. Peace be upon him who follows the guidance. After this, I call you to Islām that you may find peace and god will give you a double reward. If you reject, then on you shall be the sin of your countrymen. O people of the Book come to that which is common between us and you; that we serve none but Allāh, nor associate aught with Him, nor take others for lords besides God. But if you turn away, then say: bear witness that we are Muslims."[96]

The holy Apostle's ambassador was received warmly by the Coptic archbishop of Egypt. He agreed and endorsed the Apostleship of Muhammad Rasūlullah, but only if he would appear in al Shām (Syria).

He accorded to the ambassador a good reception and sent with him a gift to the holy Apostle consisting of two slave girls, a white mule, a donkey, some money, and a variety of Egyptian products. The two slave girls were Mariyyah, whom the holy Apostle took in marriage and who gave

---

[96] Ali, Hasan S. Abul 277

birth to Abraham, and Sirin, who was given in marriage to Hassan ibn Thābit. The mule was given by the prophet the name Duldul, for its whiteness of skin which the Arabian Peninsula had never seen before. The donkey was called 'Ufayr of Ya'fur. The Archbishop explained that he did not convert to Islām because of his fear of discharge by his superior, and that were he not a man of authority and power, he would have been rightly guided to the truth.[97]

The conquest of Egypt was initiated by the frequent incursions of the Romans into Syria, from the Egyptian side. 'Amr bin Al-'As, who traded during the period of Jahiliyya to Egypt, was well aware of the strategic position of Egypt. He frequently asked permission from 'Umar bin Khaṭṭāb to secure it, and to prevent a south-east incursion. Permission was granted, but not without hesitation, and Egypt was conquered in 20 A.H., followed by Alexandria the following year. The conqueror sent a letter to the Caliph, 'Umar bin Khaṭṭāb, on his assessment of Egypt. He observed: "The country is exceedingly fertile and green, its length covers a journey of one month and its breadth is of about ten days." A census of Egypt taken by 'Amr b. al-'Ās in 20A.H./640 A.D. to find out the number of persons on whom *jizya* could be levied, showed that the population exceeded six millions, of whom the Romans were one hundred thousand. 'Amr b. al-'Ās wrote to the Caliph: "I have taken a city of which I can but say that it contains 4,000 palaces, 4,000 baths, 40,000 Jews and 400 theatres for the entertainment of the nobles."[98]

Even before this, the Egyptians were aware of the basic and fundamental tenets of Islām, but also that they had no leader elected on those tenets to lead them in prayers and the other rituals. It was only in 20 A.H. that the caliphate was instituted in

---

[97]   Haykal. 376.
[98]   'Ali Hasan, S. Abūl. Muhammad Rasūlullah.(Lahore: Islāmic Research and Publications, 1979), 283.

the same model and principles that Allāh ordered Prophet David to lead the Jews of his time and province. It is interesting to note that immediately after the conquest, 'Amr took the following measures *to improve the condition of the peasantry,* and not to build mosques as would be expected by the critics of the Final Message, and those of his followers who have misunderstood it:

1. The soil was left in the hands of the cultivators; and the old irrigation works, which had been neglected or which had fallen into ruin, were restored; and the ancient canal connecting the Mediterranean with the Red Sea was cleared out.
2. The Egyptian Christians, who were called Copts and belonged to the Melchite sect, were treated with marked favor, in consequence of their good will towards the Moslems.
3. Taxation was regulated upon a fixed and moderate scale, and trade was fostered by light custom duties.

These measures were in addition to what was operating in Medina under the Caliphate of 'Umar. This is certain from 'Umar's declaration that, "he is not free from the responsibility and trust Allāh bestowed on him, until he is sure that the one he appoints as his representative over the Umma, did what he commanded him." One such characteristic was the open system of governance, where all and sundry are involved in looking for ways and means to improve on the common lot.[99] This is the Shura or Consultative Assembly.

The Sahābas who settled in Egypt were Zubayr bin Awwām, Ubada bin Samit, Maslama bin Khālid, and Miqdad bin Aswad. Their pupils were Yazid bin Habib, Ūmar bin Hārith, and Hayr bin Na'im Hadrami. Indeed, the number of pupils of the Sahābas

---

[99] 'Aqqadi, Abbas Muhammad,'Abqariyya 'Umar (Dar-al-hilal, 1971).

148

who settled in Egypt was fourteen. 'Amr bin Al-'As died in Egypt according to one source in 51 A.H., while other historians give the date as 43 A.H. Notwithstanding the fact that the last Message was revealed in their language, one would not expect Egypt to have played a key role in Islāmic jurisprudence, like Makka, Medina, Kufa, Basra, and other Arabs countries with a higher concentration of the Sahābas and their pupils. Indeed, it was determined that some of the ringleaders who participated in the mutiny against 'Uthman bin Affān were from Egypt.

The population of the followers of Muhammad in Egypt gradually overtook that of the Copts. Today, with a population of 84.5 million, about ninety-eight percent, the followers of Muhammad Rasūlullah are in the majority. Peace is the mother of our survival, not numbers. If, in the previous dispensations (before Muhammad Rasūlullah), the majority was the criteria for peaceful coexistence, prosperity, progress, and growth in a given location, the message brought by Muhammad Rasūlullah de-emphasized and buried that notion.

The population of Medina at the time of the holy Apostle's migration to Medina was about ten thousand. The number of emigrants, that is, the Muhājirūn, was given at less than one hundred and twenty. Yet, he was chosen to be the leader. When he died, Abūbakar Siddīq was chosen as the leader of the Muslim State, comprising about seventy thousand. The criteria chosen for his leadership were solely on merit.

The merit in establishing the Caliphate lies in establishing justice and freedom of worship and in improving the living conditions of the citizenry. Conversely, a nation or a group of people that would fail to establish the Caliphate would have their lives invariably end in turmoil and confusion. They would never enjoy peace and love for as long as the earth and heavens last. It is left to the reader to go through the history of the Muslim nations to determine if they have ever lived in the manner and style displayed during the period of the rightly guided Khalifas.

Chapter 11

ISLĀM AND DEMOCRACY

Following the style and pattern of the teaching of Muhammad Rasūlullah, the Western Christian world ought to tell us about the genesis of "democracy." There is no equivalent of the word "democracy" in the Sunna of the holy Apostle; nor does it have roots in the Bible. Even though it was inherited by the Western Christian world from the Greeks, the concept was an alien system among the Greeks. The Romans were the first civilization outside Jerusalem to benefit from the practice of the Islām brought by Jesus, the son of Maryam. If they had any system of looking after their community before that period, they did not spread it to the Far and Near Eastern communities.

Abūl Hasan Ali Nadwi describes "democracy"as it was practiced just before the sixth century A.D:

> The Romans . . . had sunk to a state of complete moral depravity. They wallowed in the inveterate vices of their corrupt and decaying civilizations. Their empires had become storehouses of confusion and mischief. The governing classes, drunk with power, indulged in reckless debauchery and sensuality. The middle classes, as is their wont, took the greatest pride in aping the modes and manners of the rich. As for the common people, they lived in grinding poverty. They filled their bellies like lower creatures and toiled and sweated like cattle so that others might live in voluptuous luxury. Not unoften {sic}

would they solace themselves with narcotics and cheap entertainments, or fall blindfolded upon carnal pleasures whenever the curse of their lives afforded them a breathing moment. Great religions became play things in the hands of debased ecclesiastics who corrupted and twisted them beyond recognition, so much so that if it were possible for their founders to return to the physical life, they would not have recognized them. In consequence of the moral debasement of the great centers of civilization and general disorder and unrest, people everywhere got entangled in their internal problems. They had no message to offer to the world. The world had become hollow from within; its life-springs had dried up. It possessed neither the light of religious guidance, for their personal conduct nor any abiding and rational principles for running a state.

One is now in a position to understand the prediction or the announcement of Prophet Jesus, the son of Maryam, in the holy Qur'ān, 61:6, of the arrival of Ahmad, the most commendable. Allāh did not send Muhammad Rasūlullah to proclaim "democracy" above all other democracies, but sent him with guidance and ad-Dīn to proclaim it above all other forms of ad-Dīn. The system of governance explained in the holy Qur'ān is clearer and more detailed than in the Holy Bible, because the Holy Bible discusses only the Prophets, descendants from Prophet Jacob, the Children of Israel. The teaching in the Holy Bible was directed primarily to Faith, the details or summary of which are available in the holy Qur'ān.

In the holy Qur'ān, 2:124, Allāh reveals His conversation with Prophet Abraham (AS) saying, "Verily, I am going to make you an Imām (a leader) for mankind (to follow you)." Prophet Abraham said, "And of my offspring (to make leaders)." Allāh said, "My Covenant (Prophet hood that is leadership by example under My Divine Guidance) includes not Zālimūn (polytheists and wrong-doers)."

The appointment of Prophet Abraham as a leader to mankind was done not simply out of presupposition and coincidence of merit, for Allāh says this, "And remember when the Lord of Abraham tried him with (certain) Commands, which he fulfilled." If Prophet Abraham did not fulfill those certain Commands, by logic and the spirit of reason and common sense, Allāh could not have made him a leader, whose example later generals were to copy and follow.

It was a ratified promise, lest one could extend it to inheritance. One has to work hard and sweat. What happened between the Children of Israel and their Prophet Samuel confirmed and supported what is in the holy Qur'ān. The appointment of Muhammad ibn Abdallāh as the Imām of the Messengers and seal of the Prophets was confirmed by the Quraysh to be on merit, for on many occasions they addressed him: "You are one of us as you know, of the noblest of the tribe and hold a worthy position in ancestry."[100]

The intent in sending Muhammad Rasūlullah to mankind cannot be explained better than by the conversation between Ja'afar ibn Abi Ṭālib and the Muslim king Negus, of Abyssinia, then holding to the Islām of Jesus, the son of Maryam.[101] On concluding his address, Negus addressed the Quraysh courtiers; "Not for a mountain of gold would I give the emigrants to Abyssinia to you."

'Amr now quickly interrupted Ja'afar and accused him of rejecting Prophet Jesus, the son of Maryam, as the son of Allāh.

King Negus requested Ja'afar to tell him what Muhammad Rasūlullah had said about Jesus, the son of Maryam. Just before they migrated to Abyssinia, Allāh, the Planner, the Wise, the Protector, and the Savior of his obedient servants, revealed the nature of Prophet Jesus, the son of Maryam. So Ja'afar began to narrate the nature of Prophet Jesus, the son of Maryam, as revealed in holy Qur'ān 19. In it Allāh stresses that Jesus is the

---

[100]   A. Guillaume: 132
[101]   Ali, S, Abul Hasan P. 123

slave of Allāh and His Apostle, His spirit and His Word, whom He cast into Maryam, the blessed virgin. When he finished his narration, the Negus and his bishops wept until their scrolls were wet and said, "Of a truth, this and what Jesus (Jesus) brought have come from the same niche. By Allāh, Jesus the son of Maryam does not exceed what you have said by the length of this stick."

If that was what formed the foundation of the call of Muhammad, justice, reason, and common sense demand that one go through his life history from that moment that is 615 A.D. to Monday 12th Rabi ul-Awwal, 633 A.D., just after the sun has passed the meridian. Let that one tell us honestly, what Muhammad and his companions did not accomplish and implement regarding his undesirable "democratic" agenda. When the holy Apostle migrated to Medina, he declined the requests of the affluent to stay with them. The first thing he did was to quench the thirst and hunger of the emigrants; he created a bond of brotherhood with the Ansars (the helpers). He consulted with his companions and participated actively in the building of his mosque. The Sahāba appointed to call the prayer time was a slave from Abyssinia, Bilāl ibn Rabī'ah. All the appointments he made were on merit.

He made himself available not only to his followers, but to all those who wanted to see him. He made himself available five times a day and once every week during the Friday prayer for a question and an answer session. Women were not barred or excluded from attending his teaching under the pretext of the separation of male and female. They were blunt and straight-forward in asking him what they should know about Islām. When the Sahābas saw 'Umar bin Khaṭṭāb wearing a gown, they asked Umar to account how he made it, because they knew that his share of the booty of the cloth was too small to make him a full gown. Likewise, when Umar was delivering a sermon on the dowry, he advised leniency, to which a woman stood up and said, "O 'Umar! You have no right to deny us what Allāh has given us."

What the Western Christian World Should Know about a Muslim

A Muslim is one, irrespective of his skin color, place of birth, and residence, who was created on that Friday in the body and spirit of Adam, who believes in obeying Allāh and that he was selected by Allāh from his community to teach one how to worship Allāh. This began in the heavens when Allāh commanded the angels to bow down to Adam. They all bowed down to Adam, except Iblis, the jinn who used his faculty of free will and refused to bow down to Adam.[102]

Mankind needs only the command of Allāh, for it was tailored to correspond and comply with his instinct, needs, and nature. Allāh claimed that He has not created mankind and jinn and placed on them a burden that they cannot carry and bear. Allāh confirms this in the holy Qur'ān 54:17 "And We have indeed made the Qur'ān easy to understand and remember; then is there anyone who will remember (or receive admonition)." This applies to the Sharī'a, that is, obedience to Allāh, in the same manner that one is able to learn the physical sciences, while another prefers to learn the arts. In this verse, "Zikr" is translated as understand and remember, implying that Allāh has prioritized understanding to remembering. It is therefore not possible for one to remember the injunctions, the Sharī'a, without understanding them.

The opposite is the prevailing situation among the followers of Muhammad Rasūlullah today. They remember--by memorizing the holy Qur'ān--without understanding it. This does not lead them to anywhere but perdition, intolerance, egotism, and impoverishment. Allāh will not accept the excuse that one is unable to understand what his prophet taught him and practiced. If

---

[102] Mustapha, Dr. Sani S. Muhammad Rasūlullah and the People of the Book: His Benevolence, Kindness, Large-heartedness and Quest for Peace(USA: Strategic Book Publishing, 2011).

Allāh could accept it, He would not have been sending Messengers in the language spoken by that community, to warn them and deliver them from bondage. Allāh explained this plainly in the holy Qur'ān, 14:4, "And We sent not a Messenger except with the language of his people, in order that he might make (the Message) clear for them. Then Allāh misleads whom He wills and guides whom He wills. And He is the All-Mighty, the Wise."[103]

In the holy Qur'ān 4:165, Allāh says, "Messengers as bearers of good news as well as of warning in order that mankind should have no plea against Allāh after the (coming of) Messengers. And Allāh is Ever All-Powerful, All-Wise." In the holy Qur'ān 17:15Allāh says, "No one laden with burdens can bear another's burden. And We never punish until We have sent a Messenger." In holy Qur'ān 27:59, Allāh associates the sending down of His Messenger with the destruction of wrongdoers and disbelievers in that community: "And never would We destroy towns unless the people thereof are Zālimūn (polytheists, wrongdoers, disbelievers, etc.)." The pharaoh was destroyed after refusing to agree to the Command of Allāh to free the Children of Israel from bondage. The Ten Commandments, the Law or Sharī'a Allāh sent to Prophet Moses (AS), which lasted for a period of about 1450 years, is full of such warnings and admonitions that the coming of a Messenger signals either destruction or prosperity.

The misunderstanding of the basic teaching of Muhammad Rasūlullah by his followers has led them to become arrogant and refractory to the Message, more so than ever. In the holy Qur'ān 7:132 the Egyptians tell Prophet Moses, in the plainest language, "Whatever Ayat (proof, evidence, verse, lesson, and sign) you may bring to us, to work there with your sorcery on us, we shall never believe in you." The Children of Israel were on many occasions honest and straightforward with Prophet Moses, for they would tell

---

[103] Let us apply this logic to our own experience. Is it possible for one to sit in an examination not covered by the curriculum that year? Could a biology teacher teach history?

him categorically in plain language that they would not believe. These incidents are not mentioned in the Old Testament, for reasons not explained. For example, in the holy Qur'ān 2:55, they say, "We shall never believe in you until we see Allāh plainly."

The followers of Muhammad Rasūlullah are misleading the Western Christian world in forcing them to believe that the holy Qur'ān is beyond their reach and that they are unclean and therefore not supposed to touch or read it. The simplest argument against these Muslim preachers is the proclamation of Allāh in the holy Qur'ān, 61:6, "And (remember) when Jesus, son of Maryam (Mary), said, 'O Children of Israel! I am a Messenger of Allāh unto you, confirming the Taurat [(Torah) which came] before me, and giving glad tidings of a Messenger to come after me, whose name shall be Ahmad. But when he (Ahmad also known as Muhammad) came to them with clear proofs, they said: 'This is plain magic.'"

Prophet Jesus, the son of Maryam, named the holy Apostle Ahmad; meaning "more commendable," while Allāh addressed him as Muhammad, also meaning commendable. What is the distinction between Ahmad and Muhammad? Prophet Jesus, the son of Maryam, named Muhammad commendable because he is his Imām and he sealed what he brought. All Prophets and Apostles before him had therefore addressed Muhammad as Ahmad. In the holy Qur'ān, it is only Muhammad among the 313 Apostles, Messengers with specific Sharī'a, that Allāh used the word "'alā." It means, according to Zamakhshari, that after the appointment of Muhammad Rasūlullah to Prophet hood, a person's belief in Allāh and the Hereafter and the former Messengers and the Books, cannot be beneficial until he also believes in him and his teaching. Therefore, there is no need for Allāh to address him as Ahmad, in the manner the Prophets and Messengers addressed him.

In this century, the followers of Muhammad Rasūlullah do not believe in the holy Qur'ān, for according to the holy Apostle, the one who does not follow and abide by its injunctions does not believe in it.[104] The first of such injunctions is the establishment of the Caliphate before one begins to pray. The followers of Muhammad Rasūlullah do not know that their prayer is void and useless if they haven't established the Caliphate. Observing the five daily prayers in a "Magsūb" land, that is, a land acquired illegally, is not allowed.[105]

One of the meanings of Magsūb, according to Lisān 'Arab, is to have sex without consent, as in the law of the Western world.[106] If one compares a "Magsūb" with an Umma without a Caliph, the followers of Muhammad Rasūlullah will not accept that analogy, despite evidence from the Sunna of the holy Apostle. It is the legitimate Right of Allāh that He should be obeyed wherever one finds oneself. There will never be an incident in one's life, where one is not governed by the legislation of Allāh. This is the proclamation by Allāh in the holy Qur'ān 75:36: "Does man think that he will be left neglected (without being punished or rewarded for the obligatory duties enjoined by his Lord Allāh on him)?" If, indeed, establishing the Caliphate is a duty, which Allāh and Muhammad Rasūlullah have defined, explained, and demonstrated, then the followers of Muhammad Rasūlullah are at a loss. There is a saying among the Muslim jurists:

وما لا يتم الواجب الا به فهو واجب

"*Wujūb*" means obligation. It is a command that is less than a Fard (an obligatory act). They meant that anything that makes an action Wājib is also Wājib. This explanation by the Muslim jurists is unnecessary, for the holy Apostle clearly commanded one to follow his actions. He described all his actions as his

---

104 See al-Ghazali. Ihyā' 'Ulūm ad-din by al-Ghazali (Cairo:Darul Fikr,1989), 322-324.

105 See Imām Shatibi, Muwafiqat (S.A.Darul ibn Affān,1997), 1:328, 386, 452-453ff.

106 See Ibn Manzur. Lisān Arab (Beirut: Darul Jil, 1988), 6:992.

Sunna. Some Muslim scholars have attempted to distinguish what is in the holy Qur'ān and its explanation by the holy Apostle. This is also uncalled for. Take, for example, the recitation of a chapter of the holy Qur'ān in prayers. The opening chapter is Fard and must be recited by all during prayers. It is Fard also to recite another chapter in the first and second Raka'. It is equally Wujūb to recite another chapter in the first and second Raka'. The holy Apostle gave guidelines only, except for the Friday and Fajr prayers on Friday. It is again Fard to follow the Sunna. Some Muslim jurists say it is wājib to follow the Sunna. Such terminology creates confusion and sectarianism in Islam, although that was not the intention.

Some Muslim jurists, who wanted to create mischief and dissuade others from following the Sunna, introduced the question of "understanding" and a predisposition to commit evil. They have, so to speak, turned the Mercy of Allāh into a heavy burden, which has broken the backs of the followers of Muhammad Rasūlullah. Allāh or His Prophet considered being predisposed to commit evil and disobey his Messenger. For example, in the commentary on Exod. 7:3-5, the Promise Study Edition says, "Throughout the Bible we read that each one of us has a choice. We can obey God (Allāh) or disobey him. And we will receive the benefits or the consequences of our decisions. Yet, it seems at first glance that God caused the Egyptian king's stubbornness. How can this be? God gives us the freedom to make our own decisions. When people choose to continually disobey God, He makes them stubborn."

These individuals have already made the choice to turn away from God. We can compare the relationship between the king's stubbornness and God's causing him to be stubborn to the following statements: "Joey flunked history class" and "the history teacher flunked Joey." Both statements are true, but the cause of Joey's failure is Joey. Similarly, the king already had a proud, stubborn attitude. God did not cause him to have this attitude. He knew the king would not readily release the

Israelites. God used this situation to show both the Israelites and the Egyptians that he is the one true God."[107] This is what Muhammad Rasūlullah explained as the Taqdir of Allāh, one of the articles of faith.

The followers of Muhammad Rasūlullah have virtually forgotten all the warnings and lessons left behind for them by him and his Sahābas. On many occasions, I pause and consider: How will Allāh judge those I have witnessed testing the Sunna of Muhammad? If the past generations were to see Allāh forgiving the followers of Muhammad for the same offense for which He punished them or threw them into the pit-fire, one would see many demonstrations in the Hereafter. I do not know what will happen that Day! For example, if Allāh incriminated the people of Shu'aibu in calling them disbelievers, simply because they refused to give full weight and measure, the followers of Muhammad Rasūlullah would not. Not all the thirty-three mentioned major sins apply to them. They regard only the People of the Book as disbelievers and go on accusing them in meddling into their affairs, preventing them from conducting their way of life according to the Sharī'a or the Sunna of Muhammad Rasūlullah. May Allāh forgive them, for they must have difficulty in understanding the holy Qur'ān, even though they memorize it completely. What a paradox!

If one were to ask them what is required for one to understand the Sunna of the holy Apostle, they would never be able to explain or give a defensive argument. What evidence do you need to convince you the followers of Muhammad have difficulty in understanding the holy Qur'ān, other than what is written in the holy Qur'ān 51:59, "And verily, for those who do wrong, there is a portion of torment like to the evil portion of torment (which came for) their likes (of old); so let them not ask Me to hasten on!"

---

[107] Exod. 7:.3-5.

What does it require for one sitting in front of Muhammad Rasūlullah to understand, learn how to perform ablution, and all the rituals of prayer? Prayer is the most difficult of all the rituals, because no one is exempted from observing the five daily prayers. Fasting, Zakat, and fulfilling the Pilgrimage are not mandatory. They speak without measuring and weighing what they say. For example, they do not know by 'ilmal yaqeen (translating theory into practice) the diurnal times of the five daily prayers. Out of exuberance and daring, they begin their fasting before the setting of the lunar month. They do not encourage the giving of charity as required in the Torah, but instead take to accumulating their wealth, with the intention of giving out the annual Zakat, which they then never give out. They paradoxically observe the Friday prayer and not the Qasr prayer on a journey.

It is unfortunate that they have failed to understand that they will never fulfill their obligations without establishing the Caliphate. They always beseech Allāh to destroy the Jews in their prayers. This is not allowed in the first instance. Secondly, they have forgotten the hadīth of the holy Apostle: "My followers will be following the examples of the Children of Israel, measure by measure and inch by inch, until if one of them will sleep with his mother, they will also sleep with their mothers." The followers of the holy Apostle are "penny wise but pound foolish." They do not believe in the Qur'ānic descriptions of disbelievers, wrongdoers, and polytheists, which is applied to them. Granted that is true, they cannot escape from being described as hypocrites.

Hypocrisy is a halfway house, an incomplete house after the Hijrah of the holy Apostle. The classic example of hypocrisy is the attitude and behavior of 'Abdullāh ibn Ubay ibn Salūl to Muhammad Rasūlullah and his Sahābas. If holy Qur'ān 108 was revealed in Makka and therefore did not apply to the followers of Muhammad Rasūlullah, they cannot deny that the holy Qur'ān 63, revealed in Medina in 6 A.H., was not describing one of them. The last stronghold of the Levi tribes of the Children of Israel had been dismantled a year before. At that time in Medina, there were no disbelievers, polytheists, and wrongdoers; there were only those praying with Muhammad Rasūlullah, but instigating his Sahābas to fight one another and be divided on race, tribe, and place of origin. Right from the very arrival of the holy Apostle in the city of Medina, ibn Salūl refused to recognize the holy Apostle. Selfishness, pride, and quests for worldly pleasures and supremacy were the reasons behind the refusal of 'Abdullāh ibn Ubay ibn Salūl to believe in Muhammad Rasūlullah.

Since one has to conduct the Jihād under a messenger of Allāh and after him under a Caliph, 'Abdullāh ibn Ubay ibn Salūl never participated in any of the military expeditions undertaken by the holy Apostle. Equally, Muhammad Rasūlullah never appointed him to lead a military expedition. The hypocrites will be worse than the disbelievers, polytheists, and other criminals on the Day of Judgment, for they will be at the bottom of the Hell-fire. The followers of Muhammad Rasūlullah should therefore study holy Qur'ān, 3:86, "How shall Allāh guide a people who disbelieved after their belief and after they bore witness that the Messenger is true and after clear proofs had come unto them? And Allāh guides not the people who are Zālimūn."

Who was the speaker in that verse? That speaker must have been a firm believer, who reflected seriously on the knowledge, attitude, and practice of the followers of Muhammad Rasūlullah and saw no sign of the Promise of Allāh in them--peace, love, security, or prosperity.

Islām As it Stands Today

Islām stands today as it stood during the time of every Prophet and Messenger mentioned in the holy Qur'an. Islām is distinct from a Muslim. The holy Apostle is confronted by the Quraysh, who say in the holy Qur'ān, 10:15, "Bring us a Qur'ān other than this, or change it." This was a rejection and an aversion to what they had learnt. It suggests their reluctance to doing away with

360 gods and worshipping the Lord of Abraham and Ishmael and inviting him to worship their gods. Secondly, when the Quraysh accused Muhammad Rasūlullah of fabricating the Message, he said in the holy Qur'ān 46:9, "I am not a new thing among the messengers (of Allāh i.e. I am not the first Messenger) nor do I know what will be done with me or with you. I only follow that which is revealed to me, and I am but a plain warner."

Thirdly, the Levi tribes of the Children of Israel instigated the Quraysh to ask Muhammad Rasūlullah to tell them the story of Prophet Joseph. This was done with the intention of embarrassing Muhammad Rasūlullah, but at the same time to make a point against them that he is indeed a messenger of Allāh, preaching the same ad-Dīn. There and then, in one sitting, holy Qur'ān 12 was revealed. What the Levi tribes told Muhammad Rasūlullah when they heard the story of their Prophet is not recorded by historians.

Technically, no one is supposed to despise one for one's belief in Allāh. Allāh in the holy Qur'ān 22:17 says, "Verily those who believe (in Allāh and in His Messenger Muhammad Rasūlullah), and those who are Jews, and the Serbians, and the Christians, and the Majus, and those who worship others besides Allāh, truly, Allāh will judge between them on the Day of Resurrection. Verily! Allāh is over all things a Witness." The holy Apostle made this clear saying, "The 'Arab is not superior to a non-'Arab except by Taqwa, fear of Allāh i.e. worshipping Allāh. A white man is not superior to a black man except by Taqwa. A yellow man is not superior to a red man except by Taqwa."[108] The holy Apostle never turned his eyes against someone, because he is not his follower. His etiquette was to consider everyone as a believer according to the prophet he is following. Therefore, as it stands today Islām is submission to Allāh, in its original form revealed to a particular Prophet or Messenger.

---

[108] Scholars of Council of Islāmic ideology. Injunctions of Islām. Islamabad. Council of Islamic Ideology. 1991. P.52

Reviewing the state of mankind at the time of Muhammad Rasūlullah, Imām Shafi'i (150-204 A.H.) observed two classes of people: the People of the Book and the disbelievers.

"People of the Book" is the term commonly used to refer to the Jews and Christians.[109] The Jews, the Levi tribe of the Children of Israel, were the only tribe out of the twelve tribes living in Medina. The 'Arab Christians lived in Najran. Generally, the term is applied to all those communities with a book from Heaven.

The disbelievers, who invented their own way of life (Sharī'a) without the permission of Allāh, made stone and wood images of their gods, inventing names for them and worshipping them. Those were the 'Arabs living in Makka and other 'Arabs living in the 'Arabian Peninsula. Some of the non-'Arab tribes bordering them also took to their form of worship and included fish, animals, fire, and stars.

The history of the People of the Book is to serve as a warning, hope, and guidance to those who come after them. To accuse such past generations of disbelief today, in the light of the holy Qur'ān, is uncivilized and unbecoming. It is important for a follower of Muhammad Rasūlullah to look at his behavior and way of life. Allāh sent Muhammad as a mercy to mankind, in that the one who hears what he narrates, believes it, and follows his actions will be forgiven by Allāh and admitted into Paradise. Therefore, accusing those classes of people who came before Muhammad of disbelief should not have arisen. They had no reliable and authentic knowledge with them on what Allāh

---

[109] Holy Qur'an 3:64. The name 'People of the Book' is mentioned twenty eight times in the holy Qur'an. It refers to no other civilization than that of the Children of Israel. Also Mustapha, Allama Dr. Sāni Sālih Mustapha. Muhammad Rasūlullah and the People of the Book. USA. Strategic Book Printing Rights and Agency. 2011. Chapter 2:3. Also Shafi'i, Imām Mustapha Muhammad Idris. Al-Risala. Beirut. Dārul Fikr. 1939. P.8

revealed to their Prophets at the time of Muhammad Rasūlullah. Even if they had claimed that what they had was an authentic revelation from Allāh to their Prophet, and refused to follow Muhammad Rasūlullah, he would have just passed over them and cautioned them to fear Allāh and tell the truth about him.

Whenever I reflect on the attitude and behavior of the followers of Muhammad Rasūlullah today, I get lost, not because I do not know what to say about them, but because they will never believe that what I say about them is confirmed by the holy Qur'ān. The holy Qur'ān is an address to you and me as individuals, and we are not absolved from what Allāh commands in regard to past generations. For example, in the holy Qur'ān, 11:84, Prophet Shu'aibu addressed his people calling them to Faith (Īman) and Islām, "O my people! Worship Allāh and give not short measure or weight." In the next verse he called them specifically to Islām, "And O my people! Give full measure and weight in justice and reduce not the things that are due to the people, and do not commit mischief in the land, causing corruption."

This call is repeated without mentioning Prophet Shu'aibu in the holy Qur'ān 6:152, "And come not near to the orphan's property, except to improve it, until he (or she) attains the age of full strength, and give full measure and full weight with justice We burden not any person, but that which he can bear."

The people of Shu'aibu compared his call to what was practiced according to their custom, going back to what their fathers used to do, worshipping others than Allāh; they believed that their property was their right (capitalism). They professed that they did not understand what he summoned them to, that he was not from the well-to-do and in addition that he was weak. They refused to obey him on the pretext that they did not understand his call. We do not have the details of their number and for how long they disobeyed him. In the long run, they were destroyed by Allāh because of their rebellion and sin.

In an Islāmic state, a Prophet or a messenger is a political leader. The call of Prophet Shu'aibu—"And reduce not the things that are due to the people"--affixed to the Sunna of Muhammad Rasūlullah, implies the following:

a. Provision of one's basic needs. When ʿAbdullāh ibn ʿUmar wanted to get married, he was delayed by the holy Apostle because at that time, Muhammad had not the means to provide him with his basic needs. When the economy of the small Muslim Islāmic state improved, he was listed among those to be given stipends and allowed to marry.

 In addition, the Muslims of the People of the Book who migrated to Medina were given their basic needs. During the Caliphate of ʿUmar bin Khaṭṭāb, he saw a Muslim of the People of the Book sitting under a shade tree. He stopped by and asked him his condition. He told ʿUmar that, ʿUmar bin Khaṭṭāb that the Amir of the Muslim Umma had burdened him with the "protection dues," or Jizyah. There and then, ʿUmar discontinued his journey, took him to the sub-treasury, and got his name struck out from the register. He was put under the register of those entitled to assistance.
b. Protection of wealth.
c. Protection of progeny.
d. Protection of the body from any harm.

Those who had disobeyed their Prophets before the time of Muhammad Rasūlullah were called disbelievers, wrongdoers, and polytheists and described variously as rebellious, disobedient, blind, deaf, and dumb. For example, in the holy Qurʾān, 5:44, Allāh says, ". . . verily, We did send down the Taurat (Torah), therein was guidance and light, by which the Prophets, who submitted themselves to Allāh's Will, judged for the Jews. And the rabbis and the priests (too judged for the Jews by the Taurat after those Prophets), for them was entrusted the protection of Allāh's Book, and they were witnesses thereto. Therefore fear not men but fear Me (O Jews) and sell not My Verses for a miserable price. And whosoever does not judge by what Allāh has revealed, such are the Kāfirūn."

In a recent sermon on an 'Arab satellite television station, the preacher explained the verse to be applying to the Jews and by implication, only those living in Medina. But did they actually separate themselves after the hijrah when judging? The Medina Covenant signed by all the parties, indeed permitted them to follow their own version of Islām, but in the case of disputes they were to refer such disputes to Muhammad. One of them was the case of adultery that resulted in the Sharī'a in Torah incorporated in the Sunna of Muhammad Rasūlullah.

Another case was that of Banu Qurayza, who broke the Medina compact with the holy Apostle. This compact was for the defense of Medina, incorporating an agreement providing the basis for the establishment of the nonfederal administration of the city. It allowed a large measure of autonomy to the units, which was consistent with the needs and wishes of the Jewish tribes of 'Arabia.

At that time, Allāh did not reveal to Muhammad Rasūlullah what to do in case the Levi tribe of the Children of Israel breached the Medina Covenant. As a result, the holy Apostle besieged their stronghold for twenty-five days; and at last, after consulting their ally Abū Lubāba, they surrendered. The Aws tribe, also their allies, intervened on their behalf for mercy according to the compact between them. Accordingly, the holy Apostle recommended an arbitration to which he appointed Sa'd bin Muadth, a chieftain of the Aws. They agreed. When he went to the stronghold of Banu Qurayza, he said, "The time has come for Sa'd in the cause of Allāh, not to care for any man's censure." Sa'd then asked for assurance from those around him, including the holy Apostle, that his judgment be accepted. After getting their assurances, he boldly declared, "Then I give the judgment that the men should be killed, the property divided, and the women and children be taken as captives." The Banu Qurayza agreed for that is what is laid down in the Torah.[110]

Commenting upon the need of a deterrent punishment for the traitors on this occasion, R.V.C. Bodley writes in *The Messenger: The Life of Mohammed*:

> Mohammed stood alone in 'Arabia, a country equivalent in area to the United States, populated by about five million people. His own dominion was not much longer than Central Park; his means of enforcing his wishes, three thousand badly armed soldiers. Had he been weak, had he allowed treachery to go unpunished, Islām would never have survived. This massacre of the Hebrews was drastic but not original in religious history. From a Muslim point of view, it was justified. From now on, the 'Arab tribes, as well as Jewish, thought twice about defying this man who evidently intended to have his own way.[111]

A Jewish scholar, Dr. Israel Wellphenson, has also reached this very conclusion that the punishment dealt out to Banu Qurayza helped to frighten and discourage the hypocrites. He says: "In so far as the hypocrites were concerned, their clamors declined after the expedition against Bani Qurayza; thereafter they said or did nothing against the decisions of the Apostle and his companions, as it was expected earlier."[112]

The Levi tribes of the Children of Israel disobeyed Muhammad Rasūlullah and were punished according to the Sharī'a. They did not hesitate but accepted the judgment. They will therefore be forgiven by Allāh and admitted into Paradise. The case of the followers of Muhammad Rasūlullah today, however, is far different, far from anything close to

---

[110] See Deut. 20:10-14, Num. 31:7-10, and Num. 31:13-15.
[111] Ali, S. Abul Hasan. The Life of Muhammad 251-252.
[112] Ibid 252.

what they profess in the Kalimat Shahadatyn. I bear witness that there is only one Law-Giver (Allāh) and that Muhammad his Apostle demonstrated and explained the Sharī'a to the extent that no one has an excuse for not understanding it. Islām today is what Islām was at the time of all the Prophets and Messengers mentioned directly in the holy Qur'ān, and those not mentioned in the holy Qur'ān. The holy Apostle says this clearly:

فما لم يكن يو مئذ د ينا فلا يكون اليو م د ينا

"What is not ad-Dīn in my time cannot be ad-Dīn in any time." In addition, the holy Apostle says, "I will leave you in a luminous state; its day is as its night. No one among my followers will desist or go against that luminous state, but will be destroyed. He, who lives long, will see people outside that luminous state. You are to be in the state you know is from me and what my Khulafā'ul Rashidin did after me."[113] The Sahābas for their part said, "The holy Apostle did not leave us until he explained everything to us in plain language and practically, on matters dealing with ad-Dīn (matters relating to the Hereafter) and ad-Dunya (all what we need to do in this world for our own good)." Those who regard themselves as not followers of Muhammad Rasūlullah should therefore think twice and come out with their evidence as to why they regard themselves as not of his Umma. This is all that has to be done for an everlasting peace in the world.

---

[113] This hadith further explains that the holy Apostle in his life time did not give anyone authority to enact a Sharī'a besides him. Also, he has indirectly confirmed that his Sahābas will never perform an Ibadat--not in the way he performed it. Thus, there is no authority in anytime except what is from the holy Apostle and his Sahābas in the matter of worship.

CONCLUSION

It is not easy to explain to you why you should do away with the wrong notion that you are not a Muslim, since the term refers to the one who believes in a Prophet, sent to his community with clear evidence of the Supremacy and Lordship of Allāh. The only way for you to surrender these wrong notions and prejudices, imposed on you without your having studied the past, is to try to use reason to justify your belief. We have to go by the usual questions: Who, How, Why, and When?

The Revelation of the holy Qur'ān, in the 'Arabic language, was not a matter of chance and co-incidence, but a matter perfectly chosen by Allāh to fit into his Perfect Design and Plan. If the People of the Book claim that Prophet Moses and Jesus, the son of Maryam, were sent to the Children of Israel in particular, the Prophets that came before Moses were not sent on that basis. Prophet Joseph was not sent to his brothers alone, but to all of the people of Egypt and those communities around them.

Initially mankind understood the advantage of living together when they built the Tower of Babel. However, that was not in the Grand Plan, Design, and Will of Allāh. It was the unawareness of our forefathers of the extent of the Mercy of Allāh that made them think of building the Babel Tower. Their migration to the East, the South-east, and then the South caused them to have multiple languages; hence, the necessity of sending to that community a messenger in their language. It was not a weakness in Allāh for him to send a warner to each community.

Wherever one finds oneself, he/she will be protected by Allāh. Differences in color of the skin, language, and place of residence have never been the criteria or the causes of conflict and poverty; rather, they are the result of man's daring to think that he is above his Lord. In the holy Qur'ān 2:213, Allāh explains the necessity of sending to mankind a Messenger, "Mankind were one community and Allāh sent Prophets with glad tidings and warnings, and with them He sent down the Scripture in truth to judge between people in matters wherein they differed. And only those to whom (the Scripture) was given differed concerning it after clear proofs had come unto them through hatred, one to another. Then Allāh by His Leave guided those who believed to the truth of that wherein they differed. And Allāh guides whom He wills to the Straight Path." This was what all Prophets did without exception.

Provided that we have the desire to understand our differences and the desire to live in peace, these attributes can help us to understand Allāh. Muhammad Rasūlullah not only demonstrated this, but also made it his way of life in Medina, even before his migration. Allāh encouraged the Quraysh and the Levi tribe of the Children of Israel on the following occasion: In the holy Qur'ān 10:94, He addresses the holy Apostle, as if Muhammad Rasūlullah lacked confidence, "So if you (O Muhammad) are in doubt concerning that which We have revealed unto you, then ask those who are reading the Book (Torah and Injeel) before you. Verily, the truth has come to you from your Lord. So be not of those who doubt (it)." This again calls for unity and understanding among the People of the Book and the followers of Muhammad Rasūlullah, not hatred and bloodshed. Can this be achieved with one community despising the other? Let us live by the example of our two eyes and all the double organs we have. Even if we can survive with the function of one, one is certainly disabled.

In the holy Qur'ān 28:49, Muhammad Rasūlullah challenges the People of the Book: "Then bring a Book from Allāh which is a better guide than these two [the Taurat and the Qur'ān], that I may follow it, if you are truthful." That was another open invitation to all those with sincere intention, will, and determination to love each other and live in peace. Did Muhammad Rasūlullah ever indicate that the holy Qur'ān was exclusive to him and his Sahābas? Why are we not listening to the Message of this gentleman? I am sure that his teaching was never denied by any sensible, rational, and free-thinking person; but through ages of prejudice and wrong ideas, some people have taken advantage of the ignorance of others and implanted the seed of hatred among mankind. This state of affairs must be addressed and looked into critically with an open mind.

If Muhammad Rasūlullah wasn't sent as a mercy to mankind, his preaching could have been the exclusive right of only a few, besides his tribe. It is not a question of exclusiveness. As the holy Apostle declared, "An 'Arab is not superior to a non-'Arab, except by Taqwa." The holy Apostle assembled his relations and addressed them, "I have been sent to you in particular and to mankind in general."

The Messengers were not sent in particular to those who want to enter Paradise, that is, to attain peace, salvation, and prosperity in the Hereafter, even without attaining the same in the world. If, according to my research, the Holy Bible explains that peace, prosperity, and salvation are only possible after obeying the Messenger and Prophet of Allāh in this world, then Jesus, the son of Maryam, could not have given the glad tidings of the coming of Ahmad, "the more commendable."

Christ's prediction was proved to be so, for it was only after Muhammad Rasūlullah migrated to Medina that peace began to spread in the 'Arabian peninsula. How did he achieve that? If he had demanded the Levi tribe to produce before him a Book from Allāh (G-d) that was a better guide for him to follow and he followed the book, he would have had no grounds on which to be followed and none of the tribes of Medina would have followed him.

On the contrary, the Levi tribe in Medina, having retained their language, could understand the Revelation and were aware of the threat in the holy Qur'ān 23:71, "And if the truth had been in accordance with their desires, verily, the heavens and the earth, and whatsoever is therein would have been corrupted." They could not deny the Prophet because they had been threatening the Aws and Khazraj tribes with his coming, as confirmed by Allāh in the holy Qur'ān 23:71, "Nay, We have brought them their reminder, but they turn away from their reminder."

The holy Apostle is addressed in the holy Qur'ān 2:120:"Never will the Jews nor the Christians be pleased with you (O Muhammad) till you follow their ad–Dīn (religion)." Say, "Verily the Guidance of Allāh that is the (only) Guidance. And if you (O Muhammad) were to follow their desires after what you have received of Knowledge, then you would have against Allāh neither any Walī (protector or guardian) nor any helper." An address to Muhammad Rasūlullah is a more serious address to his followers. Therefore, the admonishment is given not to the holy Apostle, but rather to his followers. Allāh is not referring to issues of the Pillars of Islām, but to the fundamental issue of faith, and that is nothing other than the Caliphate.

The Levi tribe of the Children of Israel's dispute with Muhammad Rasūlullah was only on his position as their Messenger and not on the issue of Islām; about the rituals. It is therefore inadmissible to consider the People of the Book non-believers, since the covenant stipulated each community be allowed to worship its Allāh. *This lesson was meant to show that the community that fails to establish the Caliphate has no grounds to observe the rituals, for their 'Ibādat will not be accepted by Allāh.*[114]

The Levi tribes, within eight kilometers radius, lived under Muhammad as the Messenger, for almost six years. Therefore, under Iradatul Kawniyya Diniyya, they were followers of Muhammad Rasūlullah. The Sharī'a revealed at that period, as

---

[114] If it were possible to write a book with one sentence, this could be that sentence.

explained earlier, was that which Allāh revealed to Prophet Moses. The followers of Muhammad Rasūlullah should understand that there was never a moment the holy Apostle "inclined" towards the Children of Israel, except to deliver the Message to them. The injunction in the holy Qur'ān 2:120, should be read and analyzed with the injunction in the holy Qur'ān 11:113, "And incline not toward those who do wrong, lest the Fire should touch you, and you have no protectors other than Allāh, nor you would then be helped."

Equally, the Jews and the Christians should better understand how the holy Apostle lived in an atmosphere of tolerance and love with their ancestors. The common notion that there was misunderstanding or that the Jews and Christians hated Muhammad or did not believe in him is contradicted by Revelation.

The Western Christian world should understand that the mercy of Allāh is ever open to and awaiting them. The holy Qur'ān, and the Holy Bible should be read together, for if I had not done so, I could not have understood the Message of Allāh in a liberal way. This is what I understand as a "secular," approach- -attempting to understand a way of submitting to Allāh, obeying and worshipping Him, in the twenty-first century.

The holy Apostle on many occasions mentioned some incidents involving the Children of Israel that are not mentioned in the Bible; they explain and give support to some verses of the holy Qur'ān. Imām Al-Ghazali and many Muslim writers have quoted such narrations from the holy Apostle. For example, when 'Umar ibn Khaṭṭāb, decided to increase the size of the holy Apostle's mosque, he approached al-'Abbas ibn 'Abdul Muṭṭallib, requesting that he sell his house adjacent to the mosque and offering him the following:

To pay him whatever amount he requested.

To build a similar house for him.

To receive the house from him as a charity.

Al-'Abbas flatly refused. 'Umar advised him to seek advice from someone. So he went to see 'Ubay ibn Ka'b and narrated

173

what 'Umar had requested of him. 'Ubay told him, "Allāh commanded Prophet David to build a house for Him." Prophet David enquired from Allāh about the house. He told him where he saw one rending his sword on a rock. He then saw a threshing field belonging to a Jew. He approached him and told him that he had been commanded to build a house (altar) for Allāh on his land. The boy asked if Allāh had commanded him to build the house on his land without his consent. Prophet David said, 'No!".

Allāh revealed to Prophet David the abundance of wealth in his possession and told him to use it. Prophet David then approached the boy and said, "I have something to offer you that will please you. I am offering a qintar of gold." The boy asked Prophet David for three qintars and kept on pressing for more, until they agreed for nine qintars. On hearing this, Al-Abbas said, "I will not accept any price for my house. I have given it as a charity to the Muslim Umma." 'Umar then accepted the house and enlarged the mosque. The Talmud version in 2 Samuel 24:18-21 of this incident is as follows:

And Gad came to David on that day, and said to him, "Go up to erect an altar to the Lord in the threshing-floor of Aravnah the Jebusite.".

And David went up according to the word of Gad, as the Lord had commanded.

And Aravnah looked afar and he saw the king and his servants passing on towards him: and Aravnah went out and he bowed down to the king with his face to the ground.

And Aravnah said, "Why has the lord my king come to his servant?" And David said, "To acquire from you the threshing-floor, in order to build an altar to the Lord, that the plague be stayed from the people."

And Aravnah said to David, "Let my lord the king take and offer up what seems good in his eyes; behold the oxen for the burnt-offering and the threshing tools, and the [wooden] tools of the oxen for [fire] wood."

All this Aravnah the king gave to the king. And Aravnah said to the king, "May the Lord your God accept you."

And the king said to Aravnah, "No; for I will only buy it from you at a price; so that I will not offer to the Lord my God burnt-offerings [which I had received] for nothing." And David bought the threshing-floor and the oxen for fifty shekels of silver.

And David built there an altar to the Lord, and he offered up burnt-offerings and peace offerings. And the Lord was entreated for the land, and the plague was stayed from Israel.

The point here is the narration of an incident between Allāh and Prophet David (technically this is the meaning of "Qur'ān"). If a Sahāba use an incident in the Torah to convince a Sahāba, then how could a follower of Muhammad Rasūlullah disregard the Torah? The People of the Book and especially the Children of Israel must support the truth by believing and supporting a follower of Muhammad Rasūlullah who is fair, honest, and unprejudiced on the cause of Allāh and Muhammad Rasūlullah. This cause is nothing other than peaceful co-existence among all those who have received Revelation from Allāh.

The Children of Israel or the present Jewish race should understand the history of Islām; in so doing, they would have the opportunity to become spiritual world leaders. The "dice" was in the hands of their ancestors; they slipped away from them and were picked up by others as a warning that no one has an exclusive monopoly on the blessing of Allāh. The majority of the followers of Muhammad Rasūlullah are conducting their way of life in a far more atrocious and defiant manner than are the children of Israel or as the Levi tribe of the Children of Israel in Medina did.

Prophet Muhammad Rasūlullah is reported to have said, *"Don't greet the Children of Israel of my Umma."*[115] Allāh did warn the followers of Muhammad Rasūlullah against following in the footsteps of the Children of Israel. This warning came before the institution of the four pillars of Islām. The greatest evil, deviation, and backsliding of the Children of Israel was their weakening of the Caliphate! They entrusted positions of responsibility to inefficient, incompetent, narrow-minded, dishonest, immoral, feebleminded, and illiterate people.

They then made the teachings of their Scriptures the monopoly of their rabbis and professional scribes, in such a manner that it was only what they deemed as right that would be communicated to their illiterate community. They went ahead and changed, directly or indirectly, every portion of their Sharī'a (Torah/Taurāt), certifying every irreligious practice as legal merely for worldly gains and pleasures. I must qualify this emphasis, for we read that when at last the Priest Hilkiah found the missing Torah, he handed it over to Prophet Joshia. Prophet Joshia then made a proclamation that all have to obey the Torah.[116] But today and ever since, the Sunna of the holy Apostle never suffered what the Torah suffered. But what are his followers doing?

The followers of Muhammad Rasūlullah, in their course of degradation, are following the footsteps of the Children of Israel in selecting their leaders against the Sharī'a of Allāh. It is to be noted that there is no difference in the Sharī'a of Muhammad Rasūlullah and that in the Old and New Testaments in selecting leaders. The crisis that began on December 17, 2010, was definitely caused in the Muslim Umma by the absence of the

---

[115] Narrated by 'Umar ibn Khaṭṭab. I did not highlight this in: Zahiri, Imām Abi Muhammad Aliyu bin Ahmad Ma'aruf Ibn Hazm Andalusia. Al-Fisl fi Milal wal Ahwa 'i Wa Nihl. Beirut. Daral Kutb 'Ilmiyya. 1996. PP. 3-423

[116] 2 Kings 22-23.

office of the Caliph. Any follower of Muhammad Rasūlullah disagreeing is advised to read his rubrics.

The present Jews will never accept that Allāh (G-d) was cruel and unconcerned with the welfare and safety of their ancestors when they were in Egypt and immediately after the Exodus. From the very moment Prophet Joshua took over the leadership from Prophet Moses, the then Children of Israel enjoyed the blessings of Allāh, lived in peace and prospered. The People of the Book will never disagree with me that their ancestors could only defeat their enemies after they returned to the teaching of the Torah.

Members of the Levi tribe of the Children of Israel should tell me how their ancestors lived with Muhammad Rasūlullah in Medina. I am beseeching them in the name of Allāh--G-d--to confirm or deny the following conversation between Huyayy bin Akhtab and his brother Yasir, reported by his daughter Safiyya ibn Huyayy Zawj, the wife of Muhammad ibn 'Abdallāh (the holy Apostle) and the mother of the faithful:

> Abū Yassar ibn Akhṭāb asked, "Is he really the same Prophet about whom there occur prophecies in our books?"
>
> Huyayy replied, "Yes."
>
> Abū Yassar ibn Akhṭāb asked, "Are you quite sure of it?"
>
> Huyayy replied, "Yes."
>
> He asked again, "What then is your intention?"
>
> Huyayy replied, "I will oppose him as long as he lives and I will not let his mission succeed."[117]

The Jews should understand that it is not possible to have peace in the world when only the followers of Muhammad Rasūlullah who do not even understand the fundamental teaching of

---

[117] Maudūdi, S. Abul Ala. The Meaning of the Qur'ān. Lahore. Islāmic Publications (PVT). 1993. Vol.1 P. 97

Muhammad Rasūlullah are given responsible positions of leadership. I believe, that the Torah is the Revelation from Allāh and that every revelation that agrees with the holy Qurʿān has a universal application, in that it is also the Sharīʿa. Therefore, the insistence that everything refer to the holy Qurʿān must be understood as an insistence that everything likewise must refer to the Scriptures.

An example will suffice: I smoked cigarettes in my early life. Smoking is not allowed in the Sunna of Muhammad technically, as it is harmful to the body. The followers of Muhammad have never promulgated a law/Sharīʿa prohibiting it. On the contrary, the Western world, having recognized what Muhammad frowned at, has now issued a Sharīʿa banning smoking in public places. What have the followers of Muhammad been doing for such a long time, that they cannot apply his Sharīʿa, until promulgated by those they consider as enemies to their holy Apostle? The followers of Muhammad Rasūlullah, in particular the ʿArabs, must obey the Sharīʿa. So where is the difference? One group is concerned about the welfare of her citizens, the other unconcerned, if not averse to, what is good for their citizens. At the present time, this is the true behavior and attitude of the followers of Muhammad Rasūlullah.

The Western Christian world must now make up its mind on what to do. The Jews must listen to the followers of Muhammad in implementing all common injunctions in their scriptures. I am sure there are a lot of Christian denominations that are interested in going over the scriptures to find what is common to all for peaceful co-existence. There have been many attempts by the Western Christian world, but unfortunately their recommendations have been unheeded.

How could they succeed, since the henchmen of the Muslim Umma are illiterate, deaf, dumb, and blind? This is evident in what is going on in the Middle-East and North Africa in their call for "democracy," but without referring their call to the scriptures. *If a follower of Muhammad Rasūlullah calls for scrapping the Sunna of the holy Apostle, he will be labeled as having committed an apostasy and as deserving to be killed.*

The issue, however, is what Allāh says in the holy Qurʻān, 63:6: "It is equal to them whether you ask forgiveness or ask not forgiveness for them, Allāh will never forgive them. Verily, Allāh guides not the people who are the Fāsiqīn (wrong-doers and disobedient to Allāh)." The truth is that the followers of Muhammad ought to understand that apart from the major sins mentioned in the holy Qurʻān 4:11-32, which are not forgiven unless one repents and amends in this world, there is another cryptic offense never considered by them--*Shirk Hafiyy*--silent polytheism. In the holy Qurʻān 39:47, Allāh says, "And there will become apparent to them from Allāh what they have not been reckoning." Explaining this verse, ʻUmar ibn Khaṭṭab said, "O mankind! There is no excuse on anyone disregarding the actions and way of life of the holy Apostle, after establishing them, in one's wrong thinking that, his action was according to the Sunna. Equally, one has no excuse on the actions he abandoned, thinking that they are not in accordance to the Sunna of the holy Apostle. Everything has been described, explained and exposed in full details. Plain and clear evidence has been produced under the very tip of one's nose. All excuses have therefore been put under the carpet."[118]

How I wish the Western Christian world would listen to me as they listened to that Iraqi who unfortunately gave them false evidence on Saddam Hussein's weapons of mass destruction! They accepted his evidence with good-will in their determination to get rid of Saddam and bring "democracy" to the People of Iraq. If one were to provide evidence that Muhammad Rasūlullah reminded the Levi tribe of the Children of Israel of the Torah and that his Mission was actually to liberate the Levi, the Aws, and the Khazraj, would they listen to him and implement his wisdom?

---

[118] See Baghdādi, ʻAbubakar Ahmad ibn Aliyu ibn Thābit. Kitāb Fāqih wal Mutafaqqih. (Riyadh: Dārul Jawzi, 1996.1. 383

Just as they ousted Saddam Hussein would they dislodge these Muslim tyrants and unjust rulers from power?

What evidence must be produced for those interested in establishing peace in the world to believe that Muhammad Rasūlullah was not a liar and did not fail in accomplishing his mission? His greatest miracle, since all Prophets and Messengers had their miracles--is certainly the holy Qur'ān. The Levi tribe, the only tribe of the Children of Israel who had contact with the holy Apostle would never deny holy Qur'ān, 27:76: "Verily, this Qur'ān narrates to the Children of Israel most of that in which they differed. And truly, in this Qur'ān is a guide and a mercy for the believers." The quality and extent of this guidance are further explained in the holy Qur'ān 17:9: "Verily, this Qur'ān guides to that which is most just and right and gives glad tidings to the believers, who work deeds of righteousness, that they shall have a great reward (Paradise)."

One guide to that which is most just and right is ifrād al mujtami' (Obeying the Command of Allāh as an example for others to follow). 'Ifrād al mujtami' began when the Prophet Abraham disapproved of his people worshipping idols. After dissociating from them, he called for them to worship Allāh; this is the demand and first step in establishing the Caliphate. Matthew Henry explains that "the children of God must not mix with those who are profane. Professors of religion, in marrying both themselves and their children, should make conscience of keeping within the bounds of profession. The bad will sooner debauch the good than the good reform the bad."[119]

Faith and Islām call on recognizing and abiding by what is known and established as authority from Allāh. Faith calls on one to abide strictly by its articles, while Islām calls on one, additionally, to strictly live according to the example of his Messenger or Prophet. If, from the Exodus to the apparent crucifixion of Jesus, the son of Maryam, the only constitutionally

---

[119] Henry Commentary on Exod.6:1-2.

accepted and practiced Law was the Torah, and Muhammad Rasūlullah himself endorsed it in calling to worship Allāh alone, the Allāh (G-d) of Abraham, Ishmael, Isaac, Jacob, and the tribes, then the conflict we are experiencing today is not as a result of the Sunna of Muhammad Rasūlullah. It is definitely as a result of the total failure of the followers of Muhammad Rasūlullah to lead their Ifrād al mujtami'i in accordance with the Torah.

There is no justification for calling one an Irish-America, African-American, or an 'Arab-American, hyphenated names as described by Riz Khan of Al-Jazeera and deplored by Helen Thomas. This is upheld by the Sunna, for when after the battle of al-Muṣṭaliq, the Sahābas fell into dispute, calling one another on the platform of their tribal and regional associations, the holy Apostle declared, "Stop that call! It is an abomination and a putrefying call!" If an orthodox Christian would prefer to willingly abide by the Sunna of the holy Apostle, although unaware of her actions, then for a follower of Muhammad Rasūlullah to prefer to live according to his tribal and regional affiliations is a crime that will never be forgiven by Allāh. The 'Arabs, especially the Egyptians, who know the most about Allāh and His Mercy, should consider this, and stop living in disregard of the Sunna of Allāh.

Allāh reminds us of the consequences of disobeying Muhammad Rasūlullah in the holy Qur'ān 63:"And let those who oppose the Messenger's commandment (i.e. Sunna-legal ways, orders, acts of worship, statements) (among the sects) beware, lest some Fitnah (disbelief, trials, afflictions, earthquakes, killing, overpowered by a tyrant) should befall them or a painful torment be inflicted on them."

Individuality is applicable in worship, only because one is not allowed to mix with the evil ones; to do so invoke disgrace and punishment from Allāh. We shall all be called into the graveyard individually, and we shall stand on the Day of Judgment as individuals. Allāh informed us in the holy Qur'ān

6:94, "And truly you have come unto us alone [without wealth, companions or anything else] as We created you the first time. You have left behind you all that which We had bestowed on you. We see not with you your intercessors whom you claimed to be partners with Allāh. Now all relations between you and them have been cut off, and all that you used to claim has vanished." Therefore, the activities of one's life in this world must be balanced against the benefits of one's life in the Hereafter.

One should pose and ask: Why is the Western Christian world interested in dealing with the followers of Muhammad Rasūlullah, especially in advising them on how to conduct their way of life? If the Western Christian world is interested in advising the Muslim world on how to conduct their way of life, it is most appropriate for them to oversee the establishment of the Caliphate. Is it not ridiculous and stupid that the West recommend to them that they do not know and the Muslim has rejected?

What is the precipitating factor in what is happening among the 'Arabs of North Africa and those of the 'Arabian Peninsula? Is it the absence of mosques, water to perform ablution, or the absence of the representative of Allāh and Muhammad Rasūlullah to lead the Muslim 'Arabs of North Africa and the 'Arabian peninsula in their five daily prayers, the weekly Friday, and the annual Īd prayers? The Torah is probably silent on this most important Pillar in Islām, although there is an allusion to it in 1 Kings 8:22: "Solomon stood facing the altar with everyone standing behind him. Then he lifted his arms toward heaven and prayed: "O Lord of Israel, no other god in heaven or earth is like you!" The inability of the followers of Muhammad to establish the Caliphate is the last nail of the coffin; however, they will never believe that, for they do not understand the holy Qur'ān.

The twenty-three years struggle of Muhammad Rasūlullah to establish peace and justice in the 'Arabian Peninsula is divided into two phases:

a. The thirteen years of his life in Makka. That was the initial period of revelation reminding the Quraysh, in the first instance, and the world in general of the Oneness of Allāh,.

b. The ten years of his life in Medina, divided under three parts:

The six years of his Apostleship as the leader of the people of Medina;

From 6 A.H to 8 A.H.--from the banishment of the Banu Qurayza of the Levi tribe of the Children of Israel to the revelation of the holy Qur'ān 9;

From 8 A.H. to his death.

The principal teaching of Islām is the establishment of the Caliphate, including association with the righteous, as explained earlier. Allāh emphasizes this in the holy Qur'ān 9:73; it is after the banning of the Banu Qurayza from Medina in 8 A.H. 'Abdul 'Ala Maudūdi's commentary is worth reflecting on:

The command enunciated the change of policy towards the hypocrites. Up to this time, leniency was being shown to them for two reasons. First, the Muslims had not as yet become as powerful as to take the risk of an internal conflict in addition to the one with the external enemies. The other reason was to give enough respite to these people who were involved in doubt and suspicions so that they could have sufficient time for attaining to faith and belief. But now the time has come for a change of policy. The whole of 'Arabia has been subdued and a bitter conflict with the external enemies was about to start; therefore it was required that these internal enemies should crushed down so that they should not be able to conspire with the external enemies to stir up any internal danger to the Muslims. And now it had become possible to crush them. As regards the second reason, these hypocrites had been given respite for a period of nine years to observe, to consider and test the Right Way, and they could have availed of it, if they had any good in them. So there was no reason why any more leniencies should be shown to them. Therefore, Allāh enjoined the Muslims to treat the hypocrites on one and the same level with the disbelievers and start Jihād against them, and to give up the policy of leniency they had adopted towards them and adopt a firm and stern policy instead.

. . . This verse enjoined that they were no more to be considered a part and parcel of the Muslim Community (Umma) nor were they to be allowed to neither take part in the management of its affairs nor consulted about any matter, so that they might not be able to spread the poison of hypocrisy. This changed policy required that the true Believers should expose all those who adopted a hypocritical attitude and conduct and showed in any way that they were not sincere allies to Allāh, His Messenger and the true Muslims. Each and every one of such hypocrites should be openly criticized and reproved so that there should remain for them no more place of honor and trust in the Muslim society: they should be socially boycotted and kept away from consulting the Community: their evidence in the courts of law should be regarded as untrustworthy: the doors of offices and positions of trust should be closed against them and they should be kept in contempt in the social meetings. In short, every Muslim should show by his behavior to such a one, that there was no place of honor or respect or trust for a hypocrite, in the Muslim society. Besides this, if any one of them was found to be guilty of treachery, there should be no connivance at his crime, nor should he pardoned, but openly tried in a court of law and should be duly punished.

This command was urgently needed at the time it came. It was obvious that in order to save the Muslim Community from fall and degradation, it was essential to purge it of all the internal dangers to this solidarity, because a Community, which nourishes hypocrites and traitors and allows the internal enemies to flourish with honor and security, shall inevitably be doomed to moral degradation and ultimate destruction. Hypocrisy is a plague and a hypocrite is the rat that carries and spreads its germs. Therefore to allow him the freedom of movement in the society is to expose the whole population to the danger of hypocrisy. Likewise, to give a place of honor and prestige to a hypocrite is to encourage many others in hypocrisy and treachery, for this shows that it is not sincerity, true faith and its welfare that count in it.[120]

Again, on Friday, the day of 'Arafat, Allāh, in concluding the Mission of Muhammad Rasūlullah, says in the holy Qur'ān 5:3, "Those who disbelieved have given up all hope of your religion; so fear them not, but fear Me. This day, I have perfected your religion for you, completed My favor upon you, and have chosen for you Islām as your ad-Dīn. But as for him who is forced by severe hunger, with no inclination to sin (such can eat these above mentioned meat), then surely, Allāh is Oft-Forgiving, Most merciful." Explaining this verse, al-Maudūdi writes:

The disbelievers have despaired of your ad-Dīn means, 'after a long systematic resistance and opposition, they have lost hope of defeating your ad-Dīn. Now they do not expect that you will ever return to the former way of ignorance, because your ad Din has become a permanent system of life and has been established on a firm footing.' Therefore, the clause "Do not fear them but

---

[120]   Maudūdi, S. Abul Ala. Vol. 4: 210-221

fear Me" means, there is no danger of interference from the disbelievers that they will prevent you from the performance of your ad-Dīn (religious obligations). You should fear Allāh and observe His commands and instructions because no ground for fear has been left for you. Now your disobedience of the Law will mean that you do not intend to obey Allāh.

"I have perfected your religion" means "I have provided it with all the essential elements of a permanent way of life which comprises a complete system of thought and practice and civilization, and have laid down principles and given detailed instructions for the solution of all human problems. Hence there is no need for you to seek guidance and instructions from any other source.

The completion of the "blessing" is the completion of the blessing of guidance.

"I have approved Islām as the way of life for you because you have practically proved by your obedience and devotion to it that you sincerely believe in Islām which you have accepted. As I have practically set you free from every kind of subjection and servitude there is no compulsion for you to submit to anyone else than Me in your practical life."

The followers of Muhammad Rasūlullah cannot deny that either they are totally ignorant of the basic fundamental teaching of the holy Apostle or that they believe in him and have the full knowledge of his call, but have rejected him. They are therefore either disbelievers or hypocrites. As to others who have been forced to be ignorant of the teaching of Muhammad Rasūlullah I hope I have aroused their interest in studying his mission, so that they will submit wholeheartedly and assist in establishing the Caliphate. Is this not the teaching in the Old Testament and the Talmud as well?

While awaiting their decision, the Western Christian world must immediately cease helping the current Muslim rulers and their scholars. There is no place for peace, stability, and progress today, if the Western Christian world continues befriending the current Muslim leaders and rulers; for according to Allāh, these

Muslims will never believe in Him. They are deaf, dumb, blind, and already in the grave, although apparently alive.

The Western Christian world, on the other hand, should satisfy themselves as to the sincerity of those Muslims well versed in the teaching of the peaceful and progressive mission of Muhammad Rasūlullah and help them establish the Caliphate. This is most urgent if the People of the Book are to listen and reflect on the Sunna of the holy Apostle. Muhammad Rasūlullah was not sent to deprive them of the full enjoyment of the bounties of Allāh, but to ensure that they receive them before they die. They will be given houses with silver roofs and elevators, doors and thrones of silver, adornments of gold, and the most beautiful, luxuriant gardens. These rewards are tied to the following demands:

Fighting oppression and injustice. This is an act common to all.

Education. Everyone must be educated to look after himself and to defend the province.

Training. Their children should be trained in such a manner that they love each other and are ready to help all those living with them.

To help their neighbors and those passing through their provinces.

To help all those in need.

To keep their promises and honor all agreements between the various tribes in their locality. [121]

In addition, there is forgiveness awaiting them. This is the history of the world from the time of Prophet Abraham.[122] Since the wealthy Helpers of Medina used their wealth in supporting Muhammad Rasūlullah, Allāh could not have disliked the wealth of disbelievers and hypocrites in supporting His Cause. Some of

---

[121] Shankīṭi, Jakni. Adhwā al bayān fī īdhā hal Qur'ān bil Qur'ān (Beirut: Dārul Ihya' Al-Tourath, 1996),46:20.

[122] This is the general overview of the teaching of the holy Qur'an- the common good and law.}

the Levi tribe of the Children of Israel in Medina helped the holy Apostle with armor. The neighboring polytheists entered into a compact, informing him of the movement of those waging war on Medina. The Levi tribe of the Children of Israel in Medina were the most aware of the benevolence of the holy Apostle. The 'Arab Christians of Najran, during their deputation, agreed that they would go back to Najran and consider his affair, and that he should give them one of his men to be with them in settling disputes among them.[123]

The amount of aid the Western world gives to the Muslim tyrants, and unjust rulers should be tailored and geared to giving the Muslim Umma appropriate, practical education. My books are addressing this issue. Today that aid has proved to be nothing but a "weapon of mass destruction." There is no need to take cover under the threat of terrorism again, although such acts are deliberate and have to be accounted for.

Some years back, the then USA Secretary of State, Madeleine Albright, complained bitterly about the poor curriculum of the Saudi schools. She was not referring of course to Western education. There has never been a Muslim ruler who looked at the curriculum of Islāmic knowledge (to secularize it). The curriculum of Islāmic education has never covered the actual teaching of Muhammad Rasūlullah. The whole system lacks reflection and practical training. That is why no one listens to a practical minded believer who points to actions not conforming to the Sunna. Therefore, the Muslim scholars cannot be from among the scholars of the current Muslim leaders, for without the support of these scholars, the tyrant and unjust Muslim rulers could not have perpetrated their tyranny and injustice and survived on monarchical rule. It is explained in the holy Qur'ān 53:38-41:"And man can have nothing but what he does (good or bad). And that his deeds will be seen. Then he will be recompensed with a full and best recompense."

---

[123] Guillaume A. P.276-277

Throughout the current uprising, none of such Muslim scholars has come out openly to explain to the youth, who know nothing about the Caliphate, that it is its absence that is responsible for their impoverishment. This is the truth, for the relationship between the Caliphate and peace, harmony, and legitimacy, explained by Muhammad Rasūlullah, was correspondingly explained in the Torah. In fact, that thread is the principal teaching and warning in the Torah.

The highest injustice in the Muslim Umma is depriving Allāh of his Right. The Western world should understand that their interference or aid to the Muslim nations will never bring peace, without solving the internal problem of the Muslim Umma: the cause of this chaos and hardships can only be solved by the practical application, of the Sunna of the holy Apostle. Muhammad Rasūlullah hesitated to accept the Apostleship, because he subconsciously knew that he was an unlettered 'Arab.

Probably, in his sincere, pure, shining, and untainted heart, Muhammad ibn 'Abdallāh had heard about the Test (the command to do circumcision to Abraham). Abraham had to pass this test before he was appointed a leader to the nation. He might have asked Allāh, "How can I get that appointment, without You testing me?"

Then Muhammad's Test began, "Read!" Displaying his sincerity, submissiveness, and honesty, he replied, "I am not the one who reads!" Gabriel again repeated the command. He again replied as before. Now, Gabriel had to punish him. He pressed his chest, the way I was taught to do on an unconscious patient for an arousal response. The pain was unbearable, but Muhammad read. This is the only way out, if we are at all interested in having peace in the world. The Western Christian civilized world must infuse into the comatose followers of Muhammad Rasūlullah the teaching of his Sunna and not the literal holy Qur'ān.

The teaching of the holy Qur'ān, for example, 22:5, has so far proved ineffective and lethal. Let us ask the followers of

Muhammad what they are doing about the teaching of the Sunna of the holy Apostle. Let them answer the following questions:

Why is it that during the hajj festival, no ruler has ever lead prayers in the two holy mosques?

Why is it that they do not observe the shortening prayer during the pilgrimage?

Why can't the Jews be given Palestine, according to their Islam?

Allāh commands Muhammad Rasūlullah to mention this internal strife affecting his followers, in the holy Qur'ān 7:65: "Say, 'He has power to send torment on you from above you or from under your feet, or to cover you with confusion in party strife, and make you taste the violence of one another.'"[124] Then Allāh said, "See how variously We explain the Ayāt (proofs, evidences, lessons, signs) so that they may understand. But your people (Muhammad Rasūlullah) have denied it (the Qur'ān) though it is the truth." Allāh comforted him and commanded the holy Apostle to tell his followers, "I am not a Wakil (guardian) over you."

If, Muhammad was forbidden to be the guardian of the then Umma, who is to be their guardian today? The Western Christian world has so far failed because they have not taken heed of this advice addressed to them. In the same way as there is only One Allāh (G-d) and one Torah, whose Messenger was Prophet Moses, whom the Children of Israel always refer to, likewise, there is only one holy Qur'ān, one Muhammad Rasūlullah, and by implication one Torah. Explaining his role to those who chose voluntarily to follow him, Muhammad drew three parallel lines. He pointed to the center one and said, "This is my way!"[125] He then pointed to the ones on each side, "These are not my way!" He told the Sahābas, "I have asked my Lord three things and He agreed on only two:

---

124 See Judges 20, for a similar Promise to the Children of Israel.
125 Baghdādi, Imām Abī Farj 'Abdulrahman ibn Jawzi Qurshiyy. Mukhtasar Kitāb Talbis Iblis. Beirut. Mu'assa Risala. 1992. 25

Not to drown my Umma. He agreed.

Not to destroy my Umma with famine. He agreed.

Not to fight one another. He disagreed."[126]

The manufacturing of armament and other lethal arsenals by the West is by the permission of Allāh, for the followers of the holy Apostle will fight and torment one another. It is not that this contradicts the command of Allāh to the Children of Israel, in 1 Kings 24, "Don't go to war against the people of Israel--they are your relatives. Go home! I am the LORD, and I made these things to happen." Rehoboam (the son of Prophet Solomon) and his army obeyed the LORD and went home.

The Western Christian world cannot be ignorant of the injustice and faithlessness of the Muslim rulers and leaders. Assassinations and illegal imprisonment has been their amusement. For example, a revelation from the archives of the Ministry of Archives showed that in 1980, Moammar Gaddafi tried to pressure the West German government to extradite Libyan dissidents or allow them to be killed on German soil, according to German Foreign Ministry documents that have recently come to light. Chancellor Helmut Schmidt refused the demand. This is not limited to Germany, but was the practice in many Western world powers. Yet, they sell these Muslim tyrants arms and ammunitions to fight and kill their own people and to engage in war with other Muslim nations.

How can the followers of Muhammad engage themselves in treachery and butchering one another when Allāh in the holy Qur'ān, 49:10 commanded, "The believers are nothing

---

[126] Shātibi, Allāma Muhaqqa Abī Ishāq Ibrāhim bin Mūsa bin Muhammad Lahmi. Al-'Itasām. Manama. Maktabat Tawhīd. Vol. 3. 299. In this hadith, the holy Apostle said, "I asked my Lord four things and he agreed only on one: My followers will never unite under falsehood." Also Baghdādi, Imām Abī Fajr 'Abdurrahman bin Jawziyy Qurshiyy. Mukhtasar Kitāb Talbisu Iblīs. Beirut. Mu'isassat-al-Risāla. 1992, 25.

else other than brothers. So make reconciliation between your brothers, and fear Allāh, that you may receive mercy." The holy Apostle explained further, "A Muslim is one in whose hands one is safe." In case of conflict against one another, they are to follow the injunction in the holy Qur'ān 49:11, "And if two parties or groups among the believers fall to fighting, then make peace between them both. But if one of them outrages against the other, then fight you (all) against the one that outrages till it complies with the Command of Allāh. Then if it complies, then make reconciliation between them justly, and be equitable. Verily! Allāh loves those who are equitable."

The problem of the Muslim Umma today began around 34 A.H. with the gruesome and cowardly murder of 'Uthman ibn Affān by irate, ignorant, and arrogant Muslim youths. Today, it is not only the Muslim youths who are ignorant and arrogant, but also the whole spectrum and breadth of the Muslim Umma. As a result of the paucity of practically oriented Islāmic scholars, the office of the Caliphate, the Trust from Allāh, fell into dispute. This led to fighting among the believers and the appointment to responsible positions of incompetent, ignorant people.

We must understand the spread of the Sunna of the holy Apostle, which within a period of thirty years covered an area of 3.5 million square miles. How many teachers would be needed to teach the Sunna, in their usual class of ten students per teacher? That was indeed the principal cause of the corruption and backwardness of the Muslim Umma after 40 A.H. Unless, ignorance of the principal teaching of the Sunna of Muhammad is tackled squarely and appropriately, there will never be peace and progress in the world.

I am not arguing that there are no competent Islāmic scholars in 'Arab countries. I have their current contributions to Islāmic jurisprudence, and I have no objection to the contents. However, what I dislike and will never agree with, for example, is for Dr. Yusuf Qardawi to fly to Cairo from Qatar and perform the

Friday congregation as the Imām. This is, by the consensus of Muslim jurists, objectionable. Allāh has determined the fate of that one, for if one knows the Sunna and refuses to follow it, he is categorized as a disbeliever! It is the heart of innovation.[127]

This is not a premise, but the reality that no one can deny today! I must stress that it is not that the Islāmic scholars in the 'Arab world, are not well versed in Islāmic jurisprudence, or that they are not available, but rather their main problem is their lack of practical skill, reflection, and motivation. With the current trend in world globalization and information technology, all that we want is the likes of Hilkiah, supported by King Josiah; 'Abūbakar ibn Hazam supported by Caliph 'Umar ibn 'Abdul Aziz; and vice versa.

The use of force has so far failed to bring peace, understanding, and love. There is no place for half-measures, compromises, partisanship, and inciting one group against the other. The world belongs to Allāh, who does not discriminate between his servants. The articles in the Pillar of faith are common to all. These articles are also the First Pillar of Islām. The Sunna explaining the Pillars of Islam is specific to his followers. This difference can never be the cause of the turmoil and confusion we are experiencing. It is the doing away with the basic teaching of the Torah, which is also in the holy Qur'ān, that is the main cause of our problem. According to the Talmud, there must be a leader in direct communion with the Lord to lead his community. An 'Arab poet of the pre-Islāmic period, Afwaha Awdī, said:

لا يصلح الناس فوضى لا سراة لهم ولاسراة لهم إذا جها لهم سادوا 128

---

[127] Shāṭibi. Vol.1. 58-368

[128] Yūsuf, Dr. Mūsa. Nizām Hukm fil Islām. Beirut. 'Asr hadīth. 1988. 25-26

Explanation: People cannot live in peace and prosperity without a leader. They have no leader by the time the arrogant and illiterate are given responsible positions of leadership.

The present generation of the Levi tribe of the Children of Israel must be active, for their ancestors were the only ones among their twelve tribes that knew Muhammad. They should lead in understanding Islām and supporting Muhammad Rasūlullah. They must dispel the notion that they are the ones standing across the mercantile throat of the followers of Muhammad, obstructing them from appointing honest, educated, peace loving persons to the responsible position of the Caliphate.

The distinction between Islām and a Muslim must be made the subject of understanding to all, for Islām is that which is from Allāh alone. A Muslim, who is a follower of Muhammad Rasūlullah, has been prevented from dealing unjustly with any of the creatures of Allāh. In the holy Qur'ān 60:9-10, Allāh makes this clear, "Allāh does not forbid you to deal justly and kindly with those who fought not against you on account of religion nor drive you out of your homes. Verily, Allāh loves those who deal with equity. It is only as regards those who fought against you on account of religion, and have driven you out of your homes, and helped to drive you out, that Allāh forbids you to befriend. And whosoever will befriend them, such are the Zālimūn (wrong-doers, those who disobey Allāh)."

The followers of Muhammad Rasūlullah should stop deceiving themselves that they are his followers. Yes, they are his followers from birth to the age of maturity. But from that moment to their death they are disbelievers and hypocrites. The true believers of Muhammad Rasūlullah are described in the following chapters of the holy Qur'ān:

The holy Qur'ān 24:62:"The true believers are only those, who believe in (the Oneness of) Allāh and His Messenger Muhammad; and when they are with him on some common matter, they go not away until they have asked his permission.[129] Verily those who ask your permission, those are they who (really) believe in Allāh and His Messenger. So if they ask you permission for some affairs of theirs, give permission to whom, you will of them, and ask Allāh for their forgiveness. Truly, Allāh is Oft-Forgiving, Most Merciful."

There are so many examples, but suffice it to mention the incident after the Hudaybiya treaty. The holy Apostle shaved his head and ordered the Sahābas to do the same. Some of them chose to cut their hair. He looked at them and said, "May Allāh have mercy on those who shaved their head (hair)." The Sahābas exclaimed, "What of us who have cut our hair?" The holy Apostle repeated again his prayer. On the third occasion he said, "May Allāh have mercy on those who have cut their hair!" They asked him why he did not include them initially. He replied, "Because you did not follow my command."

The holy Qur'ān 4:65, "But no, buy your Lord, they can have no faith, until they make you (Muhammad) judge in all disputes between them, and find in themselves no resistance against your decisions, and accept (them) with full submission." The Levi tribe of the Children of Israel in Medina never went against this verse.

The Western Christian world should submit to the Plan and Will of Allāh. They have never created the wing of a fly, which if it snatches something from them, they cannot chase it and get it back. They have never regulated and managed any affair without the approval of Allāh. What will last forever is His. Let them learn the lessons from what happened to the Quraysh, in the holy Qur'ān 13:41, "See they not that We gradually reduce the land (of the disbelieving Quraysh; that is their influence) from its outlying borders. And Allāh judges, there is no one to put back His judgment and He is Swift at reckoning."

---

[129] This verse has proved the folly and insincerity of the followers of Muhammad in rejecting secularism. Muhammad is not with them and therefore they do not have to follow him!

The Caliphate must be established in the interest of those not following the Sunna of Muhammad Rasūlullah, but who have faith in Allāh, for Allāh says in the holy Qur'ān 22:40, "For had it not been that Allāh checks one set of people by means of another, monasteries, churches, synagogues, and mosques would surely have been pulled down. Verily, Allāh will help those who help His (Cause). Truly, Allāh is All-Strong, All-Mighty." That "Allāh will help those who help His Cause" does not refer to forcing the followers of Muhammad to perform the rituals according to the Sunna of the holy Apostle, but to establishing the Caliphate. The Caliphate is the practical aspect of the article of faith.

The followers of Muhammad have no interest in establishing the Caliphate; and even if they have interest, they cannot achieve that because of their sins. One can only succeed after Allāh forgives one. It is not possible Allāh will forgive the followers of Muhammad, because they have committed the major sins that can only be forgiven after the crime is punished in one's lifetime. Therefore, for world to be peaceful there must be a change in the body guards. The People of the Book, who have faith in Allāh, must therefore, take interest in knowing the Sunna of Muhammad where the caliphate is described, and seeing that it is instituted in the Muslim countries. Yes, Allāh is able to enforce His Will, but He says in the holy Qur'ān 65:3, "Indeed Allāh has set a measure to all things." If, the Western Christian world cannot do anything in seeing that the Caliphate is instituted, my advice is this Remembrance, in the holy Qur'ān 44:89, "So turn away from them (O Muhammad), and say: Salaam (peace). But they will come to know."

Dealing with the unjust, corrupt, and ignorant rulers, but later to fight them, having fully armed them to the teeth, is a folly. The BBC World Debate on March 26, 2011, with Kate Ashton, E.U. High Representative for Foreign Policy; Senator Jeanne Sheheen, U.S. Congresswoman; and Nabīl Fahmy, a Diplomat and Former Ambassador to the U.N., had only one positive result—the importance of educating the Middle East.

As cited earlier, Beitler and Jebbin their *Egypt as a Failing State*, agree with this recommendation. And Nabīl Fahmy says, "The United States currently participates in exchanges between chief justices of other countries. Definitely, such an exchange with Egypt would enhance the rule of law providing a stabilizing influence on democratization. Other fruitful exchanges would include ones in journalism, parliamentarian, military, business, and technology. Religious elites must also establish a dialogue as part of a reformation of Islam "It is time for the 'Arab-Muslims to break the heavy shackles of the past and to try to come to terms with the West."

According to Graham Fuller moderate religious and social leaders of the Muslim world must find the courage to critique Islam and call for changes.[130] "When highly traditional or fanatic groups attempt to define Islam in terms of a social order from a distant past, voices should be raised to deny them that monopoly." I hope this book is a step in achieving that objective.

There is no curriculum for this type of education, besides the teaching of the Sunna of Muhammad Rasūlullah, starting with the Torah. I am grateful to Allāh for finding one sharing my views in a World Debate. The Western Christian world has to remove their antipathy to the 'Arabic language and learn it to help in educating the Muslim Umma. At present the followers of Muhammad Rasūlullah, if left alone, will never be in a position to bring peace to the world, because they do not trust one another and do not know the Sunna. *Without doubt, the largest congregation of the followers of Muhammad assembles during the Pilgrimage—between two and three million faithful. They do not, however, observe the journey*

---

[130] Ruth M. Beitler and Cindy R. Jebb Egypt as a Failing State: Implications for US National Security. INSS Occasional Paper 51. July 2003. Criticizing Islam has failed during its inception. All those who witnessed the revelation accepted Muhammad.

prayer. Moreover, standing on 'Arafat Day is not observed on the eighth of Zul-hajj. What evidence do you need to prove that they are illiterate?

The son of the Grand Mufti of Syria was killed. According to my understanding of the Sunna of Muhammad Rasūlullah, he was like Joseph, the one who if given authority would make his country prosper. But this was what BBC carried on his support of a tyrant: In a tearful sermon carried live on TV, Grand Mufti Ahmad Hassoun expressed support for President Bashar al-Assad, praying the killers would repent. Appointed to his post by the government, the Grand mufti is the country's top Sunni Muslim cleric.[131] According to the Sunna of Muhammad Rasūlullah, the Grand Mufti is the one supposed to be the President or any highest political leader (Caliph) to lead his people. But the Grand Mufti and virtually all the Sheikhs in the Muslim world parading as the authority of the Sunna have rejected this recommendation and command of Allāh and His apostle that: The most honored in the sight of Allāh is the most Allāh fearing.[132] The fear of Allāh is indelibly tied to one's level of education of the Sharī'a. In the manner the Levi tribes were given the role to read the Torah, the most educated in the Sunna of the holy Apostle is to be the leader of the community.[133]

I must conclude by drawing your attention, my dear reader, to the following historical incidents:

'Ātika ibn 'Abdul Muṭallab had a dream that frightened her, for it appeared that a misfortune would afflict her people. She told al-'Abbas that she saw a rider coming upon a camel who halted in the valley. Then he cried at the

---

[131] http://www.bbc.co.uk/news/world-middle-east-15152676.

[132] The holy Qur'ān 49:13

[133] My dear reader! Kindly reflect my argument with Matthew 26: 62-65; Mark 14:63

top of his voice, "Come forth, O people, do not leave your men to face disaster that will come in three days time." I saw the people flock to him, and then he went into the mosque with the people following him. While they were round him, his camel mounted to the top of the Ka'ba. Then he called out again, using the same words. Then his camel mounted to the top of Abū Qubays (a mountain hard by), and he cried out again. Then he seized a rock and loosened it, and it began to fall, until at the bottom of the mountain it split into pieces. There was not a house or a dwelling in Mecca but received a bit of it. Al-'Abbas said, "By God this is indeed a vision, and you had better keep quiet about it and not tell anyone." However, the news soon got circulated. The next day al-'Abbas went to the holy Mosque to go round it, when Abū Jahl called on him. After going round the mosque, he went to Abū Jahl who now confronted him saying, "O Banu 'Abdul Muṭallib, since when have you had a prophetesses among you?" "And what do you mean by that?" I said. "That vision which "Ātika saw," he answered. I said, "What did she see?" He said, "Are you not satisfied that your men should play the prophet that your women should do so also? 'Ātika has alleged that in her vision someone said, 'Come forth to war in three days.' We shall keep an eye on you these three days, and if what she says is true, then it will be so; but if the three days pass and nothing happens, we will write you down as the greatest liars of the temple people among 'Arabs."[134]

The significance of this incident is that the dream of 'Ātika, a polytheist, turned out to be true. Only the Quraysh were to suffer the affliction and no one else. Abū Jahl, determined for

---

[134] Guillaume A. The Life History of Muhammad. Oxford: Oxford University Press, 1987. 290-291

the affliction to befall them, said, "No, by God, we will not turn back until God decide between us and Muhammad."

Another time, when the holy Apostle was arranging the ranks of the Sahābas, he accidentally pricked the belly of Sawād b. Ghaziya with an arrow, saying "O Stand on line, O Sawād!" he said to one of the helpers who was too far forward. "O Messenger of God, thou has hurt me," said Sawād, "and God hath sent thee truth and justice, so give me my requital." "Take it," said the Prophet, laying bare his own belly and handing him the arrow whereupon Sawād stooped and imprinted a kiss where it was his due to place the point of the shaft."[135]

I hope, my dear reader, you have made up your mind on what to do regarding my thesis that Muslim disunity and disbelief, precipitating anarchy, are caused by their rulers and their preachers.[136] The majority of the Muslim Umma are illiterate, thereby allowing themselves to be ruled without heed to the Sunna. The holy apostle said, "Insecurity, disquiet and all sorts of abominations in my Umma are caused by their illiterate, ignorant rulers and preachers."[137] Definitely, if you will learn 'Arabic and read about the caliphate, the followers of Muhammad are polytheists.

According to the Sunna of Allāh and that of the holy apostle, the Western Christian world, have no grounds for helping the warring Muslim factions. This type of conflict began in 40 A.H. and will continue for as long as the sun rises from the east and sets in the west, unless the Caliphate is established. The only solution is for the Western world to support the establishment of the Caliphate.

---

[135]　Lings, Martin. Muhammad his life based on the earliest sources. London, George Allen &Unwin LTD. 1983. 146

[136]　. Ghazāli. Imām Abī Hamid Muhammad ibn Muhammad. Ihyā' 'Ulūmuddin. Beirut, Dārul Fikr.1989. Vol.1:16-17

[137]　Zuhri, Muhammad ibn Sa'd bin Muni'. Kitab Tabaqat Kabir. Vol.3.478

It is not possible to educate the Muslim world without the West actively participating to reverse the system of education they copied blindly from them. The Sunna of the holy Apostle must be taught in all Western schools (European countries), so that they can protect themselves from its false interpretation and distortions by the Muslims. The Sunna of Muhammad is nothing other than the simplified version of the Written and Oral Law.

Selling arms to the Muslim world should hereafter be stopped. It is indeed an irony that the Muslim Umma interprets the holy Qur'ān 8:60 wrongly and are ready to use all of their power to kill and threaten one another. Is this not more evidence of the folly of the Muslim Umma?

The Western world's indirect tactics in spilling the blood of innocents will always revert to them, in such forms as economic depression, plague, hurricane and earthquakes. Even if no plague affects them, they will never have peace in their minds. Supporting the Caliphate is not synonymous with believing in the articles of Islām. The Caliphate is enshrined in the article of faith, a belief common to mankind. If the Western Christian world take their hands-off the affairs of the followers of Muhammad Rasūlullah, no harm will ever come to them. They will live and become prosperous. As of this writing, no Muslim scholar in any Muslim country, irrespective of his sect, has called for the establishment of the Caliphate. Are these Muslim scholars unaware of this saying in their mother tongue, that:

وقد ثبت فى الأصول ان العالم فى الناس قا ئم مقام النبى عليه الصلا ة والسلا م، والعلماء ورثة الأنبياء، فكمـاان النبى يدل على الأحكام بقوله وفعله وإقرار،، كذاللك وارثه يدل على الأحكام بقوله وفعله وإقراره 138

Explanation. It has been unanimously agreed by the Muslim Umma that an educated one among them acts as a representative of Muhammad Rasūlullah. Muslim scholars are the heirs of Muhammad Rasūlullah. In the same manner, Prophet Muhammad

---

138 Shātibi, Allāma Muhaqq Abī Ishāq Ibrāhim bin Mūsa bin Muhammad Lahmi. Al-'Itisām. Manama. Maktabat Tawhīd. 1997. Vol.2,466

is the judge based on his statements, his deeds, or his keeping silent on an issue, as is his representative, the Caliph. He is to judge by following the examples of Prophet Muhammad. The point to note here is the emphasis "educated" and "Muslim scholars" for the qualification of Prophet hood. The holy Apostle explained the meaning saying, "If there were to be a Prophet after him that is 'Umar ibn Khaṭṭāb." A Prophet is one sent by Allāh to explain the Sharī'a. He has no Sharī'a of his own. Therefore, all of us, my dear reader, are Prophets! We are bound like them to spread the Message intact. We have the same source of knowledge.

If that is the case, then you should remember the story of the old prophet from Bethel.[139] But the followers of Muhammad Rasūlullah, although I very much doubt he taught and allowed them to listen to one another, rather than to him, have forgotten that example. Muhammad Rasūlullah is no longer an authority! Unless they are forced to explain why Muhammad is no longer an authority, there will be no peace in the world.

In the Old Testament Allāh promises Prophet Abraham that He will give his descendants the land east of the Shihor River on the border of Egypt as far as the Euphrates River. They will possess the land of the Kenites, the Kenizzites, the Kadmonites, the Hittites, the Perizzites, the Rephaites, the Amorites, the Canaanites, the Girgashites, and the Jebusites.[140] When his wife, Sarah, died in what is today Hebron, he approached the Hittites and said in Genesis 23:3, "I live as a foreigner in your land, and I don't own any property where I can bury my wife. Please let me buy a piece of land." The Hittites offered him free land, but Prophet Abraham insisted that he must buy the land. After a long argument, they agreed to sell him a piece of land for four hundred pieces of silver.[141]

---

[139] 1 Kings 13:11-34.

[140] Genesis 15:18-20.

[141] Genesis 23. We should take note of this, for the holy Apostle also bought the land upon which he built his mosque for an undisclosed

When Prophet Jacob died, his body was brought from Egypt and buried in the cave of Machpelah, the burial place Prophet Abraham bought from Ephron the Hittite. It was during the time of Prophet Moses that the Children of Israel were commanded to go and take the land of the Amorites, the non-Israelites. On their way to accomplish the promise of Allāh, they had to fight the king Sihon of Hishbon, who refused them safe passage through his country. He was killed, and the entire country was reduced excluding their livestock and everything else of value.

Other towns taken by Moses from the Arnon River to the boundary of Gilead included Aror on the edge of the gorge and the town in the middle of the gorge. King Og of Bashan, who came out to attack them, was also defeated. They then proceeded until they reached Mount Hor on the border of Edom where Prophet Aaron died. When finally they camped in the lowlands of Moab, Allāh commanded Prophet Moses (AS), "When you cross the Jordan River and enter Canaan, you must force out the people living there. Destroy their idols and tear their altars. Then settle in the land – I have given to you as your own. I will show you how to divide the land among the tribes, according to the number of clans in each one, so that the larger tribes have more land than the smaller ones. If you don't force out all the people there, they will be like pointed sticks in your eyes and thorns in your back. They will always be trouble for you, and I will treat you as cruelly as I planned on treating them."[142]

Matthew Henry's commentary is worth considering, for this was the ultimate claim of Muhammad Rasūlullah when he finally conquered Makka. Rev. Henry says:

---

sum of dirham. The place had been used for drying dates, for enclosing a graveyard, and for growing palm trees.

[142] Num. 33:50-56.

While the Children of Israel were in the wilderness, their total separation from all other people kept them out of the way of temptation to idolatry, and perhaps this was one thing intended by their own long confinement in the wilderness, that thereby the idols of Egypt might be forgotten, and the people aired (as it were) and purified from that infection, and the generation that entered Canaan might be such as never knew those depths of Shaiṭan. But now that they were to pass into Jordan, they were entering again into that temptation, and therefore:

"They are here charged strictly to destroy all remnants of idolatry.

They must not only drive the inhabitants of the land that they may possess their country, but they must deface all their idolatrous pictures and images, and pull down all their high places.

They must not preserve any of them, nor as ornaments of their house, nor toys for their children to play with, but they must destroy all, both in token of their abhorrence and detestation of idolatry, and to prevent their being tempted to worship those images, and the false gods represented by them, or to worship the God of Israel by such images or representations.

They were assured that if they did so, God would by degrees put them in full possession of the land of promise.

If they would keep themselves pure from the idols of Canaan, God would enrich them with the wealth of Canaan.

Learn not their way and fear not their power."[143]

They were threatened that if they spared either the idols or the idolaters, they should be beaten with their own rods and their sin would certainly be their punishment. They would foster snakes in their bosoms. The remnant of the Canaanites, if they make any league with them, though it were but a cessation of arms, would be *pricks in their eyes and thorns in their sides,*

---

[143] Henry's Commentary. 234

that is, they would be upon all vexations to them, insulting them, robbing them, and to the utmost of their power, making mischief among them. We must expect trouble and affliction from that, whatever it is, in which we sinfully indulge; that which we are willing should tempt us we shall find will vex. . . . It was intended that Canaanites should be dispossessed; but if the Israelites fell in with them and learned their way, they should be dispossessed; for God's displeasure will justly be greater against them than against the Canaanites themselves. Let us hear this, and fear. "If we do not drive sin out, sin will drive us out; if we be not the death of our lusts, our lusts will be the death of our souls."

Repeating the same warning, Allāh says in the holy Qur'ān 8:73, "And those who disbelieve are allies of one another, (and) if you do not do so, there will be *Fitnah* (wars, battles) and oppression on the earth and a great mischief and corruption."

The Children of Israeli's request to Samuel in 1 Sam.8:5 proved that if a community is oppressed they must rise against the oppressor. They need a leader to achieve that, one who must be honest and one who does not accept bribes or make unfair decisions. They also agreed to the choice of Samuel under Divine guidance in 1 Sam.9:2, "that he must be better looking and more than a head taller than anyone else in all Israel." But, as usual, in a community, one finds a minority or a majority who do not understand the Law or Sharī'a. They complained to Prophet Samuel (1 Sam. 10:27), "How can someone like Saul rescue us from our enemies?" They believed that a leader to rescue them from their enemies must be one in need of gifts. It did not prove to be so, meaning that according to the established Sunna of Allāh, leadership must be governed by one's level of education and one's physique as explained in the holy Qur'ān 2:247.

The holy Qur'ān has clearly drawn the distinction between leadership under oppressors and leadership under idolaters. Islām never allows oppression, because it is an act done with one's consent, affecting the life of the community and not an individual. A leader worshipping idols may not necessarily be a tyrant and an oppressor. For thirteen years, Muhammad Rasūlullah lived with idolaters ruling under loose confederation. Oppression in Makka under the leadership of Abū Jahl and Abū Sufyan ibn Harb was not on a large scale. For example, Abū Jahl refused to pay an 'Arab "*boudeon*" his goods. The 'Arab Bedouin immediately came to the holy Apostle and complained to him. He took the Bedouin to Abū Jahl and demanded there and then that he be paid. Abū Jahl obeyed.

Permission was given to wage war, that is, a struggle or "revolution" by a "group of people" against an unjust and cruel authority; it was ordained for about seventeen months after the hijrah. The permission was not spontaneous and independent of the wishes, feelings, legitimacy, and rights of the believers.[144] Their minds had already been prepared and strengthened by the Love of the Allāh of Abraham, Ishmael, Isaac, and Jacob. The question is: Why did Allāh wait until after the hijrah to give permission to wage war on the unjust oppressors? The permission began with an assurance from Allāh as told in the holy Qur'ān 22:38, "Truly, Allāh defends those who believe. Verily, Allāh likes not any treacherous ingrate to Allāh."

This verse is indeed an explanation and a proof of the continuity of Islām and that it is not possible to separate the holy Qur'ān, from the Torah. Assurance of this was given by Allāh to Prophet Abraham and his descendants *and in particular to the descendants of Prophet Jacob*. There is no amount of secularization that will separate the faith and wish of the Children of Israel in warding off evil and doing away with idols from the faith and wish of the followers of Muhammad Rasūlullah in doing the same.

The permission in the holy Qur'ān 22:39 is so clear that the only thing one can do is accuse the believers of cowardice and embezzlement of their wealth, life, and property. Allāh says,

---

[144] The holy Qur'ān 17:39

"Permission to fight (against disbelievers) is given to those (believers) who are fought against, because they have been wronged; and surely, Allāh is Able to give them victory." Allāh then explained His reason for defending them in the holy Qur'ān 22:40, "Those who have been expelled from their homes unjustly, only because they said: Our Lord is Allāh." That was exactly what happened to Muhammad Rasūlullah and his followers. Likewise, Prophet Moses was sent to free the Children of Israel in Egypt from the clutches of the pharaoh, so that they might serve Allāh as their Lord.

According to the Sunna of the holy Apostle, struggle by an Umma, or a group of people aiming to remove oppression, is not intended to dethrone a constituted "unjust" authority. The target of "revolution" in the Sunna of Muhammad Rasūlullah is "the evil" and not the person. Therefore, the first step is to prevent the evil. It is only a man of knowledge and faith who can do that. This distinction must be understood and then put into practice. The holy Apostle said, "Allāh will help a just ruler who believed in the holy Bible and all that Allāh revealed before Muhammad Rasūlullah, but will never help an unjust and treacherous ruler who believed in him."

The following conditions were stipulated by Muhammad Rasūlullah:

The "revolution" should be undertaken in the name of Allāh.

The "revolution" should be undertaken for the establishment of justice.

The disbelievers are to be fought. Disbelief here does not apply to those who believe in Allāh according to their scriptures. Muhammad Rasūlullah respected and observed "compacts" between the various tribes of Arabia before the conquest of Makka, who were yet to follow him. The holy Apostle said, "The one who recites the holy Qur'ān, but did not follow its injunctions did not believe in it."

The military expedition should be undertaken with the sole aim of defeating the tyrants.

Treachery is not allowed.

Butchering and mutilating the body are not allowed.

Only those taking arms should be fought in the battlefield.

Children, females, and the aged should not be touched.

The fleeing and the slaves should be treated with kindness.

Worshipping places should not be destroyed.

Trees, crops, and plantations should be left standing.

Cultivated land should not be pillaged.

Animals should not be killed.

Compacts must be observed.

Do not transgress in the matter of booty.

Retreating is not allowed unless as demanded by strategy.

The question is: How can you, who have believed in Allāh, do away with ignorance, the root of all evil? There is no way out but through education. Have I given you enough evidence that our suffering is due to ignorant preachers and rulers? This is the warning of Muhammad Rasūlullah: "If the two of them from my Umma fear Allāh and live according to my Sunna, the world will live in peace, prosperity. If they transgress the limits of the Sharī'a, the world will fall into commotion. They are the rulers and the preachers." That was also the saying of Jesus, the son of Maryam. When Hilkiah, the chief priest, found out the Torah and handed it over to Joshia and the Law was observed, the Jews enjoyed peace. Allāh will treat the preachers and rulers of the Muslim Umma in the same way He treated the first-born of the Children of Israel who worshipped the golden calf. They were never allowed to read the Torah. Their duty was given to the Levi tribe.

The rulers and the preachers in the Muslim Umma are described by Allāh in the holy Qur'ān 63:4: "When thou lookest at them, their exteriors please thee; and when they speak, thou listenest to their words. They are as (worthless as hollow) pieces of timber propped up (unable to stand on their own). . . . So beware of them." The Western Christian world must immediately stop recognizing the followers of Muhammad as believers, for

208

they are not. They must always see them in the way they are described in the holy Qur'an:

One to whom the signs of Allāh reached but who threw them away is described in the holy Qur'ān 7:176 as a dog.

Those who have hearts but do not understand, eyes but they do not see, ears but they do not hear is the description in the holy Qur'ān 7:179 of cattle.

One who has been given the Sharī'a, but who subsequently fails in those obligations is given in the holy Qur'ān 62:5 the likeness of a donkey.

Cartooning the holy Apostle, criticizing his wearing hijāb or niqāb, will not draw attention to their hypocrisy. They must be attacked and addressed as disbelievers.

واذا علم عن اياتنا شيئا اتخذ ها هز وا اولئك لهم عذا ب مهين

Translation: And when he learns something of Our Verses (this Qur'ān), he makes them a jest. For such, there will be a humiliating torment (Qur'ān 45:9).

SUGGESTED READING

The Sunna of the holy Apostle.

Abū Fari, Dr. Muhammad Abdul Qādir. *The Gazwa of al-Ahzāb*. Amman: Dārul Furqan,1983.

-----*The Gazwa of Hudaybiya*. Amman: Dārul Furqān, 1984.

-----*The Gazwa of Uhud*. Amman: Dārul Furqān, 1982.

Ahmad Kurshid, Ansari Zafar Ishāq. *The Islamic Perspectives. Studies in Honor of Sayyid Abūl Ala Maudūdi*. London: Islamic Foundation U.K, 1979.

Ahmad, Kurshid. *Islam: Its Meaning and Message*. Leicester: Islamic Foundation U.K., 1976.

-----*Principles of Islamic Education*. Lahore Islamic Publication,1968.

-----*Islam and the West*. Lahore. Islamic Publications,1963.

Albāni, Muhammad Nāsiri-d-din. *Ruwātul lazīna tarjama lahum Allāma Muhaddith*. Emirate: Maktabat Sahaba, 2004.

'Ali Nadwi, S. Abūl. *Muhammad Rasūlullah*. Lahore: Islamic Research and Publications, 1979.

-----*Islam and the World*. Lahore: International Islamic Publishing House, 1992.

'Aliyu, Dr. Şālih Ahmad. *Dawlat Rasūl fī Medina*. Beirut: Allprint, 2001.

al-Bukhārī, Muhammad b. Ishāq. *Sahīh Bukhārī with Commentary of ibn Hajar*. Cairo: Dārul Taqwa, 2004.

Al-Ghazāli, al-Ghazāli, Abī Hamid Muhammad bin Muhammad. *Ihyā' Ulūmud Din*,2nd edition. Beirut,{**Publishing house?**}1989.

Guillaume, A. *The Life History of Muhammad.* Oxford: Oxford University Press,1987.

Habib, Jamil Ibrāhim. *Qissa Abī Jahl.* Beirut: Dārul Kutub 'Arabiyya, 1992.

Hamidullah, Dr. Muhammad. *Introduction to Islam.* Lebanon: Koran Publishing House, 1977.

Haykal, Muhammad. *The Life History of Muhammad.* Philadelphia:{**Publishing house?**} 1976.

Concept of Islamic State. London: Islamic Council of Europe, 1979.

Jamīl, Dr. Sayyid. *The Gazwa of Nabiyy.* Beirut: Dārul Wa Maktabat Hallāl, 1994.

Kāfūrī Ahmad, 'Alīyu. *The Gazwa of Badr.* Cairo: Zuhrā' I 'lāmul 'Arabiyy, 1990.

Lings, Martin. *The Life of Muhammad.* London: George Allen & Unwin Ltd., 1983.

Madkhalī, Dr. Rabi' Ibn Hādi. *Minhāj al-Anbiyā' Fī Da'awati llāhi Fīhi Hikmat wal aqal.* Medina: Maktabat Gurabā'a Athriyya, 1993.

Maudūdi, Abūl Ala. *Islamic Movement. Dynamics of Values, Power and Change.* Leicester: Islamic Foundation, 1991.

-----*Islamic Way of Life.* Riyadh: Centre for Call and Guidance, 1967.

Qardāwi, Dr. Yusuf. Kaifa Nata 'allamu ma'a Sunnatu Nabwī.{**Incomplete**}

Quṭb, Muhammad. *Shubhat hawlal Islam.* Lebanon. The Holy Qur'ān Publishing House, 1978.

Qutb, Sayyid. *Milestones.* Kuwait: International Islamic Federation of Student Organizations, 1977.

-----*Islam: the Religion of the Future.* Damascus: International Islamic Federation of Student Organizations.{**Date?**}

Salfiy, Abū Mukarrama bin 'Abduljalil. *Da'wat al-Imām Muhammad ibn 'Abdulwahhab fi Shibh Qarat-al-Hindiyya baynal Mu'ayyadiha wa ma'anadiha.* Riyadh: Maktabat al-Islam, 1913.

Sibani, Dr. Mustapha. *Siratul Nabwi. Durus wa 'Ibra.* Lebanon. The Holy Qur'an Publishing House, 1980.

Siddiqui, Moinuddin M. *Moral Teachings of Islam.* Minna, Nigeria. Islamic Education Trust, 1980.

www.ingramcontent.com/pod-product-compliance
Lightning Source LLC
Chambersburg PA
CBHW030426290526
45786CB00001B/159